# TO MAKE A DREAM SURVIVE

To mike

Enjoy the read

## by
## GRAHAM BROOKLAND

Graham Brookland

**Grosvenor House
Publishing Limited**

The right of Graham Brookland to be identified as the author of this
work has been asserted by him in accordance with Section 78
of the Copyright, Designs and Patents Act 1988

The book cover picture is copyright to Graham Brookland

This book is published by
Grosvenor House Publishing Ltd
28-30 High Street, Guildford, Surrey, GU1 3EL.
www.grosvenorhousepublishing.co.uk

A CIP record for this book
is available from the British Library

ISBN 978-1-78148-359-6

Sir Alex with Oliver and me

# Foreword by Alex McGregor

I am honoured to be able to write the foreword for Graham's book. I signed for Aldershot in 1976 after arriving from West Ham United. It was the start of such a happy period in my life and I spent six years at such a terrific football club despite only originally signing for a year. During that period we enjoyed a fantastic FA Cup run and were seconds away from a quarter-final slot in addition to narrowly missing out on promotion to the third tier of the Football League in successive seasons. They were good days and the club was so well supported. It was a pleasure to be a part of such a great squad of players and to be able to entertain as we did.

After retiring as a professional footballer I have remained in the local area and have always retained a firm interest in the fortunes of Aldershot. It was devastating to learn of its demise in 1992 after 66 years in existence. However the loss of its professional football club showed the true devotion of the supporters in resurrecting football in the town and I am aware of the role that Graham played in the formation.

The club went from strength to strength before reaching its ultimate target of reaching the Football League in 2008 after achieving five promotions. It was a special moment for everybody, including Graham, who had played their part in the special story. Although the Football League tenure lasted only five years before the club inherited relegation and administration the fans showed their true grit and determination again to ensure that football in Aldershot survived again.

I have returned to the Recreation Ground on many occasions over the years and truly love doing so. I am always made welcome by the supporters and always so well received. They are special people who are the life and soul of the club.

Graham has been an Aldershot supporter since first venturing onto the terraces as a seven-year-old. It is comforting to know that I was his favourite ever footballer and that I was able to be able to provide enjoyment as a footballer that is still recalled with such fondness many years later.

It is a new generation of players who now provide the special memories for the supporters of today to cherish in years to come. They will be forever grateful for the fact that there remains an Aldershot Town Football Club to support. Indeed it is wonderful to learn that the club remains "Alive and Kicking".

To The Good Lady, my wife Carolyn, you've suffered too long as a football widow but I wouldn't have been able to write this book without you-seriously. I am forever grateful for your patience, understanding and support of my devotion and dedication to the football club. You have been fantastic. My son Oliver, make the most of your talents and ability. You are far more educated than I will ever be. Don't waste your opportunities and enjoy watching the Shots because I know how much it means to you.

To my Mum, David and Valerie, your kindness, support and words of wisdom have been invaluable.

To Alex McGregor-you are my all-time football hero and I am extremely honoured that you have written the foreword-thank you.

I have enjoyed writing the book. It is a factual recollection of my experiences involving 40 years as a fan on the terraces watching Aldershot FC before becoming Co-Founder of Aldershot Town FC. Every chapter captured in the book revolves around Aldershot in some form or other. Every chapter reverberates around a song that was popular at that time. I have listed each song. You can have some fun trying to recollect the artiste(s) along the way.

There is no intention to offend anybody in this book. Above all, I have written the book as I have seen it but the experiences are factual covering a unique lifetime journey with a devotion to my football team.

"Just when I thought I was out they pull me back in".
THE GODFATHER PART 111 1990

What you gonna do when things go wrong?
What you gonna do when it all cracks up?
What you gonna do when the Love burns down?
What you gonna do when the flames go up?
Who is gonna come and turn the tide?
What's it gonna take to make a dream survive?
Who's got the touch to calm the storm inside?
Who's gonna save you?
Alive and Kicking

Simple Minds- Alive and Kicking (1985)

# Acknowledgements

I am thankful to Ian Morsman for continued support for the book and genuine interest. The majority of photographs have been taken by Ian including the covers. Ian has been the official club photographer since the inception of Aldershot Town FC (1992) Ltd. He is a terrific guy, a constant support to me and, above all, a genuine bloke.

Victoria Rogers has dedicated hours of time reading through the drafts (and there have been a few!) offering advice and recommendations throughout. Support that is greatly appreciated.

Dean Martin (Kappadeano) who has always provided a loyal and reliable support to me.

Thank you also to Jon Couch for granting permission to use extracts and photos from the Aldershot News.

A most worthwhile conversation with Henry Winter proved invaluable too. Thank you for your time.

Other Photo credits: Aldershot News, Simon Haywood, Eric Marsh, Rob Worrall

# Contents

Afternoon Delight (Starland Vocal Band 1976)  1

Seasons in The Sun (Terry Jacks April 1974)  3

Sound of the Suburbs (The Members Feb 1979)/Tragedy
  (Bee Gees February 1979)  8

Driven To Tears (The Police December 1980)  11

Life in a Northern Town (The Dream Academy March 1985)  14

That's Living Alright (Joe Fagin January 1984)  19

Careless Whisper (George Michael Summer 1984)  22

Hard Habit to Break (Chicago Nov 1984)  25

The Boy With The Thorn In His Side (The Smiths Oct 1985)  29

Livin' On a Prayer (Bon Jovi October 1986)  32

Nothing's Gonna Stop Us Now (Starship May 1987)  37

True Faith (New Order August 1987)  41

The Only Way Is Up (Yazz and the Plastic Population
  August 1988)  44

Don't Want to Lose You (Gloria Estefan August 1989)  48

The King of Wishful Thinking (Go West August 1990)  52

Praying For Time (George Michael August 1990)  55

Wind of Change (Scorpions Oct 1991)  59

Always Look On the Bright Side of Life (Monty Python
  Nov 1992)  65

Weather WIth You (Crowded House Feb 1992)  68

Accident Waiting To Happen (BIlly Bragg Feb 1992)  72

Why (Annie Lennox March 1992)    75

Nothing Else Matters (Metallica May 1992)    80

Even Better Than the Real Thing (U2 July 1992)    86

Alive and Kicking (Simple Minds re-release 1992)    93

Keep the Faith (Bon Jovi Oct 1992)    98

Hope of Deliverance (Paul McCartney Jan 1993)    103

No Limit (2 Unlimited Mar 1993)    105

What's Up (4 Non Blondes Aug 1993)    110

Give It Away (Red Hot Chili Peppers Feb 1994)    114

Parklife (Blur Oct 1994)    117

Whatever (Oasis Jan 1995)    121

Boom Boom Boom (Outhere Brothers Aug 1995)    125

They Don't Care About Us (Michael Jackson May 1996)    128

A Design for Life (Manic Street Preachers May 1996)    130

How Bizarre (OMC Sept 1996)    132

Don't Speak (No Doubt Apr 1997)    138

Bitter Sweet Symphony (The Verve Aug 1997)    142

TubThumping (Chumbawamba Sept 1997)    145

Perfect Day (Various Dec 1997)    151

Truly Madly Deeply (Savage Garden May 1998)    153

Deeper Underground (Jamiroquai August 1998)    156

If You Tolerate This (Manic Street Preachers Sept 1998)    157

Believe (Cher Nov 1998)    161

Tender (Blur Mar 1999)    164

Right Here Right Now (Fatboy Slim May 1999)    168

Why Does It Always Rain On Me (Travis Oct 1999)    172

You Drive Me Crazy (Britney Spears Nov 1999)    176

Go Let it Out (Oasis Feb 2000)    183

Fool Again (Westlife April 2000)    185

Affirmation (Savage Garden Sept 2000)    189

Trouble (Coldplay Nov 2000)    191

Have A Nice Day (Stereophonics July 2001)                           197

Fallin' (Alicia Keys Nov 2001)                                      201

Gotta Get Thru This (Daniel Bedingfield Jan 2002)                  203

Whenever Wherever (Shakira Mar 2002)                                209

How You Remind Me (Nickelback Mar 2002)                            211

By the Way (Red Hot Chili Peppers Aug 2002)                        213

Time for Heroes (The Libertines Jan 2003)                          215

Something Beautiful (Robbie Williams Aug 2003)                     217

Dry Your Eyes (The Streets June 2004)                              219

Vertigo (U2 Sept 2004)                                             222

Somewhere Else (Razorlight May 2005)                               226

Bad Day (Daniel Powter Aug 2005)                                   228

Naive (The Kooks Aug 2006)                                         233

Shine (Take That Mar 2007)                                         236

Dream Catch Me (Newton Faulkner Aug 2007)                          239

Apologize (TImbaland Nov 2007)                                     243

Call The Shots (Girls Aloud Mar 2008)                              247

Always Where I Need To Be (The Kooks Apr 2008)                     252

5 Years' Time (Noah and the Whale Jul 2008)                        256

Take a Bow (Rhianna Aug 2008)                                      259

Not Fair (Lily Allen Aug 2009)                                     263

Singing the Blues (Cliff Richard and The Shadows Sept 2009)        266

I Got A Feeling (Black Eyes Peas Oct 2009)                         268

Don't Stop Believin' (Journey Apr 2010)                            271

Pack Up (Eliza Doolittle Aug 2010)                                 274

When We Collide (Matt Cardle Dec 2010)                             280

Raise Your Glass (Pink Jan 2011)                                   283

The Edge of Glory (Lady GAGA Oct 2011) or All About
    Tonight (Pixie Lott Oct 2011)                                  287

Set Fire to the Rain (Adele Nov 2011)                              293

Picking Up the Pieces (Paloma Faith Jul 2012)                      297

Skyfall (Adele Nov 2012)                                    307

Troublemaker (Olly Murs Dec 2012)                           309

Try (Pink Jan 2013)                                         312

Lightning Bolt (Jake Bugg Feb 2013)                         316

Just Give Me A Reason (Pink Mar 2013)                       324

Read All About It (Emile Sande Apr 2013)                    334

Let Her Go (Passenger May 2013)                             337

Do I Wanna Know (Arctic Monkeys July 2013)                  344

Blurred Lines (Robin Thicke July 2013)                      352

Don't Forget Who You Are (Miles Kane July 2013)             356

Wrecking Ball (Miley Cyrus Sept 2013)                       360

Somewhere Only We Know (Lily Allen Dec 2013)                367

*To Make A Dream Survive (*Alive and Kicking)               372

Let Me Go (Gary Barlow May 2014)                            375

Got No Fans (Wealstone Raider Dec 2014)                     379

Blame (Calvin Harris ft John Newman Dec 2014)              381

# Afternoon Delight

Many people never want to meet their heroes just in case they are not quite what they think they will be. I was shopping in Farnborough Gate many years ago with my wife Carolyn (The Good Lady) before I suddenly stopped. In the coffee shop was Alex McGregor. Alex McGregor, you may ask. Who is he? As far as I am concerned he is the greatest footballer that ever lived. He made 200 appearances for Aldershot Football Club between 1976 and 1982 and he was my hero. For 15 minutes or so I was hovering about not knowing whether I should go up and introduce myself to Alex. I was just pure nerves and twitching. The Good Lady asked what on earth was the problem. I said to her, *"Don't you know who that is?"* She obviously didn't even though they are both from Glasgow! I explained to her that it was Alex and he was my hero as a boy. Straight to the point as Glaswegians are, she said, *"For crying out loud just go and talk to him or let's go. Just get it out of your system"*. I duly did and was so chuffed because he was the gentleman I was hoping he would be. Just a downright nice man who I have since met on many occasions and he always has the same demeanour. Alex McGregor never disappoints in real life just as he never did on the football pitch.

Colin Bell was my first football hero. He wore the sky blue shirt of Manchester City but it was something about him that captured me as a young lad growing up in the 70s. In those days keeping track of football scores took on a whole new meaning to that of the current era. Forget Twitter, Facebook and Sky Sports News you were lucky to get two seconds on the television and the football results were always the finale after an afternoon of watching wrestling on Dickie Davies' World of Sport or Eddie

Waring's Rugby League on BBC1. Bell it was though. I wanted to be that player, I wanted to be that man!

You never had the availability of football on the television that you do these days either. Certainly no live matches (minus the FA Cup Final and World Cup). The highlights of a couple of games on Match of the Day with Jimmy Hill on Saturday night or Brian Moore's The Big Match the following afternoon. In November 1975 I sneakily watched the Sportsnight highlights of City's League Cup tie versus Manchester United on a weeknight at the top of the stairs, unbeknown to my mum and dad. Bell was seriously injured after a challenge with Martin Buchan. You could sense the urgency of the situation as he was carried off. I was gutted and in tears at the top of the stairs but couldn't share the problem with my parents as I shouldn't have been watching the match in the first place. Furthermore there were no phone-ins on the radio or the opportunity to quickly flick onto the City website to find out how the player was. It was a different world then.

My love for City was swapped, temporarily in 1974 and permanently two years later. The blue and white of Bell, Doyle, Summerbee and Co switched to the red and blue of the local Football League club, Aldershot. I had been to few live matches up to this point. A game or two at Queens Park Rangers courtesy of a friend at school but that was it. I had never been to the Recreation Ground. I did follow a Scottish team though- no, not Celtic or Rangers. Testament to my future experiences as a football fan I chose Brechin City- Why? I looked at the newspaper one day and selected them as they were bottom of the Scottish League.

# Seasons in the Sun

My love affair with Aldershot started on the afternoon of Saturday 13th April 1974 to be factual. Cambridge United were the opponents in a Third Division match. I don't remember a great deal about the game itself but the whole experience struck a chord with me. There was something special about the place. The Recreation Ground- the place that was to become so special to me. Upon entry it was unique. Picturesque with trees surrounding the confines of the turnstiles off the High Street- how many clubs actually play in their own High Street? There was even a pathway behind one of the goals too. I recall being dropped off outside the turnstiles by my dad with my brother and his friends. We stood in the North Stand and the crowd was so big (over 5000) that I had to be carried above his head in order to assess what was going on. Shots won 6-0- a decent start. Legendary striker Jack Howarth netted a hat-trick and the love affair was up and running. Tommy McAnearney's men finished eighth in the table that season. It was the highest finish any Aldershot team ever achieved.

The regular visits to the Rec really started in September 1976. I do recall watching a friendly match versus Norwich City the year before on an evening for some reason. We only went that night because my aunt lived in Newport Road, around the corner from the ground and she was pregnant and due to give birth to my cousin, Stuart, who also went on to become a lifelong supporter. He wasn't at the match that night though- mind you he wasn't born until a few months later!

My school friend Michael Bartlett was a regular, travelling with his dad to the matches, and we often spoke about Aldershot. There weren't too many others at school with an interest in

Aldershot despite the fact that we lived only seven miles away. My dad was not really a football man either. Boxing was his game and, I'm told, he was pretty decent too in his youth. He used to watch Brentford with his mates when he was a teenager but was soon banned as every time he went along to Griffin Park the Bees lost. Thereafter he spent his Saturday afternoons swimming or boxing and met his mates after the match. He worked at BOAC at Heathrow Airport in the cargo department. Funnily enough he ended up working with legendary Bees defender Peter Gelson and often spoke about him.

In the end I suppose I spoke so often about my desire to watch "The Shots" that my dad eventually took me along regularly. It became routine. Saturday mornings were all about Tiger and Scorcher, Hot Shot Hamish, Billy's Boots and, of course, Roy of the Rovers. Then onto Noel Edmonds and Multi Coloured Swap Shop. I used to set up a pretend football pitch in the lounge at home. I was the only player- Aldershot always won. Sir Alex always scored the winner- McGregor of course, not Ferguson! My dad would dash home from his shift, a quick homemade fish fingers and chips from mum's traditional cuisine and off to the Rec at 2.15pm. We'd park up just off Newport Road at the back of the High Street and walk along. It was a real buzz to me. Hordes of people, queues at the turnstiles. We always went through the same entrance and I clicked through at the same time as my dad. I'm sure the Turnstile Operator would have accounted for this though!

We then walked past an elderly lady selling tickets called Doris Hughes on the High Street steps. I later learned that she was hugely respected at the club having been heavily involved with the Supporters Club with her late husband George.

We always made our way behind the far goal to the East Bank then- it was the place to be! It was the most popular part of the stadium. It was where the noise was made and all the lads stood. You had to be a "face", mind you, to stand at the back. I loved hearing all the singing from the back of the terraces and a few new choice words into the vocabulary too. I always wondered if the lads held a regular session to improve their voices and to learn new songs.

It was great- I loved it. The first match as a regular fan was versus Swansea City on Saturday 25th September 1976. It was a 2-2 draw but it was the next match that something special occurred. Wearing the number 11 for the Shots was Alex McGregor. A silky winger from the old school. As soon as he received the ball from wide there was an air of excitement. He was just truly brilliant. The ball stuck to his feet and the defenders could never get it off him. He became my instant hero. Whenever he was on the ball you felt something was going to happen. People used to tell me that he wasn't as effective away from home- I didn't care- I only watched the Shots at home in those days and Alex was a genius at the Rec.

We used to play football at lunchtime at the Grove School in Frimley. Everybody else was Keegan, Francis, Brady, Latchford or Bremner. Not me- I was McGregor. I can remember one lunchtime collecting the ball and then waltzing past everybody in sight before scoring. All of a sudden I was a winger. It was the position I wanted to play. From Colin Bell I now wanted to be Alex McGregor.

That Christmas was special too. Well before the days of replica kits my mum and dad had somehow managed to put together the Shots kit. My favourite kit of all time too. Red shirts with a blue V neck and cuffs, blue shorts, and red socks with blue tops.

Alex McGregor (right) on his Shots debut in 1976

I was made up, not just for the kit but because they had also put the number 7 on the back of the shirt- Alex's shirt. This, of course, was well before the days of names on shirts or squad numbers. I wore that shirt all over Christmas. I was horrified when he suddenly changed numbers and thereafter predominantly wore the number 11 shirt! I was devastated but it never changed my admiration for a special footballer.

My first Shots kit from 1976 with future
Shots fan, my cousin Stuart Harris

That season wasn't the greatest for Aldershot though. They had just been relegated from the third division and after a strong start to the campaign they eventually finished 17th, winning just three of their final 18 matches. I do remember Alex scoring one of my all-time favourite goals in a 2-0 home victory versus soon to be non-league Workington in the penultimate home match. I was standing in the East Bank when he picked the ball up on the halfway line.

He strolled towards goal gaining speed as he gathered his stride, bypassing anybody in the way. He then duly lobbed out-coming goalkeeper Mike Rogan from the edge of the 18-yard box for a quite exquisite goal. It was the stuff dreams are made of. Such a shame that the talents of that era were rarely filmed.

I also recall another moment of drama in February 1977 when a comfortable 4-0 victory versus Newport County was mainly remembered due to an incident involving goalkeeper Glen Johnson. The balding keeper who was only 24 at the time but looked much older saved a thrice taken penalty from Gary Bell in the last minute before giving the referee a V sign for his troubles. He told me many years later that it cost him a few bob at the FA but he felt better for it at the time.

My dad was remarkable really. Mum was due for a serious operation and was sidelined for many weeks, firstly in hospital and then at home recuperating. He was combining everything at the time but still ensured that we could get to the Rec for the matches. He knew what it meant to me even in those early days of being a fan.

Shots finished fifth in the table in 1977/78 and went unbeaten at home throughout the whole campaign. A guy called John Dungworth had replaced Howarth by this time and returned 23 goals. It was an exciting side with names that roll off the tongue even now. I could name you that starting line-up as if it was yesterday. The following would be accurate: Glen Johnson, Mike Earls or Dave Howitt, Alan Wooler, Will Dixon, Tommy Youlden, Joe Jopling, Malcolm Crosby, Murray Brodie, Andy Needham, Dungworth and, of course, Alex. Forget your squad rotation that you have nowadays and all that loan nonsense. McAnearney only used 19 players that season and three of those players only played 11 matches between them.

This season saw my first experience of playing local rivals Reading. In all my time watching the Shots I never did see them defeat the Royals in a league match but those games used to attract healthy attendances and I recall the rivalry was intense. This emanated back to the days when the Football League was regionalised and the two teams played each other most seasons until it was nationalised in 1958. I also remember vividly Easter Monday 1978 when I was able to attend my first ever away match- the short trip to Griffin Park. Brentford were going for promotion too whilst we had beaten fellow promotion candidates Southend United 3-0 two days before. There was over 12,500 in west London that afternoon and a large contingent who had made the short journey down the M3 but the Bees had the upper hand as Steve Phillips netted a brace to secure a 2-0 victory. Little did I know that day but a future friend and Shots player Paul Shrubb was in the visitors' line-up that afternoon. For me though, I was a proper fan now- I had watched the Shots away from home! We missed out on promotion by two points in the end as Watford, Southend, Swansea City and Brentford were successful but the red and blue was etched into me now. Manchester City? Not interested anymore. Although the true test, of course, was when you finally received the Subbuteo box with your team- Aldershot FC, red and blue.

I used to create an atmosphere too using marbles putting all the red ones together in one part of the plastic stand with all the blue ones separated at the other end. It was all going great until I stained the pitch by knocking a glass of milk all over it. All of a sudden it looked like Derby County's Baseball Ground.

# Sound of the Suburbs- Tragedy!

S eason 1978/79 was one of the most talked about in the history of Aldershot FC. It was another fifth placed finish for McAnearney's men but it was the exploits in the FA Cup that were the topic of conversation. It all started in November when non-league Weymouth visited the Rec. They were seconds from creating their own shock before Malcolm Crosby netted a low strike from outside the penalty box with near enough the last kick of the match. It forced a draw and avoided the embarrassment of an upset. We won the replay and disposed of Isthmian League Barking in the second round. The third round tie at Division Two side Sheffield United saw a goalless draw at Bramall Lane. A mini upset had been caused and I can recall the excitement of knowing that I would be able to go to the replay at the Rec. It was played on a Monday night. All I can remember in the build-up to kick-off was watching Grange Hill on television and being so nervous that I hardly touched my tea before we set off to the match. The crowd was over 8000 and it was a misty evening. Dungworth was the hero, keeping up his record of scoring in every round with a late penalty, always recalled because there is a photo of the goal with Alex looking the other way at the time. The fervour from the East Bank was fantastic. Aldershot were on the map and also in the fourth round of the FA Cup where Swindon Town would be the opponents. The weather was playing havoc at this time. My brother drove up in his Hillman Imp from Bristol Polytechnic for the match only for it to be called off due to heavy snow. That was disappointing but when the match was played it certainly wasn't. 11,000 in the Rec and two goals again from Dungworth.

The Wiltshire side were out of the FA Cup; the 2-1 win ensured that Aldershot were in the last 16!

John Dungworth nets penalty v Sheffield Utd in 1979 FA Cup shock. Alex McGregor is no 11 in background looking away

We were paired against Graham Turner's Shrewsbury Town, themselves Cup kings after knocking out Manchester City in an earlier round. My brother made the journey again and again the weather was the winner due to the snow. Angry, I called the club. *"Why is it off?"* I enquired. *"Because we have a heat wave"* was the sarcastic retort from the club. I relayed the message to my family not quite understanding what it all meant. It was eventually played three nights later and it proved to be one of the most memorable matches ever to be played at the Rec.

I could tell you exactly where I was standing on the East Bank. Ironically a couple of years ago I was talking to my own friends connected with the club as we stood on our famous terrace making a promotional documentary- Paul Marcus from Eagle Radio, Ian Dawkins from Hi Speed Services Ltd and the record goal scorer of Aldershot Town, Mark Butler.

Amazingly we were all standing just a few yards away in the same section but we never got to know each other until a decade or two later. With just a minute remaining the tie was level at 1-1. I vividly recall Dungworth turning and striking the ball into the net at the East Bank end to put the home side in front. The stadium (nearly 12,000) erupted. Little old fourth division Aldershot Football Club was on the verge of the FA Cup Quarter Finals. They only had to see out the final seconds and the celebrations would start. I wasn't even concentrating to be honest as the match continued. Then all I recall seeing is the ball at the far end loop over helpless keeper Johnson into the net. The whole place fell silent.

Poor old Malcolm Crosby always got the blame as he gave the ball away in the build-up. Harsh. In fairness he was the man that ensured the run occurred in the first place with that Weymouth goal. I do remember the total numbness when the final whistle was blown. There were five people in our car on the way out of town including my school mate David Marles. Not a word was spoken from leaving the ground to arriving home. I knew then that Aldershot was in my system and it would be difficult to shrug it off! It was here to stay!

We lost the replay and I remember fiddling about with a transistor radio trying to find BBC Radio 2 on the medium wave frequency just to get updates. We eventually found out that despite Dungworth scoring his eighth goal of the competition to take the game to extra time we had lost 3-1 and the dream run was over. We missed out on promotion again that season with a second successive fifth place finish well before the introductions of play-offs extended the season.

Dungworth was sold to Shrewsbury Town in the early stages of the following season and the form dipped although a still respectable 10th finish was achieved in 1979/80. We played Portsmouth on Easter Monday at the Rec and the 12,000 attendance was a sea of blue and white throughout the stadium as the fellow Hampshire club managed to edge towards promotion. I can remember it being a touch "hairy" after the match and the pitch was invaded. My dad wasn't one to hold back if he thought there was an injustice and I recall him having more than a word with one of the local police officers on duty.

# Driven to Tears

Christmas 1980 was a memorable period. My brother had bought me a Christmas present to see my favourite band, The Police, at Tooting Bec. I was made up. The concert was a couple of days before the festive period began and I remember being so excited. Sting, Andy Summers and Stuart Copeland in the flesh- live! It didn't get any better than that. I never made the gig though! I went down with a heavy bout of the flu. My brother took his girlfriend instead. Not sure that was a good move either- they didn't last too much longer and I was a misery at home missing the concert of a lifetime- I never did get the chance to see The Police! When they reformed a few years ago the excessive three-figure entrance fees was a non-starter!

However to make up for the disappointment it was agreed that we would go to watch the Shots in action at league leaders Southend United the day after Boxing Day. In those days you played back to back matches over the festive period and Shots had defeated Hereford United 4-0 the day before courtesy of Mark Sanford netting all four goals.

Pre-M25 we took the North Circular Road around London before heading into Essex. For some reason we ended up behind the goal standing with the home supporters. I vividly remember, however, Glen Johnson winking at me in the warm up. He must have recognised us as we always stood behind the East Bank at home matches and gave the approval that we had made the journey. That's what I thought anyway! Once the match had started we were 1-0 down within a minute and eventually lost 3-0. It was a long journey back home but I got used to those in the ensuing years.

McAnearney was sacked, somewhat surprisingly in early 1981 despite the club being nicely positioned in sixth place although Dungworth had never been properly replaced and there was certainly a shortfall in the goals for column. The then club record appearance holder Len Walker, who hailed from the north east and had just returned after a spell at Darlington, replaced him after a period as a caretaker and led the team towards another close shave, narrowly missing out on promotion for a third season in four.

A transitional period ensued and I started getting the bug to watch the team away from home on a more regular basis. However I needed to earn the funds to do so. In the summer of 1982 my school mate Paul Lawrence and I started a window cleaning round around the Frimley housing estates. We earned a few bob but there was one problem. Paul did the upstairs and I did the ground floors as I didn't fancy the ladders. He wanted a bigger cut as he was doing more of the donkey work up and down the steps and he eventually went solo. I decided to set up my own car cleaning round instead and this worked just fine.

Initially every Sunday I would be seeing the regulars, cleaning the cars and earning enough money to start travelling away. I used to nip out of school early too to do some of my "regulars" who were not about at the weekend. I wasn't as successful as I should have been at school and I don't think my mum was aware of this extra-curricular activity but it was financially beneficial.

The first match of the 82/83 season was a Football League Trophy encounter at AFC Bournemouth. Paul and I travelled by train to the match and we soon learned about what life was about travelling away! Ian McDonald and Mark Sanford netted for the Shots in a 2-2 draw but I remember little about the match. What I do recall is directly afterwards. In all our bravado Paul and I were wearing Shots scarves all over the place on the south coast-proud to be an away fan. Don't ask me why as it was on a hot summer's day too. There weren't too many up from north east Hampshire for this match. Coming out of Dean Court Paul and I were walking by the large park adjacent to the stadium. All of a sudden this car screeched to a halt and these lads came charging out and started to chase the pair of us.

It was like a comic crusade as we were chased across the park straight through where a cricket match was taking place and, thankfully, at the other end of the park was a bus pulling out of its stop. Paul and I just about managed to get onto the bus out of breath but saved from a pounding! By this time we had tucked all of our scarves under our jackets around our midriff and looked more like sumo wrestlers to the bemused passengers on the bus.

We didn't have a clue where the bus was heading and it was a stroke of luck that it was making its way to the railway station.

# Life in a Northern Town

The early days of watching the Shots away was similar, travelling to places such as Scunthorpe, Halifax and Rochdale. Always watching your back and always being aware that something dodgy could occur was a part of watching the Shots away. The locals weren't always of the friendly nature. That said- I loved travelling up north. They are experiences I will always recall.

We used to go by train organised by Ian Read from the Supporters Club. Ian, at the time was just 24, but never missed a Shots match and hadn't done for years. He even cut short his first honeymoon when he got married to watch the Shots. Shots fans didn't particularly travel in numbers in the early 80s but those that did were loyal to each other. We needed to be too. We only won once on our travels in the league in 1982/83 although Portsmouth were defeated at Fratton Park in the FA Cup- that sort of made up for the long journeys home unrewarded.

A visit to Scunthorpe United's Old Show Ground provided a bonus too. Many's the time we used to hang about the away dressing rooms because there was always a possibility that a few comp tickets could come our way. We hit the jackpot on this particular occasion. Striker Howard Goddard gave Paul and me a bundle of "comps". We, of course, took a ticket each for ourselves and looked after our own but we had loads over. We then went to the end where the home fans were based and sold them at half price. For a couple of teenagers we were made up.

A visit to Rochdale's Spotland a week before Christmas was an experience never to forget. We were always a pretty close-knit group but you only needed one loud mouth. There was one guy who I just never took to- a feller named Phil from Woking. On this particular trip we arrived in the Greater Manchester town quite early with a visit to a number of local hostelries as per usual. Phil, though, was always trying to be somebody he quite obviously wasn't although I gave him the benefit of the doubt in those days as he was a few years older than me. On this occasion he was laying it on and trying to intimidate the locals. It all rebounded and I received a smack in the face prior to kick-off and it hurt too although I tried to act normal. Once we were in the stadium, there he was giving it all the large stuff to the locals on the terraces. However as the match progressed (another away defeat!) we were becoming surrounded by Rochdale fans who were obviously not interested in the match. There were less and less of us remaining behind that goal by full time but Phil, after stirring it all up, was nowhere to be seen. We needed an escort back to the railway station in a police van to avoid what would have been another unpleasant confrontation. When we arrived, there he was carrying a WH Smith's bag. Obviously aware that he was out of his depth and in line for a shiner or two from the locals he had conveniently disappeared at half-time and gone shopping. I never took the bloke seriously after that. His antics had caused me to get a smack through no fault of myself. Whilst wanting nothing to do with him his name kept cropping up years later. This ardent Shots fan had also been seen in a Leeds United shirt and then a Celtic one. I went up to Wembley once with a group of Arsenal fans for a pre-season tournament and there was Phil in a pub pre-match with an Aston Villa shirt on.

The final straw came many years later when I was viewing some photos from a match when Woking reached the FA Trophy Final in 1995 and I had to stop and think for a moment- there he was again, this time in a Cards shirt! As a football fan you see so many people of totally different personas. You learn at an early age who you can and cannot rely on. That day at Rochdale ensured that I realised that I wouldn't be relying on Phil anytime soon.

One other match does stick out from that season though. We travelled to Colchester United just after Christmas. With the poor weather in the build-up to Christmas funds were short. Some clients didn't need their vehicles cleaned over the festive period. This was, of course, unreasonable. I needed funds to get to Layer Road. Paul and I were struggling so we went to extreme measures on Boxing Day evening down the Brackendale Road area (posh part of Camberley!).

We embarked on some carol singing. In the pitch dark we were asked by one old lady what we were collecting for- *"SOS"* we replied – *"Save Our Shots"*. We weren't even in any adverse financial difficulty as a club in those days. The lady told us to hold on. We waited and then heard this clamour of aggressive barking. She unleashed her dogs on us from the back gate. We scarpered in opposite directions in what was a scary experience as we ended up out of breath pretty quickly.

Hull City was an experience too. The February 1983 visit to Boothferry Park and the Fourth Division leaders also saw Aldershot News sports reporter Nick Collins travel with us as we left Aldershot Railway station at 6.45am. Collins has gone on to carve out a terrific career, highlighted in his role as Chief Football Reporter with Sky Sports, a job that he has carried out for many years now. He was a decent bloke too but I am not sure if he will remember his journey to Humberside alongside the worldwide venues that he has travelled to in his career. There were only 17 of us as we embarked from Kings Cross up to Doncaster before changing. Hull was a lively place too and we went 2-0 up against all the odds. The locals were not amused. There were just four of us standing on the big away section on the side of the stadium directly next to the vociferous home following segregated by a feeble fence. The coins started piling over the top. *"No wonder you lot are always skint up here"* bellowed supporter Eamonn Smith, one of the four. The coins were soon cleared up though, never to return to their rightful owners.

It was a shame the match wasn't played a couple of months later- the £1 coin had been introduced by then!

All the way to Hull in 1983
(3rd from right with Ian Read
second from left)

By this time in addition to my car cleaning round I also earned a few bob working in McDonald's in Camberley. I never made it though. The highest position I ever encountered was preparing the "fries". To make it at McDonald's you need to be on the front tills. I never achieved that accolade. During the pre-season of 1983/84 I experienced a problem. I had been given a shift on a Saturday whilst we were due to play a friendly at Gillingham. I couldn't have that.

Missing a match at any level was a non-starter. I tried to change the shift but my line manager, a guy called Leroy, wasn't having it. I never turned up for the shift and never worked at McDonald's again. I did, however, make the match at Priestfield.

We also went to Orient in the League Cup in September 1983. A day up in London and a few of us were in tow including Duncan Rendall, my best mate from school. He wasn't a regular but just up for a few pints. An entertaining 3-3 draw at Brisbane Road and after the match we were all walking up Leyton High Road heading for the tube. All of a sudden we were set upon by the locals and it became nasty. I pegged it up the road and survived any problems.

Duncan believed it best to carry on walking to try to convince the locals that he was one of them. They weren't convinced and he got a pounding! Welcome to the world of watching Aldershot on the road, Dunc!

Standing on the East Bank and mixing with lads who were older and a touch more streetwise there was always a touch of trepidation at times, but as time develops and you learn that you have plenty in common everybody accepts each other as "one of the lads". When you have a group of young men together there are always one or two toe rags and this was no exception. However you develop your own circle of friends of people you can trust and avoid the "toe rags". "Weasel" was my nickname and my reputation increased after a Supporters Club disco at the Lakeside Country Club in October 1983. I can't deny that I had a skin full and ended up being wheelbarrowed home caked with mud from top to bottom after being chucked into a pond. Keith and Colin Crow, fellow Shots fans to this day and good lads who lived opposite, knocked on the doorbell at 2am and scarpered.

When my mum opened the door there I was comatose and drenched. She was hysterical and my dad sorted the situation out. His warning the next day lives with me to this day. *"Son, you can come home in that state once, possibly another time too, but there will never be a third time"*. The next day one of the Crow boys knocked on the door to see how I was. They received a tongue-lashing from my mum and told to disappear pretty rapidly. One thing was for certain though- word had got about and by the time I got into the minibus for the Tuesday evening League Cup tie at Notts County I was in- *"one of the lads"*. Weasel had made it!

# That's Living Alright

We faced our most challenging away match of them all on Saturday 14th January 1984 and a visit to Hereford United. Times were hard again and we didn't have enough for the journey to Edgar Street. "*We could hitchhike*" said Paul, the night before in the pub for a pint straight after watching Auf Wiedersehen Pet on the box. Hitchhike we did. On a desperately cold and bleak morning we set off on foot from Frimley at 7.30am and our first lift was from a milk float outside Martins Newsagents in the High Street. We were taken along to Blackwater where another couple of lifts took us to the M4 junction at Reading. We were making good time and somewhere along the line I recall being taken all the way into Wales to arrive at Chepstow. This proved a problem though. We walked past Chepstow Racecourse, not really knowing where we were going. The snow started and it was freezing cold.

These were pre-mobile phone days, of course, and we didn't even know if the game was on or not. We were in the middle of nowhere and must have walked for a couple of hours without any joy and were getting tired and fraught. The match was looking a distant prospect and we didn't know what to do next. We were in the "valleys" by now. Then, just as it looked as though we were in trouble, the "thumbs up" paid dividends. But when we looked at the car that stopped we started to laugh. Our lifeline was a Robin Reliant driven by a Welsh preacher. He asked us where we were going and we told him- Hereford United Football Club. He informed us that he was not a football fan but that if we promised to read the Bible, he would take us to Ross-on-Wye. We agreed to do so. There we were with the preacher, Bible in hand, with Paul in the front and me crouched in the back trying to keep a straight face. The preacher kept to his word and we were then taken on the final part of the journey to Edgar Street by a Bulls fan actually going to the game. We arrived at 1.30pm. When we got to the social club at the ground we met the official party of supporters who had travelled to the game by coach.

Mary Sweet was one of the most natural and warm hearted supporters the club ever had and a lady that I took a great deal of advice from over the years. She was such a pleasant kind-hearted person who also had that air of authority too. She was your "Aldershot Nan". When she found out about our hitchhiking escapade she told us in strong terms that we would not be doing the same to go back to Frimley. Mary offered to pay the £4 each to Ian Read for the return journey on the Supporters Club coach. We lost the match 2-1. I never did ask Paul if he did keep to his side of the bargain set by the preacher in the Robin Reliant!

Len Walker's side did well that season. A combination of Dale Banton and Les Lawrence upfront proved deadly in the second half of the campaign and we weren't far off promotion, finishing fifth again. Indeed there was a period around the February/March time when we were always at least three up at the interval, going on to defeat Mansfield Town, 7-1, Halifax and Chester 5-2. An Easter Saturday defeat at Reading probably put the kibosh on matters not long after a terrific victory at Swindon Town.

I was certainly an outspoken individual at this stage. I recall another time that season and a 0-0 draw at home to Crewe Alexandra. I wasn't too impressed with referee Daniel Vickers' performance and wanted to let him know about it. I remember running onto the pitch at the end of the game and remonstrating with the official before Shots skipper Joe Jopling got hold of me and just said, "Leave it, son". That was enough for me and I came to my senses.

One away journey towards the latter part of the season was a visit to Birkenhead and Tranmere Rovers. This was always a dodgy place to go and this time proved no different. Pushing for promotion, there was a larger visiting support than usual. A problem occurred in the crowd and the police became involved during the match. The bottom line is that the home supporters found it hilarious to spit at our fans from the upper tier above from where we were gathered. One of our directors was a retired Major from the Army- Alan Dobson. In fact, at the time, he was the Secretary of the Army Football Association a place I would become familiar with over 20 years later. He was a formidable character and a former Grenadier Guard. He was also not one to remonstrate with. He came down to see what the problem was.

His presence only made it worse. He challenged a supporter, an unkempt old boy (although he claimed he was only 38) called Alun Edmunds. He was always unclean, had a fag hanging out of the end of his mouth usually washed up with a can of bitter. Indeed I can smell him as I am writing! When Alun tried to explain to Dobson what was going on he was immediately put down by the Major who said, "*When you address me you call me MAJOR*"! Alun duly responded. "*Yes, and when you speak to me in future you call me Chief Petty Officer Edmunds*".

# Careless Whisper

T he passion that I had for the football club was something that just grew in rapid proportions. I was incensed about a letter that was written in the local paper by a local resident that was detrimental. I wrote back defending the club and promoting the positive aspects that it held within the local community.

A letter was written to me by the then secretary, Mike Cosway, stating that the Board of Directors had viewed the letter and that I would be invited to meet Len Walker and the players in recognition of the letter and they would be in contact. Alas the follow-up was never made and it left me angry to be honest. It made me realise in later life to make sure that involvement and promises made to supporters were carried through. You never know who may be affected and the influence that these kind of matters can have on individuals. It annoyed me and could have been avoided. In truth I didn't expect a letter in the first place and would have thought no more or less of the club if I hadn't received one.

I had become more involved by this time, joining the Supporters Club Committee. Little was I to know the importance of how this decision would map my future out and the close connection with Aldershot that would never leave me. My first responsibility was to sell Golden Goal tickets outside the Radio Shots building.

These days a terrific supporter called Ricky Cope sells them from the same spot and I will only ever buy them off him as he reminds me of when I used to do it. An infectious enthusiasm. In those days the cars used to drive up from the High Street gate and I used to stop everybody irrespective of who they were.

It was my first introduction into learning that the more sophisticated the car the less likely it was going to be that you were going to get a sale from whoever was in it. Many would turn their noses up or look down at me as though I wasn't there.

There was plenty of dissention between the football club and the Committee at this time and by the start of the 1984/85 season the Supporters Club had been banned from the ground by the Chairman Reg Driver and his board of directors. Indeed the football club attempted to set up its own "Aldershot Football Club Supporters Club 1984". It never got off the ground and we, as our own committee, operated outside the Rec on match days before entering the turnstiles prior to kick-off. It all got rather unpleasant to be honest. The whole reason why the Supporters Club had been banned was primarily down to the fact that the club shop was not open prior to one of the pre-season friendlies but this was just an excuse.

Supporters Club banned from the Rec in 1984. With Ian Read (thumbs up) and fellow Committee members Dave and Caroline Brewer

The deeper matter was down to a whole host of personality difficulties with the Board and senior members of the Supporters Club Committee who had been in post for many, many years in the days when the Supporters Club used to operate from its headquarters at 127 High Street. They were a thriving organisation at the time but the trust was lost, especially when HQ was sold and the Supporters Club funds were used to build a new social facility called The Sportsmans Club. The Supporters Club were supposed to have a strong vested interest in the facility but, as time progressed, its involvement became more and more diluted as the football club appeared to take control of it. This didn't sit well amongst some of the longer-standing committee members.

My later take on it was that there was a mistrust on both sides that would never have been sorted out. Knowing what I know now I would have banged their heads together. We were all attempting to do the best for the same cause- Aldershot Football Club. There were some good people on both sides.

It was more than just a squabble between supporters though. There was a full-blown attempt of a takeover at the club that was making progress and by November time this had been completed. The Driver regime was ousted and replaced by Godalming-based solicitor, David O'Connell and his consortium which included the likes of local businessman Cliff Jenkins, Tim Elliott and supporter Terry Owens, all names that would appear in the future. Included in the Driver regime was Bob Potter, a local entrepreneur who was best known for owning the Lakeside Country Club which became home to the BDO World Darts competition from 1986. My first introduction with Potter was on Saturday 29th September 1984 as Darlington came away from the Rec with a 4-3 victory. I had been giving my usual outspoken verdict, from the seats of the North Stand, and on this occasion it was during the match. Potter took offence and told me in no uncertain terms after the match what he would do to me if he heard me speak in similar tones in the future. I responded stating that I didn't think the actions of *"threatening me by coming over the wall to sort me out"* were befitting of a club director. I had been a bit lippy, mind.

# Hard Habit to Break

Whatever, I still travelled to Rochdale on the Tuesday evening to see Martin Foyle and Peter Foley score the goals in a 2-1 victory in front of just 960 spectators. I was there on the Saturday too and the long haul up to Blackpool although I never did see the match.

A weekend away in the Lancashire hotspot caught up with me. If my memory serves me right a night out on the Friday evening with fellow Shots fans saw me a touch the worse for wear. In fact I felt awful throughout the night and into match day. I had never experienced such sickness.

We all met in a pub in Blackpool town centre at 11am on the day of the match but all I remember is sitting slumped in a chair unable to do anything and unable to keep anything in. All I was doing was drinking water.

By the time we arrived at Bloomfield Road I was laid out in the middle of the road as the team coach pulled up. Our popular Scottish coach, John Anderson, approached the fans I was with to ask what was wrong with me. When it was explained to him he took me into the dressing room and I lay on a massage table whilst Len Walker was giving the team talk. I was still there at half-time. With five minutes remaining there was all kinds of commotion going on as the dressing room door was forced open urgently.

Being stretchered in was substitute Clive Day who was concussed. The Blackpool medical man looked at me and said in no uncertain terms, "*Who the hell are you and what are you doing here. Get out now!*" or words to that effect. I think he thought I was some kind of drunk who had managed to make his way into the dressing room. I was manhandled out of the dressing room and told to get lost or something off!!

I always stated that it was the cod in white sauce that caused the damage in the bed and breakfast the night before and nothing to do with those pints of Oranjeboom!!!

Although league form was poor Len Walker had taken the team through an exciting League "Milk" Cup run in the early part of the season. This included exciting victories versus AFC Bournemouth and Brighton and Hove Albion before recording a goalless draw in the third round at Norwich City.

This meant a replay at the Rec where nearly 10,000 saw a non-event in a match that should never have been played, spoiled by heavy fog. City won 4-0 and went on to win the competition. It was the last time such a crowd was ever present at the Rec as future ground grading issues ensured that the capacity was continually lowered. At one stage a stadium that had seen just short of 20,000 people packed in as recently as 1970 was limited to 3,000 for a period of time.

With the arrival of O'Connell and Co in November time a new manager had been brought in to replace Walker. Ron Harris came with a good pedigree, especially as one of the most famous players ever to wear the blue shirt of Chelsea. Unfortunately a lot of the on-field progress was overshadowed by events off the pitch. Since the boardroom shenanigans it had all kicked off behind the scenes by this stage and all kinds of share transactions were taking place. One notable piece of business that Harris completed was the loan arrival of Teddy Sheringham from Millwall.

Not sure if the future England striker mentioned his six-match stay at the Rec in his autobiography and I have to be honest and state that I don't remember his time as an Aldershot player either. We only scored three goals in those six matches and also lost 6-0 at Stockport County!

There were more fun and games at another visit to Scunthorpe United in 1984/85. A Gary Peters goal wasn't enough on the pitch as we lost 2-1 but afterwards a few of us were walking back when we got charged by these Scunthorpe fans in the train station. A few pegged it but a few of us stood our ground.

Startled at this some of the locals turned around and made for a quick exit. One unfortunate soul had committed himself and ran straight into me, Ian Read and another friend and committee member, Dave Brewer. He got more than he bargained for and then banged his head on the pole as he made a retreat. *"F\*\*\* off, tosser"* he was told as reinforcements arrived with a couple of our fans actually crossing the train track to back us up. As I said, we used to look after each other.

I recall being part of a number of Shots supporters that ran on the pitch at the end of a league match at home to Chesterfield. Spireites goalkeeper Chris Marples had decided that, after receiving a torrent of vitriolic abuse during the course of the game, he would respond by gesticulating to those fans expressing interest in him gathered in the North Stand. As soon as the referee blew his final whistle everybody was over the railings in pursuit of Marples, who also doubled up as a county cricketer for Derbyshire. He thought at first it was all light-hearted banter before the realisation set in and he scarpered towards the tunnel and only just made it! God knows what would have happened if we had caught him.

A few weeks before this we entertained Colchester United supporters in The Sportsmans Club. We were due to play them in a football match prior to the main event in the afternoon. The weather put paid to both matches but the United fans had travelled.

We hosted them, provided food and drinks before playing them at pool and darts instead. Imagine how horrified we were to learn that those same fans had then gone over to the Rec and snapped the goal posts in half. It set off an ugly scene in the club and we were pleased to see the back of them thereafter.

Harris, O'Connell and Co. signed off the season with a convincing 5-0 victory at home to Rochdale on a Friday evening. It was pretty common knowledge at the time that it appeared that there would be a further dismantling of the Board of Directors at a forthcoming AGM with Messrs Driver, Potter and Co. set to return after acquiring the required amount of shares at extortionate rates for a takeover. At the time I strongly opposed this along with the Supporters Club Committee and recall leading a demonstration on the pitch at half-time which was supported by the vast majority of the Shots faithful. Alas the takeover was eventually completed. Harris was gone and Len Walker returned with the previous regime taking back control of the football club. I was angry because I didn't think that the O'Connell regime had been given adequate opportunity to succeed and thought that a return to the previous regime was a backward step for the future of the football club. Typical of the way the club communicated to the fans in those days not a mention was made about the takeover in the first match day programme of the 1985/86 season.

Former Chairman Reg Driver with Len Walker and John Anderson behind

If this all wasn't bad enough, August 1985, and a day after we had lost at home to Burnley, proved the end of something special too- a good football career- or a football career anyway.

Playing for the Supporters Club at Ordnance Road just behind the Rec I was running along nowhere near the ball and my right knee just gave way. The whole works- anterior cruciate ligament, cartilage and medial ligament too. I was in agony and couldn't straighten the leg at all. It probably wasn't helped when one of the managers of our opponents on the day forced me to stretch my leg to straighten it. Two weeks inside the Cambridge Military Hospital too. None of the keyhole surgery in and out in one day as you have in current times. It was never the same again and every time I tried to play thereafter the knee just gave way after a couple of matches and I could never play frequently. Did it ruin a promising career? Well, I believe we were in the Aldershot and Farnborough Sunday League Division 6 at the time and I often wonder if I could ever have made it at Division 5 level!!

# The Boy With the Thorn in his Side

I, along with many other Shots fans, was incensed about the boardroom situation and called a meeting along with Ian Read and others. The result of the meeting was the formation of the "Aldershot Action Group". The Sportsmans Club was obviously a no go. I spoke to the landlord of the nearby Volunteer Pub at the time to see if it was possible to meet there. He was happy before a late change of heart on the afternoon of the meeting meant that his venue was out of action too. Eventually we held it in the Cannon Pub, opposite the Rec.

A hostile venue at the best of times, it was absolutely packed on the night and I recall standing on a table in the pub conducting the meeting as a rage-filled 18 year old to talk about how we would oppose the Board of Directors. I remember after the meeting Martin Creasy of the Aldershot News, who had attended, warned me to be careful; it was good advice. However we proceeded with the Action Group and we were certainly not popular within the hierarchy at the Rec.

The first league match of the 1985/86 season was testament to the mess the club was in. The lowest ever opening day attendance, 1,411 versus Exeter City, also saw a programme with few sponsorships sold in any department. It was a messy first few weeks of the season. The home attendance the following month, 1,027 versus Port Vale, was the lowest ever in the history of AFC. The following match versus Scunthorpe United saw an increase of 29! In October Ian Read and I were invited to do a radio interview in Guildford at County Sound Radio to talk about the club's plight and our opposition to the Board of Directors.

After a scathing attack on everything to do with the club on the morning of a home match versus Wrexham the team duly went on to win 6-0. Problem! What problem?

I must confess to causing all kinds of problems though. Helping to graffiti the Rec with typical "Driver Out" or "Sack the Board" slogans to making nuisance calls to Driver at all times of the day or night to get the point across. I lost count of the times I used to nick my mums bed sheets at home and spray can them or the walls with slogans too. I felt particularly bad about all of this many years later because I learned that one of those whose job it was to erase the graffiti from the walls was Richard Aggett, husband of club administrator Rosemary Aggett, who was to become a dear friend of mine and who I class as the bravest lady I have ever known and a stalwart of football in Aldershot.

Many's the time that I and friends would exit "Last Orders" to find the nearest phone box to make the phone calls. It eventually worked against us though. The Aldershot Action Group was gaining momentum and we placed an advert in the Aldershot News with relevant phone numbers included. Low and behold in the middle of the night our home phone buzzed. We were on the receiving end now and this happened regularly over a period of time. Our numbers were in the public domain and it didn't take a rocket scientist to work out who was making the calls. That old adage that I later learned- what goes around comes around- was certainly making its point in this respect. I know what a nuisance I was to Reg Driver and Co. during this period. My name must have been mentioned with plenty of expletives from those that ran the club. In fact I know that it was. It got to the stage where I became so disillusioned with the club that I actually stopped watching some matches for a brief (very brief) period of time. I couldn't handle the lethargic atmosphere, drastic drop in attendances and, above all, lack of communication or appreciation of the situation from the powers that be. I had some friends who watched West Ham United and tagged along with them to some games but I was always so desperate to find out how Aldershot had done after the match that I used to dash to the nearest phone box outside Upton Park (praying that it was working) to make the call to find out the result.

Learning that I had missed a 6-1 victory versus Stockport County was the final curtain for me and I was back for good.

Another protest was held on the final match of the season for the visit of Preston North End. We had asked all fans who opposed the Board of Directors to watch the match from the East Bank. Ian had led this demonstrating with a megaphone outside the turnstiles encouraging fans to do as we asked to make a stance. I can recall making the "Sack the Board" banner and standing behind it on the East Bank with a sizeable crowd behind it. Prior to kick-off I was threatened by a steward that I would be escorted from the ground after dropping a meat pie wrapper on the terraces and not picking it up. He asked and I refused. Mind you it might have done me a favour if I had been escorted. The support for the cause was in good numbers. However Shots won the match comfortably 4-0. By the end there was only the usual suspects standing behind that banner including myself and Ian Read. Most of those loyal at the start had quietly slipped away goal by goal.

Locally-based dentist Colin Hancock had recently become Chairman and was not best pleased by the banner. In fairness to him, though, he had started to communicate with supporters via the programme and looked to be actively interested in bridging the gap.

# Livin' on a Prayer

E ven Hancock, a suave sophisticated character who originated from the east Midlands, could never have predicted his first full season at the helm. 1986/87 will go down as the most successful in the history of Aldershot Football Club and nobody expected it. Few would have believed this possible at the commencement of the campaign either. In total 64 matches were played. Indeed after opening the first three league matches without victory only 1,443 spectators clicked through the Rec turnstiles for the visit of Lincoln City.

A comfortable 4-0 win and a hat-trick from Mike Ring set the tone but promotion was never a serious proposition until the last couple of months of the season. This was primarily due to the introduction of the play-offs. Hancock had already indicated at this stage that the finances of the club were difficult stating in the October programme versus Hartlepool United that *"The financial situation has always been a problem and I am seriously concerned about the ability of the Club to meet its current operational expenses as well as reduce the established debts in the time that our creditors' patience will permit."*

Prior to this Len Walker had steered his side to some tremendous cup success too. After defeating Torquay United and Colchester United in the first two rounds of the FA Cup we were paired with a tie versus top flight Oxford United; the first time a Division One club had visited Aldershot in the competition since Aston Villa in 1964. There was plenty of excitement abounding with fans looking forward to the match until the club put its spanner in the works.

Since the Bradford City disaster in 1985 new safety standards had been set at sports grounds. The club were looking for an increase in its capacity but, in the meantime, had decided to substantially increase the cost of the ticket prices to £11 and £9; during this period it cost £2.80 for normal entry to a Football League match at the Rec- a 300% or so rise! On the same day neighbours Reading were at home to Football League leaders Arsenal and the highest price for a ticket was £7.

The decision caused pandemonium amongst fans with the vast majority opposed to the hike in the prices. I needed no motivation to air my views on the matter and was vehement in my dissent to the situation. I went to town in the local paper advising families to forget the football and *"take your kids to a pantomime in London and get value for your money"*.

Ticket sales were incredibly slow for the all ticket match but the club chose to keep a brave face. Their argument was that if the fixture was away from home it would cost Shots fans the same including the travel and admission prices. What a load of nonsen-se. The point they missed was that this was a great opportunity to galvanise the club with a feel good-factor on and off the pitch. I was adamant that I would not attend. Many said the same. Indeed the actual attendance given at the time was 1,966 although this was later increased to 2,034. Whatever it was it made little difference because at the time it was the lowest ever FA Cup third round attendance in the history of the competition. To me it said it all. However, what had been lost in the equation itself was the actual match. The occasion ended up in being one of the greatest in the history of the club. Aldershot won 3-0 in John Aldridge's last ever match for Oxford before he joined Liverpool. Was I up Redan Hill watching half of the pitch with many other Shots fans? No. I stayed totally away at home in Frimley with my only way of keeping in touch being via Grandstand and Ceefax! I recall seeing Glen Burvill and Colin Smith's names on the score sheet on the television and then the afternoon developing into something spe-cial. Did I feel part of it? No. It remains a big regret that I didn't attend the match. Not because of the principle because I firmly believe that the reasoning for the increase was wrong.

Many years later talking to the players of the time I soon realised that in all the publicity surrounding the day it was the players who missed out. Yes- they were giant killers because of the result but due to the sparse attendance it never really felt the occasion it was for them. I learned that boycotting is all well and good to get a point across but not if it is your own team's players that suffer because of it. There was a lot of division between those who attended and those who didn't. I believe I made the wrong decision.

A "proper" attendance of just under 5,000 was present for the fourth round visit of Barnsley but we missed out on playing Arsenal in the last 16 as the Yorkshire club progressed comprehensively at Oakwell in a replay. Another day off work in vain.

Soon after the FA Cup exploits one of the most sensational outcomes to a football match at the Rec was recorded after a 1-1 draw with Fulham in the southern section quarter-final match ensured that the tie would have to be concluded by a penalty shoot-out. Aldershot eventually won 11-10; a record at the time that was included in the Guinness Book of Records for many a year afterwards. In total there were 28 spot kicks in the shoot-out before Ian McDonald fired the winning kick home. The only problem for me was that I wasn't there. At that time I was working as a barman in the One Oak Pub in Frimley. This made sense really as I was saving a lot more money being behind the bar than in front of it and, as a bonus, customers used to buy you drinks as part of the round!

I was at a tremendous southern area semi-final victory at Swindon Town where we came back from a 2-0 deficit to defeat the Wiltshire side 3-2 amongst chaotic scenes at the end. We scored all three goals in the final 34 minutes of the match after home keeper Fraser Digby had been sent off. It was fair to say that the locals in the 8,450 crowd were less than impressed but I kept my fitness regime up nicely being chased through the car park afterwards. We just about made it back to the car unscathed.

The regional final saw the visit of Bristol City to the Rec for the first match in a two-legged affair. For the first time in our history a visit to Wembley was a possibility and discussed amongst the Rec faithful. I had watched Brentford in 1985 in the final versus Wigan Athletic and knew what it meant for supporters to play at Wembley.

This was in the days when playing at Wembley was at a premium and meant something special to players and fans alike, not as nowadays when they roll out the carpet for the Dog and Duck Cup semi-finals and it actually becomes a chore for followers of some clubs and expensive too.

Joe Jordan's side were due to visit the Rec on Tuesday 7th April 1987 and I had ensured that I swapped shifts at the One Oak to the following night and was all ready for action. Then, due to the heavy rainfall, the match was postponed on the Tuesday and put back 24 hours. I was livid. I couldn't get out of my shift and had no way of finding out how we were getting on. I had to wait until the Frimley-based Shots fans returned to the pub post match to learn that we lost 2-1 in front of a capacity 5,000 gate. I did attend the second leg at Ashton Gate.

We were always on a downer in front of over 16,000 fans where many, by the end of the match, were already congregated on the edge of the pitch waiting to join in the celebrations; we lost 4-1 on aggregate.

The team then went on a decent run of form which included victories versus Swansea City and Halifax Town (both 4-1) and comprehensive away successes at Cambridge United, Burnley and Lincoln City. One trip to Hartlepool United was bizarre. The result was a 1-1 draw.

Indeed all I can recall from it was that central defender Steve Wignall saw the red mist at some stage and must have charged 20 or 30 yards before head-butting a Pools player. He was dismissed and we actually ended the match with nine players. My main recollection was that we made it a weekend. Five of us travelled up by car but didn't stay the Friday night in Hartlepool but in Whitehaven in Cumbria. The reason- we had latched onto an old boy in the One Oak pub called George who lived in the town but had been down a few months previously visiting his family. A lovely feller whose claim to fame was that he had been the "Cumbrian Dominoes Champion". Although he couldn't have been that good because I actually beat him in one game and had never played the game before! In our naivety we thought that a trip across country would take an hour, two at the most. We left our bed and breakfast at 10am on the Saturday morning and eventually arrived on the blustery north east coast ten minutes after the match had started. Over five hours travelling time!

Despite there being 5,000 at the Bristol match the club were forced to make the final few home league matches all-ticket for some spurious reason. All this did was deny necessary income at the time. Aldershot fans have never truly been tuned into all-ticket affairs. Indeed for a run-of-the-mill league game many people wait until the actual day of the match and weigh up the weather and other considerations before making the decision to attend or not. The all-ticket stamp denied them that choice.

As a result the attendances were lower than they otherwise would have been. However that didn't stop Len and his side pulling out all the stops. Despite a last day defeat at home to Cardiff City we had made it into the first ever play-offs.

These were exciting times especially as we had an abundance of experience in our squad including the likes of former Everton midfielder Andy King, former West Ham United winger Bobby Barnes added to the likes of McDonald and Wignall.

# Nothing's Gonna Stop us Now

Pre Wembley finals, both play-off matches were played on a two legged basis. They also included the fourth from bottom team from the division above; a factor I liked but only lasted a matter of seasons before it was deemed that all the play-off teams should be from the same division. On this occasion Bolton Wanderers were that side.

Gary Johnson netted for the Shots in the home leg on a Thursday evening in May to set up a return at Burnden Park. Walker was forced to make a host of changes with key players unavailable due to injury. However a truly heroic performance from the Aldershot side with goals from Glen Burvill and Darren Anderson ensured a 2-2 draw and we had made it to the final where the famous Wolverhampton Wanderers were the opponents.

There were only five days from the Bolton match to the first leg of the final at the Rec which was played on Friday 22nd May. I ensured that I was off work that night from the One Oak.

I may have missed Bristol City but nothing was going to stand in the way of this match.

I worked at the pub with Paul Lawrence, he of Hereford hitchhiking fame. The landlord of the pub, a guy called Ian Heggie, had said to Paul that he couldn't take the time off for the Wolves match. Paul pleaded with him but there was no change of view. I thought the Ian was being unreasonable and needed to assess the bigger picture. We spoke about the matter and I told him of how much this match meant to any Aldershot fan let alone Paul and I who travelled the length and breadth of the country in pursuit of our team.

Ian had a think about things and approached me on my next shift me to see if I could get a ticket for the match. I presumed that it was for Paul and that he was going to surprise him when he turned up for work on the Friday. I bought the ticket and said no more. I was flabbergasted when I eventually learned that the landlord had the audacity to attend the match himself leaving Paul on his own in the pub. He had never been within a million miles near the Rec and had no interest in Aldershot Football Club, apart from when we were the butt of the jokes. Upon his arrival at the pub Paul duly walked out of his job never to return! I would have done the same.

The Rec was packed on the night. Another capacity crowd and it was all a bonus really. Few expected a return from Graham Turner's men; the same Turner who was Player/Manager of Shrewsbury Town just eight years previously on the most agonising night a Shots fan could experience. Turner had the strike partnership of Steve Bull and Andy Mutch at his disposal and a vociferous group of supporters desperate for a return of the glory days of decades gone by.

The conditions couldn't have been any wetter on a ghastly Friday evening in north east Hampshire. The tight surroundings of the Rec just didn't suit Turner's men and goals from Ian McDonald and Bobby Barnes gave Aldershot a shock 2-0 lead to take to Molineux on the Bank Holiday Monday.

Shots took 2,000 fans to the Black Country and I can remember the feeling of expectation travelling in one of the large convoy of coaches. The atmosphere was tense and intimidating with just under 20,000 present at a decrepit old stadium that had clearly seen better days. I wasn't too sure where those fans came from either.

When Wolves entertained us in league action earlier in the season just 3,357 creaked around the famous old stadium. Indeed most of the ground was unsafe including a full side and behind one of the goals, all closed off. Those that were there though made some noise and we were under the cosh for the majority of the first half but still held the lead.

Even with 10 minutes remaining you felt that if Wolves managed one then they would go on and win the match. However it didn't happen and Barnes even had the cheek to net a late winner for Walker's men.

Aldershot were promoted for just the second time in their history. It took an age to get out of Wolverhampton as the home supporters had aired their dissatisfaction with proceedings with just about anybody they crossed. It was particularly unpleasant and we were kept in for over an hour before everything was cleared. However cue the celebrations.

Upon returning to Aldershot players and fans mixed all along the High Street and by the pubs. Aldershot was overgrown with pubs in those days unlike the barren and sparse dwellings of the current time. On this night they were packed. My only regret of the day was refusing to enter The Sportsmans Club. I had not been welcome in the establishment for a period of time due to disagreements with the management. They issued an olive branch on the night and I refused. Petty minded of me really. Mainly due to the fact too that it was probably the only place in town that would have a "Late One" with the police insistent of spoiling the party by ensuring all the drinking houses were emptied on time.

However the achievements of Len Walker and his staff should never be underestimated. Len came in for plenty of "stick" at times and, when I reflect on matters, they were totally uncalled for. Don't get me wrong, I am no innocent party in all of this. I used to be heavily involved in some of the chanting and totally regret this. Len's stock as manager has grown stronger with each passing year. Knowing what I know now about what he had to endure I appreciate how well he did as a boss. Every year he had to bring a player in for peanuts and sell them off for a considerable sum just to keep the club afloat. From Steve Claridge, Bobby Barnes, Tony Lange, Martin Foyle, Adrian Randall, the list is endless. He managed to achieve this.Len was badly treated towards the end of his reign at the club which followed a couple of years later. He deserved better.

I have got to know Len better in more recent times than I ever did when he was manager. I remember sitting on a table with him at a function at the Lakeside Country Club a number of years ago and I apologised to him for some of the actions I took in my youth. He is a good man and was an excellent manager. There was a time when he deserved an opportunity for a fresh challenge when the situation he faced became intolerable. It must have been a massive frustration not knowing if your players were going to be paid or not at the end of each month but he worked through it despite the consistent choruses of discontent from fans who, at the time, were unaware of the full picture. Of course there were occasions when it wasn't so great. I remember a painful 6-1 home defeat versus Darlington in the early 80s followed by a turgid home loss to Hartlepool the following Saturday but, hey, that is football and I believe that the board of the time deserve praise for not caving in to the calls for Len's head. It was the right call.

I'm not sure even Sir Alex Ferguson could have coped with the nonsense that went on in the final years of AFC. Aldershot Football Club was promoted just twice in its 65-year history.

Len Walker captained the first team in 1972/73 missing just one match that season and managed the team the second time around. He was involved in around 1,000 matches as player and manager. He deserves his place in folklore. Len could have been helped throughout his tenure, like so many at the time, if the club had been able to communicate better. It used to bug the life out of me that many years later when I was secretary of Aldershot Town FC that Len, no longer in full-time employment within the game, would deliver the match programmes to the Rec earning a few bob as a delivery driver having been involved for over 20 years as a player, coach and manager of Aldershot Football Club. His knowledge and expertise deserved better.

# True Faith

The start of the following season (1987/88) was typical of the frustrations the football club faced with "red tape". The euphoria of looking forward to third tier football for just the fourth season in its 61-year history was dampened by necessary ground improvements. This meant that the opening home match of the season versus Mansfield Town was postponed after Hampshire County Council had withdrawn the required certificate as some of the safety works had not been completed to their satisfaction. In fairness to the club it had been forced to make some huge structural changes to the stadium costing an excessive six-figure sum. This included the installation of ridiculous fencing behind the East Bank and part of the North Stand to keep supporters off the pitch. The club never wanted this in the first place. Many years later as the "Phoenix" club we ended up having to pay a considerable amount to have the fencing removed. The club had also moved Saturday kick-off times to 3.15pm as *"The Football League have been concerned about kick-offs being delayed because of the late arrival of spectators"* they said. I didn't think this would be a problem at the Rec and it wasn't!

When the action did commence the first half of the season was a whirlwind. Victories were recorded on travels to Fulham, Preston North End and a rare success at Southend United coupled with convincing home victories versus Brentford and Bristol City.

Of particular annoyance to me was missing the first time visit to Sunderland for a league encounter in October due to my own pub job. I could get out of most but, alas, not this one.

The club's relationship with the Supporters Club had smoothed somewhat and we were back operating within the stadium by this time. I was the Press and Public Relations Officer before moving on to become Secretary. There was a succession of Chairmen with Derek Bayly, Bill Warren and later Ian Read. The club still had contentious issues however in the public domain and soon after an embarrassing FA Cup exit at Sutton United (a performance hailed by boss Walker as "pathetic") it banned the local newspaper, The Aldershot News and Mail.

The Christmas period was one of triumph and a belief that the side was capable of achieving more. A Boxing Day defeat up the road at Brentford was soon forgotten two days later when Keith Peacock's Gillingham were mauled 6-0 at the Rec. We were 5-0 in front at the interval and were invincible on the day. The win cost the affable Peacock his job. New Years' Day saw another convincing win, 3-0 versus Bristol Rovers, and the following day an honourable draw was achieved at Brighton and Hove Albion's Goldstone Ground.

Aldershot were in the top half of Division 3 but that was as good as it got. I was in the Railway Arms in Frimley after returning from Brighton and in walked in the Board of Directors including Driver and Hancock. I know now that the Board was in conflict at this stage. There were some who knew that with an injection of two or three players there was a possibility the club could compete for the play-offs. However the majority view was that this could not be afforded.

Whatever the truth of the matter was from this period onwards Aldershot Football Club declined rapidly and never recovered. The remainder of the 1987/88 season saw just four victories recorded in 22 matches. Included in this was a major highlight as Sunderland were defeated 3-2 at the Rec in front of 6,042 spectators.

Just before the Sunderland match I recall losing it totally in a league match at Gillingham. To be honest it was never a venue I particularly looked forward to going to. We were 1-0 up and looking good for a "double". However in the space of the last six minutes we had two players in Paul Roberts and David Barnes sent off, a controversial penalty awarded against us before conceding a winner for The Gills in the fifth minute of injury time. The referee, Harrow headmaster David Elleray, needed a police escort off the pitch. Not one of my favourites if I am being honest but his autobiography was good although this match was never mentioned!

It was looking bleak as we entered the last month of the season until successive 3-0 home victories versus Mansfield Town and Port Vale. We were five points clear of danger with just three matches remaining; two of those away at fellow relegation threatened sides. I recall waiting for the team coach to arrive at Rotherham United's Millmoor Stadium on the penultimate Saturday of the campaign. When the players disembarked many of them sprinted over to the local bookies opposite. This struck an uncertain note with me and, sure enough, we lost the match 1-0. Victory would have secured safety.

A goalless draw at home to Preston North End two days later on the May Bank Holiday meant that our destiny would go to the last day of the season at Grimsby Town. It was simple- if the Mariners won the match then they were safe and we would be in the scrap for the play-offs. Any other result and we would be ok. We managed to get to Lincolnshire, a full car in my yellow Fiat 128! It was an intimidating atmosphere at Blundell Park but Tommy Langley gave us an early lead. It was all square at the interval and we were holding our own pretty well. Then for some inexplicable reason our substitute, Paul Roberts, hauled down a Grimsby player just minutes after replacing Ian McDonald. It was a certain penalty.

Fortunately we had the ever-dependable Tony Lange between the sticks and he managed to save the spot kick from Marc North. It was a fraught final few minutes but we eventually crossed the line. There was some nervy times after the match as the home fans tried to wrestle down the perimeter fence that separated the visiting supporters from the pitch. We didn't care. We were safe and another season of third tier football beckoned.

# The Only Way is Up

Those of us who had more intrinsic knowledge of the club knew that the jigsaw was falling apart. There was more movement in the boardroom with local businessman Terry Lewis taking over as Chairman and Reg Driver becoming Managing Director/Secretary before being ousted at an EGM held in November 1988. I thought this was a good move at the time.

Years later when I got to know more about how a football club functions first-hand I realised that it was the worst possible move. You need continuity and familiarity. Although not a favourite on the terraces Reg was well-respected within the local community, Rushmoor Borough Council and at the Football League where he was a huge influence.

Attendances were cut in half and when we did eventually record our first win of the season at the seventh attempt only 1,527 people witnessed the win at home to Wigan Athletic. A Steve Claridge goal saw off Sheffield United in November but it was all a touch painful by then.

The best memories of these days was of our own Supporters Club team which was reasonably successful. We originally set this version up in 1984 after a group of us became friendly with our counterparts from Doncaster Rovers who were led by a terrific friend called Paul Mayfield. We used to travel to south Yorkshire for weekends that coincided with the first teams playing and we used to have plenty of fun. Weekends in Doncaster were not for the faint-hearted mind and we used to experience all kind of scrapes. Good memories though! We went on to play many other teams, Fulham and Darlington spring to mind, but we also entered a team in the local Aldershot and Farnborough District Sunday Leagues. I was the Secretary of the team and got to quickly learn the trials and tribulations of such a role with the local league authorities quick to come down on me if something was untoward- not phoning in a result on time or not returning a cup won the previous season. I used to sweat if I knew that I needed to contact the League Secretary for any reason knowing that I would be on the receiving end of some verbal exchanges.

There were some benefits though. Alan Edmunds, who I referred to earlier from our Tranmere trip in 1984, was a local referee- not a great one either. He only did it to pick up a few quid at the weekend. Many's the time he would be in charge and if I had given him too much verbal he would threaten to send me off. I would just remind him that I was also responsible for paying the match official and if he did so he wouldn't be getting his money!

With events on the pitch grim enough it appeared that the powers that be in government were becoming destined to make entry into football matches as hard as possible too. Don't get me wrong it wasn't a great period for football with hooliganism remaining evident added to the disasters at Bradford and Heysel just a few years previously. However Luton Town Chairman and Conservative MP David Evans had stated publicly that it was time that football fans changed their habits and started to arrive well in advance at matches like they did at Drury Lane or the Royal Albert Hall.

A man obviously not tuned in to standing on a cold uncovered terrace in winter, he was behind a proposal to introduce a Membership ID Card "Football Spectators Bill" for all supporters that was put forward by the Minister for Sport at the time, Colin Moynihan. I was vehemently opposed to it as were 92% of Shots supporters and the vast majority of fans across the land. What was more alarming is that a third of our fans were adamant that they would stop watching football if the bill was passed. I, along with committee member Barry Underwood, initiated a dossier representing the views of Shots supporters that was sent to Moynihan, Evans and all local MPs including our own, Julian Critchley in Aldershot. The irony of it all was that there were more arrests in percentage at horse racing meetings than at football matches.

The bill was eventually passed but never introduced due to a later football tragedy and subsequent report. In fairness to Critchley he actually abstained from the vote but never responded to my invitation for him to be the guest of the Supporters Club at a match to learn more about the experiences of being a lower league football supporter. The other six local MPs voted in favour; none of them had ventured into the Rec though.

I touched on the subject in my programme notes of Saturday 15th April 1989 when league leaders Wolverhampton Wanderers were the visitors. It is ironic that I wrote *"The vast majority of you have never felt threatened or unsafe at The Rec and feel that Aldershot Football Club have done more than should have been necessary in safety measures around the ground. Many supporters feel that the fences in the East Bank and surrounding areas were not required. It must be stressed though that Aldershot FC were forced to implement these measures and it was not out of choice"*.

Later that very afternoon we were to learn of the biggest disaster in the history of English football when 96 supporters lost their lives at the FA Cup semi-final between Liverpool and Nottingham Forest at Hillsborough. Pre social media days, I was told that there was a problem during the match whilst we were watching Wolves continue their successful season with a 2-1 victory including a goal from Steve Bull. It was only when I got home that the full impact of what happened was realised. It is criminal that a generation on we are only now finding out the full truths and facts about what really happened.

Every programme viewed, every family account, it was a truly shocking sequence of events and I hope that those families that have dedicated their lives to prove what actually occurred receive the full justice their efforts deserve. I hated at the time that some sections of the media had provided some pretty distasteful stories without factual evidence. "Tabloid Trash" I called it and that is exactly what it was. An awful, awful day not just for football but for society in general where power and greed covered up truth and reality.

Matters on the pitch for Aldershot had not improved either and we couldn't even put one over on our traditional rivals on

Easter Monday when a last-gasp late injury time penalty from Stuart Beavon earned Reading a draw at the Rec.

As the season petered out to certain relegation the financial difficulties became ever more apparent. Items were being removed from the Recreation Ground headquarters to satisfy creditors and the club needed money and fast. As a Supporters Club we supported the newly-formed "Save Our Shots" fundraising scheme initiated by Terry Owens, the director who had been part of the brief O'Connell regime.

# Don't want to Lose You

The start of the 1989/90 season was bad enough. I had written off my beloved Fiat 128 in a pretty horrific crash in Feltham. I was eventually able to replace it with a Renault 19 which was the biggest piece of junk I ever encountered. So bad that it eventually broke down prior to a pre-season friendly with Lou Macari's West Ham United. Not only was I without a car I had missed a pretty good match against decent opposition. The season didn't get any better either.

The club was put into administration just before it started. That dreaded word- ADMINISTRATION- I despise it. Colin Hancock, by this time, was actually the only director and had helped to steer the club through murky waters, paying the wages himself. He had shown his own commitment to the cause and we backed him. Colin had explained that at one stage it nearly ceased to exist during the summer of 1989.

Considering the off-field difficulties the team fared reasonably well during the first part of the campaign. Steve Claridge and Dave Puckett were pretty formidable as a strike partnership too.

Presenting a Player of the Month Award to goalkeeper David Coles during the 1989/90 season with Colin Hancock (left) and Dave Brewer

We drew Sheffield Wednesday in the League Cup second round. It felt a touch eerie being in the away stand at the Leppings Lane end at Hillsborough just above where the disaster occurred six months earlier. We earned a goalless draw but the hope and anticipation soon evaporated when we lost the replay 8-0.

The second part of the campaign was a disaster and we slipped down the table at an alarming pace. This was in conjunction with losing six of the last seven matches 2-0 and losing 15 times since an awful 5-1 reverse at Maidstone United on New Year's Day. I started to become frustrated with proceedings and continued to question the players' performances in my programme notes.

I stated in an article versus York City in March 1990 that the players weren't putting in 100% to the cause and not appreciating the fans. I said, "*Why was Chris Powell, yet again, the only player to come over and acknowledge the Aldershot supporters at the end of last Saturday's game at Colchester.*

"*Supporters travelled by coach, rail and car, spending up to £10 to get to the game. Hard earned cash and no sign of appreciation by most of the players.*

"*Anyway, thanks for the acknowledgement Chris- we do appreciate it and maybe next time the other 10 might have the courtesy to express their gratitude. Support is dwindling as it is, you don't want it to dwindle any further.*" As it happened Powell, who returned to the Rec many years later as manager of Charlton Athletic, is one of the best ever loan players to wear the red and blue.

This even led to Chairman Hancock putting an article in the following programme expressing how unhelpful criticism of the team and manager was. I am certain this was a follow-up to my previous article. I was on a rant by this stage. I had plenty of sympathy for Hancock though who I truly believe was hung out to dry really because he was provided with little or no support from elsewhere.

I transferred my aggression from the pitch to the "local suits" for my notes in the penultimate programme versus Maidstone United as the club's situation was now extremely perilous. "*Colin obviously has no further available cash injections to plough in; understandable as well, when he has received no support or back-up from the local council and the local "prosperous" businessmen. Yes they know who I mean. I'm talking about all the wealthy "suit brigade" who attend all shareholders' meetings talking about how much wealth they have and using our club as a political football. Well chaps, yes the ones who have done all the talking at these meetings over the past six years of bickering, it's time to put your money where your mouth is. I've been at these shareholders' meetings over the past few years and have been very disillusioned at the accusations, finger pointing etc by people who I'm not totally convinced even attend the football and at the end of the day that is what it is all about. I'm not finished yet. What about all the flash cars we see entering the Rec on a home game day? You know the private number plates attached to Rollers and Mercs. Yes, the number plates which probably cost more than my own car. Do they really care about the club as they drink at the club's expense in the Directors' Lounge or are they just present for a free booze-up"?* I raged. There were no takers. Perhaps those it applied to hadn't read their programme- or, indeed, hadn't even purchased one!

Whilst public meetings were being held to try to secure the future of the football club I had a further dilemma on the pitch. At least we had secured our Football League status by seven points with Colchester United slipping into the Conference. We would have required an application for re-election had the old method still been in place. My problem on the pitch stemmed from the end of season Player of the Season Awards which were being held in the Sportsmans Club on the evening of our final match of the campaign versus Cambridge United. I had contacted Len Walker to request the presence of the players.

He responded stating that it was pretty unlikely considering the criticism that had emanated towards them during the season, particularly from me. He provided me with the opportunity to ask them in person.

I was taken down to the dressing room with much trepidation knowing that I could be in for a rough ride from some of the lads. Len introduced me and outlined who I was. I looked at the players and there were some "daggers" looking at me in return.

When Len gave me the floor I explained about the presentation evening and the importance of the players attending the function.

One or two laughed whilst big burly centre half Darren Anderson responded directly to me loudly- "F\*\*\* off you C\*\*\*". I responded to him immediately- "*I take that as a no then*" and left the room pretty swiftly. In fairness a few of the players did appear on the night but there was one further problem. Steve Claridge had left the club in February and was appearing against us that afternoon for his new team. Some of the players had expressed concern that he was going to win the award bearing in mind that he had been gone three months. They told me they wouldn't be happy if this was going to be the case.

During the game itself I remember behaving like an idiot in the North Stand as our winger Ian Stewart was sent off, clambering onto the perimeter fence, shouting all kinds of abuse before turning around and looking at my 14-year-old cousin Stuart Harris who I had taken to the match. He looked at me and must have been thinking "*What planet are you living on?*"

Claridge actually did win the runner-up award with Dave Puckett picking up the main honour. Third placed Adrian Randall wasn't present to receive his award. "*I'm not sure I will be able to get there. Do I have to go?*" he asked me. I was a bit concerned at this considering that he had been playing for the first team in the afternoon and the Sportsmans Club was directly opposite the entrance to the stadium. I don't recall Anderson being present either which was probably beneficial to me.

# The King of Wishful Thinking

T he seriousness of the club's financial situation had reached alarming proportions during the summer of 1990. Indeed there were times when the likelihood of starting the following season was bleak. Just prior to the Cambridge match a public meeting had raised some funds to keep the club afloat with a pressing £120,000 Inland Revenue debt requiring settlement.

There were some big hitters at the meeting including many of those that had been on the Board of Directors over the previous decade. Attended by over 500 people at the Royal Aldershot Officers Club £44,000 was raised immediately.

Representing the Supporters Club at the time I said, "*It's near enough begging but it's got to be done*". It did, however, need much more than this. The Sportsmans Club was closed as the club was unable to pay the brewery and time was running out.

A succession of possible consortiums or my favourite saying during these dark days, "*There is an interested party*" came and went without the sniff of any parting wedge.

The Aldershot News actually broke the news at the start of August 1990 that the club had folded with a heading "*ALDERSHOT FOOTBALL CLUB BORN 1926 DIED 1990*".

At this stage Colin Hancock was in last-gasp talks and the season was just three weeks away. Then it came- the saviour of Aldershot Football Club- a 19-year-old property developer called Spencer Trethewy. It was reported that he would be putting in an initial £100,000 followed by £60,000. The winding-up order was cancelled and the club was back in business.

A celebration match versus AFC Bournemouth was arranged at short notice and Trethewy and his fellow new Directors were lauded to an appreciative crowd. We may have lost the match, heavily if I recall rightly, but it didn't matter because we still had a football club. Trethewy wrote in his programme notes for the opening home match of the season versus Scunthorpe United, *"I am confident that with your support the club will never be in the same situation again, that the team will reach the target I have set them and do not accept second best. I honestly believe that Aldershot Football Club has a great future"*.

We were all told that the big debts had been cleared and the future was rosy. It was a difficult opening to the season which was to be expected due to the uncertainty of the summer months. Experimental Friday night football was proving a success though and it meant that you always saw the Aldershot goals on the following day's popular "Saint and Greavsie" show.

Trethewy, an alleged teenage tycoon, received international headlines and even appeared on the nation's most popular talk show of the time hosted by Terry Wogan on BBC1. He swanned around in flash motors and certainly enjoyed the publicity. To be honest I couldn't have cared less at the time. He could do whatever he pleased if he was going to stump up the funds to keep the club I supported afloat. The first time I met him was the only time I had any official dealings with him. He attended a Supporters Club AGM and I met him to walk him around to where we had the meeting in the Vice Presidents Club behind the South Stand. It felt strange. I welcomed this lad who was five years younger than me and had arrived in a stretch limo. It was all surreal but I never had any suspicions that something wasn't right though.

Then came the bombshell in November- Trethewy was exposed by the News of the World as a fraud, reportedly owing money to a variety of outlets. It also stated that he had not invested any of his own money into the football club. The instalments paid to the club had been loaned to him by Club Doctor Alan Gillespie and long-standing supporter John McGinty. Trethewy was suspended as a Director by Hancock and eventually was gone. The bleak times were back at the Rec and the club became a bit of a laughing stock.

I felt sorry for Colin Hancock regarding this matter. He had put his trust in Trethewy and it is easy for people to ask many years later why hadn't due diligence been provided on him but from Colin's point of view the club needed funds and needed it pretty damn quick. I am sure I would have done the same in his position.

As far as I am concerned Spencer Trethewy's intervention kept the club afloat for another 20 months or so. He caused me no ill and I never really got to know him.

That said, I cannot take him seriously as the destruction and deceit he caused for close friends to me, especially John McGinty, leaves an especially sour taste in my mouth and certainly did for John and his family. We all make mistakes but boy this was a huge one which damaged trust and integrity. Spencer later became manager/owner of Farnborough Football Club and changed his surname to "Day". We sadly lost John in 2009. I wonder what he would have made of it all. I don't need to wonder though- I know. Trethewy ended up in prison in for multiple charges of deception in 1994.

At the time John said "*It was all fantasy. He lived in a fantasy world. He was a con- King Kong. He hadn't lived enough to be what he said he was*".

# Praying for Time

At least I had seen us finally beat our old adversaries Reading for the first time during this period, albeit a 3-1 win in the Leyland Daf Trophy. This was also three weeks after witnessing one of the worst nights ever experienced as a Shots fan- a 10-1 reverse away to Southend United in the same competition. That made it 24 goals conceded against the Essex club in two seasons and five matches. I was furious and made my feelings known by the tunnel at half-time. I think it was our striker Charlie Henry who received the worst of my vitriol only for the fact that he was the nearest player to the tunnel. Only later was I made aware that, again, the players had not been paid.

We lost our Boxing Day match bizarrely to the weather, against Darlington, as the Rec was flooded due to a downpour on the morning of the match- Elleray was due to be in charge of this one again. I said in the programme notes at the time, *"Welcome to our close rivals for this traditional local derby. Who arranges these fixtures? Another gem from the Football League"*. In addition to the aborted Darlington match the players were due to spend their New Year's Day at Carlisle United. On the proposed Darlington day I do, however, remember being in our "Radio Shots" building which was the headquarters of the Supporters Club on match days. An elderly gentleman approached me and asked why the match had been called off and I explained to him. He said it was a shame because he only ever got to see the Shots over the Christmas period and always looked forward to it. He told me that he was a former player. I asked his name and he replied – Stan Cullis. It didn't really click with me at the time but I had been speaking to one of the most famous footballing icons of his generation. Stan is sadly no longer with us but has a stand named after him at Wolverhampton Wanderers for whom he made 152 appearances. It would have been far more had the Second World War not intervened. Stan also spent 16 years as manager during their most successful period. He was an England international but importantly he also played for Aldershot during the war years. He wanted no fuss, just came along to watch the match from the stands. It was probably indicative of the gentlemen who played football during that era.

There was some good fortune on the pitch in early 1991 when progress in the FA Cup versus Tiverton Town and Maidstone United paired us with a home FA Cup tie versus West Ham United in the third round. Due to ongoing safety concerns with the Rec the match was switched to Upton Park; this would never be allowed nowadays of course. The financial benefits were huge and the incentives for Len Walker's side immense. It also avoided the potential for controversy as the club would have been forced into considering increasing the admission prices a la Oxford in 1987.

From my point of view I was pretty excited about the match too. I worked for an insurance brokers, Leslie and Godwin, in Aldgate on the edge of the City of London. There were a few "Hammers" fans in the office. I was ribbed something rotten and they all thought that it would be a goal fest.

They also thought Aldershot was "out in the sticks" and living in Hampshire we were all "carrot crunchers".

We took 3,500 fans to east London and made a huge noise in a near 24,000 attendance. We congregated in the Hole in the Wall pub outside Waterloo Station in the build-up to the match. All I remember from that is the atmosphere in the pub suddenly turning nasty. All of a sudden a fight broke out involving other Shots supporters. Our group wasn't involved but got separated as the mood became untidy and volatile. I remember watching those fighting and my brother getting forced into a corner, trying to escape those wanting to use their fists. The red mist hit me and I charged through the centre of where those who were fighting were gathered to allow my brother the space to escape the nonsense. We didn't hang about too long afterwards. Never a dull moment. The players did us proud too and we earned a 0-0 draw. I enjoyed venturing into work on the Monday morning and was probably early for a change. What the draw also did was earn a replay which would also be held at West Ham as we were originally the home team. It wasn't so good the second time around and we lost 6-1 but a six-figure return should have been good for the club.

In between the two West Ham matches we had a league match at Scunthorpe United. I was driving on this occasion and we were pushed for time as we arrived at the new Glanford Park stadium. We were looking for a pub and thought that the new complex would provide a hostelry. We were met by a steward at the stadium car park. He told me that I couldn't go through as I had no pass. I replied stating that I was a player and late for the team talk and that I would be fined if I didn't get there pretty quickly. He sympathised and let us all through in my car. We soon learned that there was nowhere for visiting supporters to get a drink. We decided to drive back out and find a local pub. There was surprise on the steward's face as he saw my car driving towards him again. I wound down my window and just said, *"It's alright mate, I've been dropped from the team"*.

The team continued to struggle on the pitch. We were 4-0 down at home to Hartlepool within half an hour and eventually lost 5-1. In March Colin Hancock ended his tenure with the club handing over the Chairmanship to Colchester-based businessman Mike Gill-Anderson.

Understandably Hancock needed to spend more time on his business affairs that had been adversely affected. In truth he could do no more.

It was no better for me either. I developed a bout of glandular fever and, importantly, couldn't take my future wife, The Good Lady, on our first date- taking her to Heathrow Airport as she headed home to Glasgow for her birthday weekend. She thought I was pulling a fly one and wasn't actually interested in her. Also of huge consequence at the time was the fact that I couldn't make the away match at Peterborough United either on Easter Saturday. A defeat at London Road followed by a 5-0 reverse at Torquay United on Easter Monday made for a pretty miserable holiday period.

After eight successive defeats there was a change in management as Aldershot were bottom of the Football League.

After over 20 years of service in a variety of capacities Len Walker was replaced as manager by former England international Brian Talbot. Three victories in the final nine matches meant that we finished one point above bottom side Wrexham. However there was no relegation from the Football League this season which was handy.

# Wind of Change

Aldershot entered what would result in their final ever season in the Football League with a visit to Turf Moor but for the tenth away match in a row defeat was incurred with a 2-0 reverse versus Burnley. The defeat pretty much summed up the season though. I cannot begin to explain the desolation being an Aldershot Football Club supporter provided during those dark days.

At the start of 1991/92 I was elected as Chairman of the Supporters Club. At this time I had no inclination of what this responsibility was to consist of. Gill-Anderson had added to his board of directors with the addition of Aldershot-born businessman Trevor Gladwell as his Vice Chairman alongside a couple of other directors.

At the AGM where I was elected as Chairman we invited Gill-Anderson, Talbot, Secretary Steve Birley and the experienced former Wolverhampton Wanderers defender George Berry to the meeting. The usual spiel that I became accustomed to over the years was spurted out- *"new stadium on the horizon and an assurance that all outstanding debts would be paid."* blah blah blah! What I have learned in football is that the current regime always blames the previous one for its problems. Anderson did state on the night, however, that Aldershot were actually in a better position than most third and fourth division clubs. As usual my committee and I believed the best in Gill-Anderson and, in fairness, we had no reason to doubt his integrity at the time. How wrong we were all to be.

At 66-1, alongside Halifax Town, to win the division we knew it would be a tough ordeal from the outset but Talbot had quietly appeared to have manoeuvred well in the transfer market bringing in a great deal of experience with the likes of Keith Bertschin and even Frank Stapleton (who played one match) into the squad alongside Berry.

Indeed Stapleton featured at Wrexham in a 0-0 draw in north Wales in mid-September time. The word was out that he had played and three days later Halifax Town visited the Rec for another Friday evening experiment. Stapleton was expected to play and an additional 600 supporters came through the turnstiles to witness the appearance of the former Manchester United and Arsenal legend in a Shots shirt. The only problem was that he didn't appear due to personal reasons. He never wore the famous red and blue shirt again!

Indeed the only fact I recall from the Halifax match is that we were robbed and the name of referee Ray Biggar became an even bigger talking point after an evening that saw the dismissal of goalkeeper John Granville followed by Charlie Henry.

I started blaming all and sundry in the following programme notes after the 3-1 reverse and also asked the management for an explanation as I wasn't convinced the players had been "putting it in" for 90 minutes although I do recall that both sending offs were farcical. I concluded, *"Let us hope that Friday 20th was the last black Friday"*. I couldn't have been more wrong.

Around this time I travelled around Europe by train with friends and missed some matches. The most notable recollection of this period was being in Prague on the day we were away at Chesterfield. I had one of those old transistor radios with me. We were standing on the terraces of Sparta Prague who were entertaining Slovan Bratislava.

After signing autographs for all the locals due to the fact that my mate was wearing his Arsenal shirt we stood behind the home terrace and I was fiddling about with my radio trying to see if I could get any English stations to find out how the Shots were getting on. I hated not knowing what was going on if I wasn't there. All of a sudden I managed to tune into the BBC World Service and the first words I heard were, *"News of a goal at Saltergate. Chesterfield 0-1 Aldershot. Dave Puckett the scorer for the Shots"*. I went mental and all the locals turned around to look at me and must have been thinking, who on earth is this clown! Reception of the station was then lost and only picked up again standing on Charles Bridge overlooking the Vltava River a couple of hours later. Catching up with excitement I waited for the late James Alexander Gordon to read the full results. James' legendary tone ensured that as soon as the first team score was announced you knew the rest. There it was Chesterfield 2 and I knew we had lost…Aldershot 1. The day was spoilt!

By the time I returned to England it was noticeably all falling apart. Only two victories had been recorded in the 18 matches prior to the visit of non-league Enfield to the Rec in the FA Cup first round and the first signs of a rift in the Boardroom were detected when Gill-Anderson threatened to resign. Funds were so tight that Birley, who hailed from Devon, was sleeping in his own office to save the pennies. The players had started to travel to away matches by car instead of on a team coach.

The signs were becoming ominous. Just prior to the visit of Blackpool, and a 5-2 home reverse, Gill-Anderson was ousted as Chairman by the Board of Directors in a vote of no confidence and replaced by Gladwell. I was angered by this as just a month previously all appeared to be well in the Boardroom after Gill-Anderson and Gladwell had showed a united front at our Supporters Club AGM. Gill-Anderson, however, remained as a director although appeared to have disappeared off the face of the earth.

The defeat versus Blackpool led to manager Talbot threatening to put his players "on the dole" as 12 of the squad's contracts were due to expire at the end of the season. Whatever his thoughts on the long-term future the short-term was priority and Enfield had to be beaten in the FA Cup.

It was a competition that had mixed experiences for Talbot. He had won the tournament in 1978 and 79 with Ipswich Town and Arsenal but the previous season whilst in charge at West Bromwich Albion he had seen his side capitulate 4-2 at home to non-league Woking at The Hawthorns. Former West Ham United defender Paul Brush scored the only goal of the game to give Enfield a shock victory in a match that saw Graham Westley feature for the Middlesex side- more about him later! A successful cup run was essential. Chairman Gladwell stated after the match that the club owed £92,000 to the Inland Revenue.

It was too much for Talbot, an honourable man, who worked exceedingly hard to try to turn the fortunes of the club around but was always on a loser to be honest. There was far too much damage to repair. His style of football wasn't met with universal acclaim by the Shots fans but he worked with what he had.

He went on to successful times at Rushden and Diamonds leading the club into the Football League but I am sure he saw that the writing was on the wall as soon as the Enfield match ended. A former Chairman of the PFA he had had enough and duly walked away from the club with a parting shot, *"Fans have got to realise the situation here. It is very serious."*

The popular loyal clubman Ian McDonald was given the arduous role of "Caretaker Manager" assisted by Steve Wignall. By now the funds had run out and nobody was getting paid. A near impossible task but all the emphasis was on activity off the pitch at this stage.

Former Chairman Hancock offered support alongside some of the ex directors including Bob Potter and Reg Driver. Gladwell attended a meeting of concerned supporters in the Sportsmans Club and told those present that he could not guarantee the future of the club and that the bickering in the Boardroom was becoming too much to deal with. Writs were flying all over the place and, as usual, when money becomes involved, people became protective, unstable and, eventually, unreasonable.

A supposed deal with Cambridge United was done for the club to recoup just £25,000 for the deal with Steve Claridge instead of the huge sell on fee they would have received if the former striker was sold on later down the line.

A deal was also done for midfielder Adrian Randall to sign for Burnley for £40,000 although the club could have earned a fortune the previous season had the Amesbury-based player agreed to sign for Sheffield Wednesday for a reported fee of £250,000. It could have made such a difference to the club at a crucial period. Another of Len Walker's golden signings though-he only parted with £10,000 to AFC Bournemouth in December 1988 for Adrian.

As Chairman of the Supporters Club there was also discontent amongst fans who had previously agreed to part with £95,000 in May 1990 in return for shares of which they had never been notified about or been provided with an authorised share certificate. Gladwell confirmed that he had no knowledge of the shares issue. It was a sorry mess.

Irrespective of past dealings though we set up a Trust Fund from the Supporters Club to try to raise more funds for our ailing club to survive with a guarantee that every penny would be returned should the club fold. I also pleaded with Gladwell to accept Colin Hancock's offer of support. I had attended a meeting at the Lakeside Country Club with Hancock and his former Directors in attendance. I was sat next to Bob Potter who turned to me and just said, "*What a bloody mess?*" There was no alternative for Gladwell.

At this time I had had enough of everything. The following Saturday we also entertained a group of supporters from Burnley but I had to approach the landlord of The Crimea pub for help after the guv'nor of our own supporters club, The Sportsmans, had refused to help us with a request to cater for a buffet for both teams (approximately 40 persons) in the build-up to the main attraction in the afternoon. I was livid. Here we had a club skint and there I was trying to give them business all to no avail. We experienced more problems that night for our Christmas Disco. I politely reminded, or maybe not so politely, the hierarchy of the club that the Sportsmans was actually our headquarters and, as an organisation, we had donated £9000 to build it it the late 1970s. As often happens in football if you get the wrong clientele involved exclusivity becomes the norm and that is what the Sportsmans Club became. It became a touch "snobby" and not a club run by the supporters for the supporters. I must confess I had more than the odd "dust up" there when the frustration got the better of me. A number of years before as a teenager an altercation ensued at the bar with me and one of the regulars. He started on me and within seconds we were both on the floor grappling. Everybody else joined in and when order was restored I noticed that my jacket had been ripped and the arm was hanging off. It was two days after Christmas and the jacket was a present. When I returned home my mum and dad saw the damage and my dad went ballistic. Never one to shirk responsibility and to stand up for what was right he was in touch with the landlord of the Sportsmans and the bottom line was that next time I was in the club I would be refunded the cost of the jacket or the matter would be taken further, especially as the guy who set on me was in his forties. I returned to the Sportsmans the next day and a sheepish landlord gave me the agreed £30. I was made up, I didn't particularly like the jacket anyway and had a few quid in my pocket. Furthermore I was under 18 and shouldn't have been drinking in the club anyway but that was never mentioned.

# Always Look on the Bright Side of Life

T he New Year of 1992 started with a new Chairman out of the blue with the arrival of Crystal Palace director Simon Hume-Kendall subject to his resignation from the south London club.

The club even publicly announced that the arrival of the new Chairman would include

*"Clearing all outstanding creditors and leaving the club with sufficient capital for the remainder of the season and the complete 1992-93 season during which time it is anticipated that fortune should alter sufficiently for the club to enjoy successful times ahead".*

It all sounded as though maybe the club was turning the corner but it wasn't so. The club was losing £6000 per week and by this time were bottom of the Football League with wages now unpaid.

Hume-Kendall came up with a number of differing options to attempt to keep the club afloat. The club bank account was eventually frozen and it was reported that Hume-Kendall, whose name had remained as a director at Crystal Palace, was on his way after stating that there were hidden debts that he was unaware of. The level of communication from the club was appalling and the signs by this stage were particularly gloomy.

McDonald was doing a sterling job trying to keep his players focussed despite payment not being provided and with some of his players able to sign for other clubs should the opportunity arise which, for many, it did. *"What on earth is going on?"* I blasted in the programme notes versus Walsall in early February. The usual rhetoric at the directors of the time continued, *"WE NEED ANSWERS! To me the best directors at any football club should*

*NOT be seen and should NOT be heard, just get on with the task in hand, quietly and efficiently. I'm always seeing your (the directors), names in the papers- so now tell us the truth- what are you doing to prevent Aldershot Football Club from closure?*

*"To those of you who can say to us, the supporters, something constructive and beneficial then great! We're 100% behind you. To those of you sitting in the Directors Box where the answer is "nothing" then do the honourable thing- RESIGN NOW! YOU SERVE NO PURPOSE AS A DIRECTOR!*

*"Shall I tell you why I'm angry- I'm furious because after reading in the local press that the negotiations taking place would ensure the players and office staff receiving their wages, I then find that on 31st January no wages were forthcoming. NO WAGES- it's a miracle these players even entered the playing arena at Rotherham last Saturday. I'll tell you something for nothing, if I had a job and was to be told that my salary was to be halved or not paid at all- I WOULDN'T BE AT WORK THE NEXT DAY. It's unacceptable that you are playing with people's livelihoods and guess what?*

*"I bet the drinks are flowing in the boardroom today- yes, both before and after and yes, I wouldn't be surprised if the Directors Box is the busiest part of the Recreation Ground this afternoon, with all the complimentary tickets flowing around. My view, and that of the Supporters Club- "WE SYMPATHISE 100% WITH THE PLAYERS AND OFFICE STAFF. WE'RE 100% BEHIND YOU, YOU'VE BEEN TREATED UNFAIRLY AND UNREASONABLY.*

*"All the supporters of this club are sick, tired and disillusioned with the events that have occurred here. It's become repetitive and apparently progress-less. But yet we're all still here backing the club against all proper reasoning. Why? Because we want to see the club survive, continue and one day eventually prosper. We're on Death Row- IT'S SERIOUS! I appeal to the Board of Directors- there's been too much dirt thrown around for far too long! For Christ's sake come clean and let us know the truth. YOU ALL OWE US THAT AT THE VERY LEAST".*

I wasn't too happy as you can see with this latest turn of events. We had all had enough. By this time the Supporters

Club was paying for the away coach travel for the players and management.

I realised the full instability we had at the club and the demeanour of the characters involved with a simple conversation on one of these journeys. I can't recall which match it involved but I was sat on the team coach with Gladwell and the club Chaplain at the time, a guy called the Rev John Maxwell. They were involved in a conversation that suddenly became heated. Suddenly Gladwell closed in on the Vicar and shouted at him- "*Why don't you f\*\*\* off Vicar?*" I couldn't believe what I had heard and witnessed. Imagine my horror when Rev. Maxwell responded and shouted back "*No, why don't you just f\*\*\* off!*" That was it for me. I finally realised what we were up against.

With the players either leaving or training at home to save on the petrol costs the situation was dire and every match started to be advertised as "possibly the last ever Aldershot match".

The Supporters Club committee was collecting funds to help save the club whilst on match days bucket collections with donations from the fans became another source of income but this time it was solely to be given to the players to give them a little something bearing in mind they were not being paid.

We played Gillingham on a Tuesday evening in mid-February. The Rec was packed and I am certain there were far more inside the stadium than the 2,986 figure recorded as the official gate. The East Bank was full to bursting. Once all the monies were collected I always ensured that they were given to Ian McDonald in order for him to distribute to the players. I can recall being up in the club offices at half-time and Gladwell was insistent that I gave him the money as he needed it. I told him no – only one man was going to be given the funds and it wasn't him. He got really shirty with me and became aggressive. It made me even more determined to ensure that I wouldn't leave the money inside the building. I took it out and arranged to give it to Ian separately after the match.

There was plenty of emotion too as the fans congregated by the Directors Box on the pitch to show their universal support of the players during the desperate situation. This became a regular occurrence over the next few matches.

# Weather with You

T here were more public meetings, aborted proposed takeovers and mystery investors but time was running out. Even George Berry said *"The players are sick and tired of it all. Every week there are new deadlines and every week the agony is prolonged. If it wasn't for the players, staff, vice presidents club and supporters then Aldershot would die because the directors aren't doing anything. This whole business is disgraceful. Don't the directors realise they are mucking around with people's lives? From week to week we are told lies. If Aldershot are going to die then let them die with dignity. We are becoming the laughing stock of the Football League. The fans will not put up with this for much longer and the sympathy vote is waning rapidly. And as for the so-called rescue packages- it seems that empty vessels make the most noise".*

Berry was right, the situation was dragging on. The club was given a deadline of 18th March 1992 to resolve an outstanding debt to the Inland Revenue with a petition to be heard in the High Court.

McDonald was just about able to field a team of players, with regular departures due to the financial situation. He wasn't having any luck whatsoever. When Mansfield Town visited the Rec on Friday 21st February he welcomed fans in the programme with *"Welcome to Final Word Part IV- it seems like only yesterday that we were apparently mourning the last game against Walsall yet here we go again".* For this match the players had been told by Gladwell that they would receive some wages prior to kick-off. However 35 minutes before kick-off they were told that there was nothing available and they would have to continue to play for nothing. They arranged a quick meeting and only agreed to fulfil the fixture for three reasons: McDonald, Wignall and the fans. Our collections usually accounted for about £75 per player but many of the players resided in the midlands and further afield so the payments were usually eaten up pretty quickly. I know that our efforts were appreciated though.

Once the Mansfield match started Dave Puckett scored a cracker with just four minutes on the clock. I remember the match pretty well mainly for conceding a penalty that never was followed by the dismissal of Berry who was sent off by referee Kelvin Morton for dissent after the spot-kick was converted. We eventually lost the match 3-1. The following day on the Saint and Greavsie Show our plight was mentioned and the goals showed.

Jimmy Greaves, a footballing legend in his own right, was quite condescending regarding our plight and the fact that Berry would not be getting any wages to pay any fines for his dismissal. I thought it was unnecessary but as I have learned in life when the "chips are down" you become an easy target.

The following week we travelled to play-off chasing Scunthorpe United and McDonald's men gave a terrific account of themselves despite going down 1-0. Again the players only agreed to play out of loyalty to the management team and fans. At the end of the match the loyal fans chanted for McDonald for a lengthy period. He duly obliged about half an hour after the end of the match, wearing just a towel to applaud the fans.

By this time I had been made redundant from my job in the City of London. I did a bit of temping and got a job as a driver at British Car Auctions in Blackbushe. After crashing into the vehicle in front queuing up to parade the car I was driving I was told in no uncertain terms that my services would no longer be required. A stint (two days actually) at Diners Club followed before I was informed that I would be timed by the Team Leader on how long it took me for a toilet break!

I realised that I had a problem utilising my time wisely because I was not only watching the lunchtime editions of

Neighbours and Home and Away but also the repeat versions a few hours later at tea time.

I offered the club my services on a voluntary basis (well it had to be- nobody was getting paid) and worked in the offices answering phones and doing general admin to help out.

The day before our away match at Barnet I took a call and it was Bees manager Barry Fry. He wanted to speak to McDonald who wasn't available. He asked me to take down his number and I couldn't find a pen to jot the information down. I asked him to wait whilst I tried to find a pen and he responded, "*You've got f\*\*\* all at that club. When you come to Barnet tomorrow night come and see me and I will give you a load of pens*". I told him that I would do.

The evening at Underhill was a farce. Ian Mac was now having to field more and more youngsters and Shots were easily defeated 5-0. I remember being in the Barnet Social Club after the match and it all became an embarrassment. Players were arguing, not having any money to get home. A "whip round" involving people such as programme printer Karl Prentice was undertaken just to give the lads some pocket money but it was all grim viewing to be honest. Feeling pretty dejected leaving the club I, and the friends I was with, walked in the dark out of the stadium. Who did we walk past going the other way but none other than Barry Fry? I thought about it and then chased back after him and caught him off guard. He must have wondered what I wanted as I called out to him. He stopped and I told him that we spoke on the phone and that he was going to supply me with a load of pens. He thought about it and said, "*Oh yea, I remember. Um- sorry I haven't got any at the moment. I haven't been down the bookies today*". We both laughed and went on our way.

Further defeats followed at home to Northampton Town, Blackpool and Lincoln City but by this time the gates had been cut in half and only 1,300 to 1,400 loyal souls were turning up waiting for the inevitable.

Ironically Northampton had just been given a reprieve after incurring a £1 million debt whilst Blackpool fans, on a cold, windy and gloomy Tuesday evening, raised funds to help save the club. Their Chairman Owen Oyston presented John McGinty and myself with a sizeable personal cheque to help fight the cause too. There were only 3700 at Bloomfield Road on the night. The Seasiders were league leaders as well and seven of our squad were just 20 or younger.

# Accident Waiting to Happen

After previously having some sympathy with Gladwell and his crowd I finally lost patience with the lot of them. He even went public to state that he was unaware that the club were playing a league match up at Scunthorpe the previous weekend. I actually wrote the secretary's notes for the Northampton match due to the departure of Birley but in my own "regular" fan notes I blasted *"ANOTHER DAY, ANOTHER WEEK! BUT STILL NO PAY! It disgusts and appalls me that our club is now being subjected to such humiliation as we find ourselves in this turmoil without, as yet, being convinced that there is light at the end of the tunnel. Who's the Chairman then?*

*"Our friend Trev reckons he didn't even know there was a game at Scunthorpe last Saturday; that, so he says, is the reason he didn't attend. Ever heard of the sports pages of the daily papers then Trev? Or (0252) 20211- straight through and they'd have told you the game was on. If these "so called directors ran their businesses the way they run OUR football club there would be more people queuing up at the Unemployment Benefits Office than there already are".*

In the same programme director and soon to be Chairman, Mike Davey, informed supporters that a loyal fan was going to remedy the situation and pay the players and staff the outstanding amount due and ensured that the situation "must never happen again." He even went on to state that there was a realistic chance of saving the club.

He concluded, *"Please don't say you have heard it all before, because you HAVEN'T and I certainly would not be wasting my time if I did not honestly believe it had a chance of success".*

The Lincoln match was the last ever home fixture. We lost 3-0 and people were beyond caring by now. We knew what was going to happen and were powerless to prevent it. All the words and wisdom from those at the top were just that. It was all hot air. Aldershot Football Club was going to die and how many outside the town and its surrounds really cared?

No football supporter ever believes that their club will cease to exist. If your club is in dire straits then there is always that hope and optimism that somebody will come in to be the great saviour. Not at Aldershot Football Club though! On Wednesday 18th March 1992 Mr Registrar Buckley wound the club up in the High Courts and it all took less than a minute.

The club could, however, fulfill their fixture at Cardiff City two nights later as it was away from home. Davey, by this time, went public and said that he was confident that he could secure a mystery backer! Change the tune, I'd heard it all before.

The visit to Ninian Park was an emotional occasion for all concerned. I arrived at the Rec on the morning of the match to be told that unless the money for the team coach was stumped up in advance then it was going nowhere. In those days we could only take £100 out from the Supporters Club Building Society account at any one time.

I had to travel to the Farnham, Farnborough and Aldershot branches to get the required funds and also provide to Ian McDonald the "pocket money" from collections to help the players. Time was pressing and I had to get a speed up to get the monies needed, especially from the Farnborough branch where I recall being in a lengthy queue. When I finally got back to Aldershot with the required money the players were all giving me grief. *"Hurry up- we've been waiting for you. We need to get going".* Thanks I thought- If only they knew!

We stopped off at a hotel in Cardiff for the pre match eggs and toast and I remember England and Liverpool legend Emlyn Hughes being in the same hotel and taking a real interest in the club's plight and wishing everybody the best of luck.

We lost 2-0 on the night but the emotions pouring out from the few hundred Shots fans who travelled to Ninian Park will live with me forever. There wasn't a dry eye in the house when the referee blew the final whistle and the home supporters were superb in their reactions too. It was a quiet journey home on the team coach and when we arrived back in Aldershot I remember departing the coach in silence and having fish and chips with Ian Read at Tony's Bar in the High Street at about two in the morning reflecting on the facts that our club was no more and not quite believing what we had experienced! It wasn't meant to be like this.

I went back to the Rec over the weekend and the sadness still haunts me now as I recall watching grown men standing on their spot on the terraces where they had stood for years on end, as man and boy, many with tears streaming down their faces. I couldn't accept the hurt and couldn't accept the desperation.

On Wednesday 25th March 1992 it hit home for good as the club was officially wound up.

With Steve Wignall and Ian McDonald as the doors are due to close in March 1992

A few days later the remaining staff and players were given their redundancy papers by the club liquidators. A photograph of them all was taken on the centre circle and I watched them with such sadness from the North Stand. This was the confirmation-Aldershot Football Club was dead!

# Why?

1992

So what was the cause of the downfall of Aldershot Football Club? There has been much debate and insinuation over the period of time since the demise but nobody has ever really got to the bottom of the reasons why. However if you look back into the aeons of history Aldershot was always a club living on the edge since its inception in 1926. A club that spent the majority of its existence in the bottom level of the Football League, it temporarily punched above its weight. If you analyse the attendances over the years they were pretty healthy in the 1940s and 50s but that was when divisions were regionalised and the club played the likes of Reading, Southampton, Crystal Palace, Brighton and Hove Albion and QPR.

Reg Driver was the stereotypical Chairman of his time, a local fishmonger. He was approached to become involved in the club in the early 1970s during the tenure of Jimmy Melia. He was reluctant to do so but due to his family's respected involvement within the Aldershot Football Association he agreed. Reg had been the Chairman of the Association and involved with the Hampshire FA too. He was soon alarmed at the financial situation the club found itself in despite the supposed lucrative years soon after the cup matches versus Carlisle United and Manchester United which drew the highest ever attendances at the Rec of 19,138 and 18,509 respectively in 1970. Added to that a bumper pay day in the FA Cup as Liverpool were the opponents at Anfield in a third round tie in 1971 attracting over 45,000.

He made some decisions that may have been unpopular amongst supporters and also dismissed Melia but he also tightened the purse strings to ensure that the club could ease its financial burden moving forwards.

He led the club as Chairman to its first ever promotion in 1972/73 and, despite relegation three seasons later, he was in charge for the golden period of the late 1970s and early eighties which saw, in my view, the best ever side to represent Aldershot.

This was also a great period to be a Shots fan too. There was money in the bank, a new changing room complex and office facilities had been built. This was in addition to owning a number of houses in the town where players and management could live. It also possessed a thriving commercial department, at the time one of the most forward thinking in the country.

The early eighties started to see a decline in attendances in dramatic fashion and, for some reason, Aldershot seemed to be one of the hardest hit. Those regular three and 4,000 crowds soon dipped to below 2,000 by 1981/82 onwards. The club was snookered in a way. The houses had to be sold off, a key member of the commercial department departed with some sceptical that he was earning too big a wage. My philosophy is simple on this- as long as the club benefits best then the income earned by personnel is irrelevant. Even when Len Walker led the club to a close promotion quest in 1983/84 the attendances were pretty pitiful for most of the season compared to previous years.

When the realisation set in that finances were grim and there was nowhere else to turn the takeover of the club by the O'Connell regime gave the supporters a lifeline to cling onto but this was, of course, short lived. The Driver and Potter regime returned six months later and it wasn't a popular move at the time.

In truth that saga of the mid 1980s was the beginning of the end despite Len Walker's momentous achievement of leading the club to promotion in 1986/87 against all the odds. Financially it was always a struggle and good people like Colin Hancock tried to rectify the situation but only, eventually, at huge cost to himself.

I met Reg Driver many years later at his house at my request after I stepped down as Secretary of the future Aldershot Town and had a fabulous five-hour heart to heart with him. Just the two of us and his bottle of Bells. I was driving, however, and politely declined. I learned enough upon leaving his house to be certain that had he still been involved at the club in 1992 it would never have folded. I remember in the hostile days when the Driver regime was at its most controversial the amount of so called fans who said to me. "*We won't be back until he has gone*". Where were they when he was finally ousted?

Don't get me wrong, Reg had his faults. He wasn't the most pleasant when he'd had too much to drink and his communication skills certainly needed tidying up but I am of the firm opinion that he had the best of intentions for Aldershot Football Club. Well respected within the Football League, local businesses and with Rushmoor Borough Council he would have used his negotiation skills to full effect to avoid the terminal demise. The saddest part for me overall is that I don't believe he stepped into the Rec again after his departure in 1988. I attended his funeral in 2011 and was truly saddened to learn of his passing and wrote the following obituary which few would have believed a few years before:

*"Many supporters of Aldershot will recall those days in the mid-1980s vividly. I was a teenager at the time and a fierce critic of Reg and the Board of Directors and when I look back it must have made his life extremely difficult at the time. There were demonstrations and I was a big part of orchestrating them. Reg and I would have many an argument and there is no disguising that fact.*

*"However, if I knew then what I know now and with the wisdom of experience I would have done everything possible to get both of those consortiums together for the good of the football club because there were some good and influential people involved in both camps. I am sure with better communications it would have worked.*

*"During my time as secretary of Aldershot Town what I did learn about Reg though was how highly regarded he was by many people for his administrative skills and abilities. Make no mistake about it he was an influential man.*

*"When I decided to step down as company secretary in 2002 and after much discussion with Rosemary Aggett who served both clubs superbly in an administrative role I knew that my time would not be complete until I met with Reg to talk about those events of the mid 1980s and the hostilities that it created.*

*"I was surprised when he agreed to meet me as I didn't think he would be interested but he was. I spent one of the most fascinating evenings I have had involved with Aldershot at Reg's house and we spoke openly and honestly about all the events that occurred until the early hours of the morning.*

*"I learnt so much that night and admired the fountain of knowledge that he had about football and Aldershot in general especially learning about the early days of his involvement with the club.*

*"I left his house with great respect for the man. You can never change history and the circumstances will always remain but what I do know is that he worked tirelessly for Aldershot Football Club. He gave 16 years of his life to the club and many, many more years to local football including the Aldershot FA where he was also well respected.*

*"I am truly saddened to learn of his passing. On behalf of Aldershot Town Football Club we extend our deepest sympathies to the family of Reg at this difficult time."*

To me the above account sums it up perfectly.

I also know that those involved towards the final agonising months before the club folded were certainly out of their depth. Reg Driver was never in this category. The days of the local trade chairmen are a rarity in football these days. Actually that is rather sad.

Although Aldershot Football Club was no more there was still time for football and this proved crucial. Ian McDonald could not have chosen a worse year to have his testimonial. I was on his committee and actually wrote the match programme which I enjoyed doing. There was all kinds of red tape surrounding his actual testimonial fixture versus Southampton. Indeed the only way the match could be played was by the kick-off time being brought forward to avoid usage of the floodlights which meant that the attendance was less than 2,000.

It must have been a strange experience for Ian but Saints brought a strong team to the Rec including the likes of Alan Shearer who was actually replaced by Nicky Banger who would have his own role to play at the Rec in later years. I am not too sure many players have had to fulfil such an occasion representing a club that no longer existed. He deserved the occasion too after making 423 appearances, netting 62 goals between 1981 and 1992. It should not be forgotten also that Woking FC were extremely supportive with another match being staged at Kingfield where Paul Gascoigne handed the match ball over.

# Nothing Else Matters

1992

W hat about the future of football in Aldershot though? Was there any possibility that football could remain in the town at any level?

A few weeks before the eventual demise of the club Terry Owens had approached me to see if I was interested in helping to form a new football club. I responded precisely to Terry- *"Not really, we are doing everything that we can to save the current one"*. I knew Terry vaguely due to his involvement with the Save Our Shots campaign a few years before which had raised funds to keep the club afloat. He had done a pretty good job with it. He also had some previous as being part of the O'Connell consortium that swept into power briefly in 1984/85- he could take the credit of attracting the club's first ever main sponsor- Midas Press- during that season too. A flamboyant character, he liked being in the public eye and centre of attention. However he was also Aldershot "thru and thru" and that was enough for me.

Terry had attended some of our Supporters Club committee meetings trying to raise the profile of his fundraising efforts and we all used to have a little chuckle amongst ourselves as we knew he would always leave by telling a joke. They were never that great but we were polite. He could be a divisive character to some but it was all pleasant enough though. He also stated that he had played for Guildford City and Frimley Green in his prime- I was never convinced of that fact. Show me the medals, Terry!

As soon as the developments of 25th March 1992 sunk in Terry was back in touch. Were we interested? You bet we were now. A meeting was set up with our committee for the Crimea Pub opposite the Rec for the following evening.

I called our committee members to inform them of what was occurring and we held the meeting. It was the first of many I would have with Terry over the next few months. Little was I to realise how crucial these meetings would be.

You see it was all a game at the time. I hadn't a clue what possibilities there were but my committee and I were adamant we would do anything in our capabilities to ensure that there would be a football club to support.

Terry had made enormous strides though and was advanced in what possibilities there were. Due to being made aware that the chances of AFC surviving was slim he had made inroads as early as February 1992 regarding the formation of a new club. He had already made contact with the Conference, Beazer Homes (Southern League) and the Diadora (Isthmian League). I knew there was no chance of the Conference accepting us but knew little of the other options. There were also other consortiums interested in forming a new club including former Chairman Gill-Anderson whose behaviour was a touch erratic to say the least.

I used to watch a bit of Camberley Town in my early teens when Aldershot were away. In fact I can remember being chased up the road by an Epsom and Ewell fan once outside Krooner Park. In addition I watched Farnborough Town many times too and there was never any competition between the clubs and most Aldershot supporters were keen on seeing the 'Boro' do well. Many former Aldershot players ended their days at Cherrywood Road and I remember seeing many including Richard Walden, Brian Lucas and, of course, Alex McGregor, line up in the yellow jersey. With the realisation that football in Aldershot would return but at non-league level I needed to freshen up on my own knowledge of the game and, more importantly, how these clubs operated. I took in plenty of matches. I recall travelling to Andover and seeing them invoke a six-goal demolition of Canterbury City and a guy called Paul Odey scoring four goals. I also took in Stevenage Borough playing at Maidenhead United in an Isthmian League Division 1 match.

The discussions with Terry continued most evenings. Nick Fryer, who was the Supporters Club Secretary, was also involved in these meetings and we soon linked up with a guy called Peter Bridgeman who was to become the first ever secretary of the club.

A further meeting at the Crimea involved Colin Hancock and ended up at Terry's house in the early hours. I liked Colin and he was greatly affected by the demise of AFC. He wanted involvement in the new set-up but we were quite adamant that we had to start with a clean slate and have new people involved in the running of the club. Colin understood and we wished him well.

Nick instigated a petition to ensure football in the town continued and over 5,000 people signed up to it. Nick and I are of the same ilk. We are pure Aldershot people who want nothing but the best for the football club and not particularly interested in the politics that surround it. Sadly as the club progressed and the nearer I became to the inner sanctum it became impossible to avoid the politics; something that caught up with me over 20 years later. I hated it.

There was some good work being undertaken behind the scenes with Terry at the helm. We called a public meeting on 22nd April 1992 at the Royal Aldershot Officers Club.

This was the catalyst to know if we were onto something or not. 100 or so in attendance and we may as well have packed up. However there were over 600 people packed into the room which was also full of hope, enthusiasm and belief. I have to say too that we had it extremely well organised. Even the little things such as having photos of former Shots legends throughout the room and also the playing of You'll Never Walk Alone. No ipods in those days. I had to tape the song from vinyl and we played it on some ancient recording machine and just prayed that the song would be audible.

At the meeting the supporters were introduced to those that were working tirelessly to ensure that they would have football at the Rec come the start of the 1992/93 season, irrespective of the level. My brother David was involved at this stage. I had brought him into the equation after the realisation of the necessity of business and financial sense. He had spoken to me, aware of what was going on and offered to help on a voluntary basis. A chartered accountant and supporter who had attended his first match in the late 1960s he fitted the bill perfectly.

So much work and research occurred during that summer to set the wheels in motion. Farnborough Town FC, especially the likes of Dick Molden, were also helpful offering advice and explaining how they operated their club. One of the major achievements to secure a future was to ensure that football returned to the Rec. David, Terry and Isthmian League Chairman Alan Turvey attended a meeting of Rushmoor Borough Council to put forward the business proposals and the green light was given. This was essential in my book.

By this time a limited company (No: 2711473) had been formed with two shares worth £1 each. Terry owned share number one with me holding the certificate for number two. A number of years later it was always my ambition that I would eventually hand that down to my son Oliver to keep it in the family. The first ever Board meeting of Aldershot Town FC (1992) Ltd was held at Terry's house on 18th May 1992 in the presence of my brother, Terry and me. Terry was formally elected Chairman.

We set the club up correctly. A small part-time playing squad (none of this Rangers having an alleged £7.8M playing budget in the fourth tier of Scottish football!) was announced. Many people believe that Steve Wignall was the first manager of

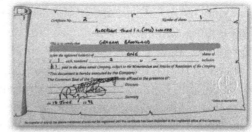

One of the two shares that formed Aldershot Town Football Club (1992) Ltd.

the club but factually that is incorrect. Prior to the public meeting Ian McDonald had accepted the position of Player/Manager with Steve in the position of Player/Coach/Physio. I was never too sure who would treat him if he had been subjected to an injury whilst on the pitch though!

We also agreed that the Board of Directors would be consist of eight directors including representation from the Supporters

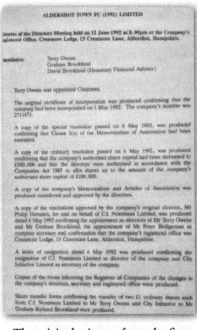

**The original minutes from the first ever meeting of Aldershot Town FC (1992) Ltd**

Club who would have equal rights. Each director would have to contribute a minimum of £2500 to be a board member but nobody could own more than 20% of the shares. Famous comedian and actor Arthur English, who was born and bred in the town, accepted the position as President. Terry and I actually sifted through the applications for proposed directors before inviting them onto the Board.

We also honoured and acknowledged those that had served the club previously with Honorary Patrons and Life Members in recognition of service given. There was even an ex-players ticket issued for players of the AFC era (within reason of course- 100 or so matches minimum). A questionnaire was produced and within days many sponsorships had been placed in addition to a large take-up of share capital.

At this time I also set up a premium rate phone line called Shotsline. I had always had an interest in broadcasting and remember often calling the original phone information line run by a guy called Tony Millard operating a service for Brighton and Hove Albion. It fascinated me and I knew that setting it up could be invaluable to the club. I wasn't wrong either. Operating the "Shotsline" changed my life really and set me up as the main link between players, management and supporters for the next 21 years.

Perhaps the phone call I made to a guy called Dave Boddy who operated a company called Sportslines at the time was one of the most important I ever made in my life. By the time it closed down in 2009, as the world wide web started to take precedence, Shotsline had earned over £300,000 and its success made the national stage on many an occasion. In its first season alone a staggering 61,374 calls were made! I worked it out that I probably conducted in the region of approaching 10,000 interviews during my time involved at the football club.

Primarily this was because in those days there was no internet, social media, Facebook or Twitter. The matches were not even covered on the local radio stations. Before being provided with an old style "mobile" phone the size of a tree trunk I used to have to submit my match updates via public telephones.

Sometimes I would have to visit three or four phone boxes before finding one that was working to provide the actual match report!

We had one match in Wales at Newport AFC in 1994 which Arthur English would never forget. It was a cup game played on a Sunday. Arthur settled down to listen to one of my live commentaries from his home but dropped off soon after kick-off time. He eventually woke up towards the end of the match. Out of pocket too at 48p per minute. Fortunately we won the game 3-1. I don't think Arthur listened to my commentaries again though! It even brought a laugh at his funeral a few years later.

My brother had prepared a profit and loss account based on an average home gate of 850. I can recall us all sitting in the home dressing room one Saturday afternoon discussing what kind of attendances we would get. Difficult really as we still didn't know what league we would be in- if at all!

Work was occurring at 100 miles an hour but it was exciting to be involved. A problem materialised with regards to the managerial position as Ian McDonald had been offered the position as Reserve Team Manager at Millwall under the leadership of Mick McCarthy.

Ian had always stated that if a full-time position in the Football League came up then he would have to consider it. He duly did and we wished him well.

# Even Better than the Real Thing

1992

Ｔhere we were with two months before the start of the season not knowing if we would have a club competing within a league, no manager, no players and no stadium confirmed. We held a meeting in Terry's garden and invited Steve Wignall to attend where we offered him the job. Steve states in his excellent autobiography, "You Can Have Chips" that I looked a little nervous and he was right. Here was I just 25-years-old swapping the easy passage of airing my views from the terraces over many years to being on the verge of appointing a manager to a new football club. All of a sudden there felt a pressure that I was now representing supporters on a far bigger scale and everything would be scrutinised. We had to ensure that we got the decisions right and, importantly, be transparent with our communications with the fans. Steve also says in his book that mine and Terry's *"enthusiasm for the new adventure was more than infectious."* Steve Wignall was now officially the manager of Aldershot Town Football Club.

I conducted my first "Shotsline" interview with the new manager and laugh as I look back on the occasion. I used one of those old monotone portable tape recorders to conduct the interview with a grinding in the background throughout our conversation. I clearly recall one of Steve's quotes though- *"It's a new club, fresh club, CLEAN club. We've got honest people working in it."*

Some people thought that it was a gamble appointing Steve as the manager. No non-league experience and somebody who had been a professional for over 20 years.

True, but I thought it important that we had somebody at the helm who had been through the pain of the demise of AFC and also knew what the supporters had gone through too. A Liverpudlian by birth, Steve was a proper football man. Disciplined and fair but a good clubman too. Somebody who knew right from wrong. He fitted the bill perfectly having played under the likes of Brian Clough and Frank McLintock and as tough a centre half as I have ever seen. All we needed now was confirmation of the Rec and league status.

In between these times Terry and I drove down to Southampton where an auction was being held disposing of all the "AFC Memorabilia". We had some money behind us now with the additional support of John McGinty, one of the newly appointed directors who had also been involved in the fundraising to save the old club. A jovial, likeable Irishman who owned his own removal business in Bordon, he liked a sing-song and was great entertainment. He would provide his own legacy many years later. At the auction were some familiar faces including popular former striker Dave Puckett. The main item purchased was the Boardroom table which heralded much history at the Rec. For some reason it was a necessity for it to return to its home although I never really quite worked out what that reason was.

I remember the journey for another reason too. I was still getting to know Terry at this stage but had done a fair bit of research and spoken to some other close confidantes to find out a bit more about him. *"He loves himself"* seemed to be the most consistent response. *"If he was chocolate he'd eat himself"*.

As Terry picked me up for the journey down to the south coast he said to me, *"I've just prepared a compilation on a tape that you might be interested in listening to"*. I didn't have a choice, he put it straight on and there it was. The guy singing on the tape was none other than Terry Owens himself. Danny Boy was his encore but there was Sinatra, Engelbert Humperdinck. You name it and it was on that tape. All the way down to Southampton. When we got into the car on the return journey – *"Do you want to hear more of my songs?"* he asked. *"Nah... you're alright Terry!"* That is what I learned about Terry. Yes he did rate himself and he certainly had an ego but then most people I came into contact in the Boardroom developed one over the years whether they think they did or not. I wasn't really bothered to be honest. It grated with some but not me. Few could have pulled off what he had at this time.

Whilst we waited for confirmation of what league we would be admitted to Ian McDonald's testimonial season continued with a fixture at Camberley Town FC on the May Bank Holiday. This was the first time I had taken The Good Lady out publicly. It nearly proved a disaster.

For the whole period from arrival to departure at Krooner Park all I did was speak to supporters wanting to know what was going on, some begging that football had to survive in the town at whatever level because they didn't know what they would do if there was no Aldershot! I was told The Good Lady was seconds from leaving the match whilst being on her own for so long. We had a good evening in the end at the Royal Standard pub opposite the ground and I suppose it was actually a good introduction to having a boyfriend/husband involved in a football club as she got used to it pretty quickly.

By the time the second public meeting occurred in mid-June we had already held the inaugural Board meeting which had been held at the Hogs Back Hotel. We were organised and able to inform another massed gathering of where we were and it was encouraging. We had been granted a three-year licence from Rushmoor Borough Council. Originally this was to be shared with Farnham Town who were to play at the Rec too during 1992/93 but they pulled out prior to the season starting and we actually nicked a number of their better players.

Arthur English had designed the new colourful phoenix badge. The most important piece of information was that we had been accepted into the Diadora Isthmian League Division 3. Aldershot Town was officially "Alive and Kicking". Ironically the most discussed matter at the meeting was whether the admission prices should be £3 or £3-50.

We also had to find a new sponsor. It was decided that we would hold a raffle to find the winner. Each entrant paid £250 and received a variety of benefits but the overall winner would be the official main sponsor for the season. We all laughed when the lucky recipient was a guy called Ray Yeowell who was the proprietor of the local florists in the High Street. The sponsors' name was emblazoned on the front of the team strips for our inaugural season- Pam's Florists!

Terry Owens was the conductor without a shadow of a doubt. His ability to plan, coordinate and structure and to have an excellent foresight into accepting various possibilities and outcomes was crucial to the formation of Aldershot Town. What I was able to provide was a youthful enthusiasm but also a pure understanding of the needs and requirements of the supporters. I was also proud to chair such a superb set of people within my committee who were focussed and committed to the cause. The summer of 1992 was just an enjoyable experience I would never swap for anything. It was tense because we had a dream to fulfil and deadlines to meet but it was, above all, just fun. It was a privilege to be involved and the experiences will never, ever be taken away from me. I know what was achieved against all the odds. I know who those people were who still stand on the terraces now who put everything into making sure that it worked but never brag about what they did to cement a return of football to the town. Without the supporter you are nothing and we proved this

The inaugural 1992/93 squad Aldershot Town squad

I was fortunate to lead a fantastic Supporters Club Committee in 1992.

in 1992. Without the efforts of the Supporters Club during this period there would be no Aldershot Town FC now. Fact!

Indeed in the first season as a Supporters Club we had instigated a Super Shots Lottery which saw over £7000 donated to the club in the first 12 months, formed a new social club from a squalid environment behind the South Stand in addition to a new club shop.

The Shotsline was also the Supporters Club's responsibility as were the refreshment huts.

One obstacle that we did have, however, was the total apathy of the local newspaper, The Aldershot News. As part of his duties Nick Fryer had been appointed as Press Officer by this stage and he and I had continuous opposition and sarcasm within the Sports department, headed by the Sports Editor Peter Hutchinson but ably assisted by his juniors, Nick Cherrie and Richard Fleming. To be honest they all thought it was a bit of a joke, a fairy tale and had no belief that it would work. If anything it just made us more determined to succeed. The volatile relationship was to continue for many years though and would continue to raise its ugly head. The overall Editor, John Elliott, was often invited to attend matches to try to improve the relationship but the sports department was a law to itself.

The first ever fixture was back at Krooner Park on the first weekend in August; a four-team competition involving Camberley Town, Fleet Town and Frimley Green. Inquisitive Shots fans turned up in their droves desperate to see their new heroes. All local lads such as Mark Butler, Tony Calvert, Stuart Udal and Chris Tomlinson soon to be added to with the likes of Steve Stairs, Steve Harris and Shaun May from Farnham Town. Butler scored within five minutes versus Fleet Town and there was just a sense of pride and joy in the occasion as we won the Simpsonair Trophy. In fact something just felt good about the whole scenario.

The opening match at the Rec was a friendly against a famous old non-league club who had also hit hard times but were on the way back- Romford! In 1949 the Essex club had narrowly lost the first ever FA Amateur Cup Final versus Bromley in front of 95,000 fans at Wembley.

They folded in 1979 but had a group of devoted people also keen to resurrect football in the town and they had done so for the start of the 1992/93 campaign starting in the Essex Senior League.

There were 820 present for this friendly match and I recall little about the 3-0 victory. This was a massive day for all of us behind the scenes because we needed to get everything right. Turnstiles, catering, social facilities- these were all the responsibility of the Supporters Club.

I was in charge of the social club. The reason- because I had done that pub work at the One Oak a few years previously and had some experience. You may laugh at this but I can recall how proud I was when the jukebox arrived and I spent time cutting up cards, adding the names of the song and inserting them into the front of the jukebox (singles in those days!) all with the new club crest on them. "Alive and Kicking" was there too by personal request. It would become our club anthem.

The problem with the Romford match was that it was the hottest day of the year by far. As the fans started arriving the bar became packed. We had a problem though. The pumps were not working in the way that they should have been. Every time we started to serve a pint it ended up looking like an ice cream. A flake would have topped it off perfectly.

After a few minutes I was in panic mode and needed to think this through otherwise we were in serious danger of falling flat on our face. I contacted the landlord of The Crimea over the road- Tommy Graham. He came over immediately and within minutes had sorted it all out. I was forever grateful to Tommy for that especially as he must have been pretty busy himself on the day. He saved the day and, ultimately, our embarrassment. That's how it was though. The local community wanting the club to succeed. We actually only got our licence through the support of another local publican, Dave Passmore, then landlord of The Rose and Crown in Grosvenor Road, latterly Tiffany's.

I stated in my notes versus Romford, "*There is no prestige in being involved in the running of a Diadora League team. Oh no! No directors on an ego trip here. It's all about sheer hard work, determination and above all commitment. That is why I believe the club can prosper and be successful. For one thing, the club is now operated by a board of directors who all have one thing in common. They are local people who have followed Aldershot Football for many years combined.*" It was true too and something, in the main that we had planned on how we operated for the first few seasons anyway. As time goes on, however, changes occur and not always for the better.

# Alive and Kicking

1992

Saturday 22nd August 1992 was THE special day. It was what we had all worked towards for the whole summer. It was the day that all Shots supporters were so excited for. A year before the opening day of the season had seen a visit to Burnley's famous Turf Moor. Here we were now eagerly awaiting the arrival of one of the founding members of the Isthmian League in 1905- Clapton. This was what it was all about though. This moment confirmed that football was back in Aldershot.

The fact that it was five levels below the Football League basement division was immaterial. We had something to work with. Prior to kick-off Terry and I unleashed some fireworks from the North Stand end of the ground. The players on the pitch will, to this day, tell you about how they had to run to avoid the fireworks as they landed on the playing surface. Health and safety was not so prominent in those days. We were then introduced to both sets of players and a carnival atmosphere surrounded the Rec on this most special of days. That budget figure that we had agreed on was blitzed too with 1,493 in attendance; this was also the lowest crowd of the season but also more than attended the final Football League home match at home in March 1992 for the visit of Lincoln City.

Steve Wignall appeared to have assembled a decent playing squad. Indeed the starting line-up that day was full of local lads and the captain of the British Army team, Kev Parkins plus former Farnborough Town favourite Keith Baker who had joined as Player/Assistant Manager. At 37 years of age he still had the demeanour and calmness of a player that possessed the ability to be playing at a much higher standard. Stuart Udal was a local lad who had played for Tongham and Ash United and had actually come through a trial held at Bourley Road. To me he became what wearing an Aldershot Town shirt was all about. He wasn't the most naturally gifted player to ever wear the red and blue but he never shirked responsibility and never gave less than 100%. Only three players made more than Stuart's 236 appearances and he played with pride and vigour. Captain Dave Osgood had played at a higher level locally too.

Added to the return of former Aldershot and Farnborough District schoolboy Brian Lucas who had made 138 appearances as a professional for AFC between 1980 and 84, we looked to be in good hands. Chris Tomlinson, son of groundsman Dave, was also included. He actually played on that fateful night in Cardiff just five months previously.

After 27 minutes or so we were 2-0 down and there was a sense of alarm around the stadium. I recall looking at my brother with more than a touch of trepidation about me. Had we underestimated this? Was this going to be a damn sight harder than we thought?

Fortunately, as they did on 231 occasions between them in the years ahead that strike partnership of Butler and Stairs came to the rescue. 3-2 in front at the interval we eventually won 4-2 and Parkins even had a storming 25-yard strike disallowed late on. A significant presentation was also made to celebrate the occasion. Clapton Chairman Mike Fogg presented to Terry Owens a flagon of Rum. He had one proviso to this though- the rum was not allowed to be opened until the day the name of Aldershot returned to the Football League.

That evening in the social club I swapped from behind the bar to the other side. We celebrated until the early hours of the morning, relieved that our club was up and running. In those days it was whoever was last out of the bar, lock the door. It was usually Butler and Stairs too. The place was a goldmine because it became a place where the fans could mix with the players and everybody enjoyed each other's company.

Butler was the typical football supporters dream. A lad born in the town who lived within walking distance of the Rec. In addition he had grown up on the East Bank terraces watching the likes of Dungworth, Jopling, McGregor and Brodie and was also present for the famous play-off victory at Wolverhampton Wanderers. He loved the fact that he could walk down Victoria Road to matches with fans patting him on his back. Good job too as he would never have been able to drive home afterwards!

For Aldershot fans so far there had been little difference to the environment where they had always witnessed their football. The only unusual aspect of the Clapton match was that we had won-something that they hadn't witnessed in 1992 at whatever level. But it was at the Rec which was still a Football League stadium. Indeed the average attendance in the Isthmian Division 3 the previous season was just 90 or so.

The only way of acquiring all the results of the other matches in the division in the early days was by physically phoning them up to enquire the score. This was ok to an extent but if the phone was in the middle of the social club then it became a game. Often would be the case when I would get through and ask *"What was the score please?"* and the voice at the other end would just say *"9-0 mate"* and put the phone down. Repeating the exercise there would be no introduction this time just *"9-0"* and that was it. You got used to where the difficulties would arise and where not- usually to the east of the country and the county of Essex!

The real awakening came on Tuesday 2nd September and a visit to an Essex club, Collier Row's Sungate Stadium. It was also my 26th birthday and I recall being a touch embarrassed as "Happy Birthday" was sung out in the bar by the Shots fans. The official attendance for the match was 444 and 400 were travelling Shots and they were certainly viewing their team in surroundings never previously experienced. Collier Row played in a suburb of Romford. It was a small, compact venue with a terrible playing surface and everything possible to intimidate the opposition was provided by one of the more fancied teams in the division who had won their opening two matches.

The referee that evening was Steve Bennett and in a tight encounter we came from behind to win 2-1, courtesy of a late Butler winner. The celebrations at the end were as though we had won the FA Cup. That is what it meant to be a Shots fan in 1992.

The atmosphere in the bar afterwards was one of pure joy. Everybody wanted to be involved and be a part of a unique story of a town that refused to accept its football team going into oblivion.

There was a glitch off the pitch in September, when despite drawing with a team from a higher division in Leatherhead in the Diadora League Cup, the match was recalled for some unsavoury incidents off the pitch when a group of Shots supporters let their club down. It was more so in high jinks activities than anything else but some of them crossed the line and I wasn't having it. The police became involved and consequently so did I as the Chairman of the Supporters Club and director of the football club. I hadn't spent my whole summer working to set up a new foundation and image of the club for it to be pulled apart by a small number of individuals who should have known better.

What disappointed me somewhat is that statements that I gave regarding the matter ended up in the hands of some supporters who were directly involved in the events. It was shambolic that this was allowed to happen and affected my trust with working with the police for a period of time. As it was, because of this I recall some supporters calling me a "grass" at certain matches. I fronted this out with those concerned because I would have done whatever was required to ensure the good name of the club remained intact.

It was, however, a fact that due to the larger than usual attendances that the visit of Aldershot Town guaranteed in the early days every club had a duty to ensure that they were prepared on all fronts to make the day as successful as possible. The gate money some of these clubs received would have previously paid for a season's activity and the more welcome the reception the more money they would also receive behind the bars.

There was no looking back in the early part of the campaign and we won our opening 10 league matches. I believe this was so crucial to set a foundation for the club. A difficult start and I am sure that inquisitive supporters who had turned up just to see what it was all about would have disappeared in their droves. As it was the opposite occurred and by the time Royston Town visited the Rec on a Tuesday evening in mid-October over 2,100 were present; another record league attendance at that level. It was a fantastic occasion with the fans as noisy as I could remember for some time. We played well but couldn't find the net until Butler netted the winner with 12 minutes remaining. A year before and there would just have been total apathy and disdain but not now.

By this time Wignall had recruited the services of a former colleague from the Football League days as the popular Paul Shrubb arrived as Player/Coach from neighbours Cove whilst the arrival of Andy Nunn started a long connection for the defender with Aldershot Town who would eventually enjoy a romance with the club that included coaching roles before becoming the Head Groundsman.

I also remember a visit to Feltham and Hounslow Borough in the middle of that 10-match winning sequence and recording a 3-1 victory courtesy of a brace from Brian Lucas on the Middlesex club's artificial turf. Feltham is where my family moved from in the late 1960s to Frimley and a town where for some reason I have always retained an affinity with. I do remember travelling with Barry Underwood to watch them play another match at their dilapidated Arena stadium one night still trying to get a feel of the level of football. We arrived at the car park and the steward said to me- *"You can park your car here if you want but I can't guarantee it will be here after the match!"* That summed up Feltham perfectly and, unfortunately, many years later the club had to move away from their home venue due to increased vandalism at the stadium.

# Keep the Faith

1992

The 100% record ended in the most unexpected of circumstances. Bracknell Town arrived at the Rec having won just once in their opening 11 matches and were rooted to the foot of the division. In the weeks building up to the match they had been defeated 9-0 at Royston Town and 7-0 at Tring Town in the FA Vase. If ever a home win was a certainty this was it- wasn't it? The Robins even had their defender Tony Carter sent off before the interval but somehow it took a late Steve Stairs goal to earn a point in a 2-2 draw and whilst the unbeaten record was secured the 100% run was over. We always joked with midfielder Tony Calvert that it was his inclusion in the team that caused the problems. One of the most larger than life characters ever to wear the Aldershot Town shirt Tony had been unable to play the first few weeks of the campaign due to being suspended courtesy of a Sunday league match the previous season. Bracknell was the first match that he started replacing the previously ever present Shaun May and was he ever reminded of it in future years! In fairness he actually scored our equaliser in the first half of the Bracknell match.

Tony suffered a serious life changing illness many years later and I was saddened to learn of his plight because he is just an infectious character that would have you in stitches of laughter whatever the occasion. His dad, Colin, was also one of the nicest, kind-hearted blokes I have ever met and a skilled tradesman who was always on hand to help the club out whenever we needed him in the early days. He saved the club a fortune. Dedication that I never forget.

As another indication of how clubs managed to raise their game against us in those early years Bracknell then lost their next match, at Thame United 9-0. The 2,241 attendance that day broke another Division 3 record. Hard to believe that it was over 1,000 more recorded than would attend a Football League and five levels higher encounter versus Northampton Town over 20 years later. On the pitch the Bracknell draw did not appear to hinder the players and they continued to push themselves away at the top of the table.

An evening at Camberley Town brought back memories of yesteryear. It seemed incredible that Aldershot were playing their neighbours in a league match. Here was a Camberley team that I had watched as a youngster when Shots were away and remember the likes of Richard Parkin, Mickey Clarke, Brian Ives, Alan Turner and Keith Blount.

Indeed I recall watching a local derby at Farnborough Town on Boxing Day 1978 where the Surrey side defeated the 'Boro' in an epic 4-3 victory. They were some side too. Eventually many of the Camberley players switched the few miles across the county border to Farnborough. That was the beginning of a decline in fortunes on the pitch but they had, for me, provided some good memories. 13 years later and a Krooner Park record attendance for a competitive match of 2,066 (at a venue that averaged just 83 the previous season) saw goals from Osgood, Calvert and Tomlinson in a 3-1 victory.

We had a scare in an away match at Thame in mid-November though. A beautiful village in the Oxfordshire heartland it was always a pleasure to visit their welcoming Woodside Road Stadium and over 600 Shots fans had made the journey on a crisp afternoon to watch a side that had started the day in third position in the table. It wasn't going to plan though. We were 2-0 down entering the final 10 minutes. Boss Wignall had brought on Nunn and Lucas to try to change the outcome. Captain Osgood reduced the arrears with nine minutes remaining and in the final minute that man Lucas managed to net the all-important leveller. Everybody went mental when Lucas scored. That togetherness and solidarity between fan, player and management shone through again. The friendliness didn't extend to the two managers and Steve had a real issue with Thame boss

**A young Oliver with first ever ATFC boss Steve Wignall**

Bob Pratley at the end of the match when they went to shake hands. The boss of the Oxfordshire side was less than courteous to Steve and it bugged him.

The Thame match was important to me for another reason too. After putting out an article in the match day programme regarding the Shotsline, local businessman and supporter Philip Torjussen came forward and offered to sponsor me a mobile telephone through his company Telefonix- to cover the matches so I could update whilst they were in progress. I was made up and ever grateful to Philip who became not only a close friend but a tremendous sponsor of the club although some around the boardroom table needed constant reminders of exactly what Philip did contribute to the club. Sometimes it's not just monetary contributions, it is the hidden costs that are soaked up by the sponsor that the club never sees.

Philip Torjussen contributed thousands to Aldershot Town over the years and ensured that I had the apparatus available to ensure that the Shotsline was the most listened to service in non-league football and in the top five nationwide at all levels including the newly formed Premier League clubs. The leafy suburbs of Oxfordshire saw my dulcet tones set the stage at regular 15 minute intervals for the first time. Indeed our results at the time were not even included on Teletext. This is why the Shotsline was so successful. Fans knew that there would be an instant service. Yes it was a premium rate line but I like to think that over the years it provided a premium service. Through the years we introduced live commentaries and it was pure fun!

I loved those commentaries and the listening figures prove that the fans enjoyed them too. Indeed supporters still come up to me now and say that they always knew how we had got on when they rang the Shotsline for the result by the tone of my voice before I had read the result out. Indeed there was one match I covered between Collier Row and Thame United, our two main rivals. It was an evening match in Essex. The fact is that I wasn't even at the game, I was in the One Oak pub in Frimley. I made arrangements to speak to one of the bar staff every 15 minutes for an update by payphone in the foyer of the pub. I then rang the Shotsline to provide an update and had friends in the background shouting *"Come on The Row"* making out that they were at the match. It must have worked. The game itself finished 0-0 but we received over 500 calls on the night! Great days!

The first defeat was finally recorded in the third round of the Diadora League Cup at Premier division Hendon in mid-December, at the 24th time of asking. There was no disgrace in this, a 2-1 defeat by a team who were in seventh position three divisions higher. Leading up to the match we didn't have a goalkeeper either due to illness and, in Mark Watson's case, cup tied. We had to borrow Steve Osgood, who actually played in that final match at Cardiff City, from Windsor and Eton for the night. Another memory recall for the Hendon match was the attendance of 679. It looked far more and it caused our club to make a direct protest to the Isthmian League because as a cup match we were entitled to half of the revenue. This was not the only time we would have cause to take such a matter further and I hated it because we were shafted by some clubs. During my time as a full-time club official we never doctored an attendance figure. With the history surrounding the demise of AFC in my view we had a duty of care to our supporters to ensure that everything that we administered was done so properly and correctly without any opportunity for comeback later down the line. I would not have it any other way.

1993 started in a familiar way to 1992- a league defeat! However the previous calendar year's loss at home to Crewe Alexandra was in the Football League and was Aldershot's 13th in 21 matches. A year later and five divisions below a 2-1 reverse at Clapton was the first ever recorded by Aldershot Town in the 22nd match. The East London side were at the wrong end of the table and fighting a relegation battle. It was a dour afternoon at the Old Spotted Dog Ground, a venue that had seen better days. Stairs had put us in front at the interval and there appeared to be little danger of us conceding that treasured unbeaten league record as experienced substitute Gursel Gulfer was introduced.

I'm not sure if Gulfer had featured for Clapton before and I'm not certain if he ever did again but he certainly placed his name in the history books with a brace on 65 and 78 minutes. We were stunned. Defeat was experienced for the first time in league action and it hurt. I recall interviewing Clapton boss John Arnold after the match and he was elated. It showed to me how much it meant to beat Aldershot and as disappointed as we all were I was genuinely pleased for him. It also made me think that this would be a situation that we would need to deal with as we rose through the leagues because there were some pretty switched on clubs within the Isthmian League at higher levels who would just love to add the name of Aldershot Town as a scalp.

# Hope of Deliverance

1992

In January 1991 Aldershot had tested the versatility of West Ham United twice in the FA Cup third round attracting over 43,000 to the two matches. What Aldershot fan in their right mind would have contemplated the fact that two years later to the month their big match of the season would be against another side from the edge of the East End, Collier Row Football Club? It was a fact though. Row were second in the table and, although 14 points behind us, they had four matches in hand.

This was a vital period of the season. On the morning of the match groundsman Dave Tomlinson called me. *"Graham, it's wet. We've got a problem"*. Whenever Dave called I took it seriously. The groundsman's view is paramount to me on any pitch situation.

Many's the time Dave would have unintentionally ended my Saturday morning "fry up" with a phone call. I always used to come over straight away and, as we did on many occasions over the next 10 years, we got a team of helpers together, mainly from the Supporters Club committee, to do our damnedest to get the match on. Even Terry Owens and Peter Bridgeman were out there with their forks. That is what we all did though in those days. We mucked in together. You cannot beat that commitment but, in truth, it costs nothing but for some reason I learned that the higher up you progress the less likely people involved within a football club appear to want to get their hands dirty, as though they are above all that.

The teamwork for this match worked though and referee Vic Smith gave the green light. We were behind at the interval but, ironically, Dave's son Chris netted the equalising goal at the East Bank end after the break. A point apiece and a staggering attendance- 2,873! This was incredible for a match being played at the ninth tier of English football. It was 1,000 more than the previous evening's Football League match between Wigan Athletic and Reading. The following Tuesday evening Wimbledon entertained Everton in a Premier League match and attracted just 166 more through the turnstiles.

If the Collier Row match was all positive, the following week was possibly the lowest point many Aldershot Town fans will recall as an Isthmian League club- a visit to Bedfordshire and Leighton Town. There was nothing pleasant about the place from the time we arrived off the team coach at Bell Close. There had been crowd disturbances at the home match in September, all emanating, I may add, from the visiting supporters which I had witnessed at close hand from my seat in the press box which was in the South Stand in those days. There had been rumblings about the return match which had been made all ticket but none of us could have expected what actually occurred. The atmosphere was just putrid. The welcome from the home officials was downright shameful. It had started in the week leading up to the match when their manager Bill Harrison had said in the local press that Aldershot *"Are a Diadora League side now and it's time they acted like one. We shouldn't have to bend over backwards for them"*. When the match got underway the 700 Shots fans in the record attendance of 1,522 had one half of the ground. However the two sets of fans were segregated by weak fencing. Home fans were watching the game pouring pint after pint down them and then it all went off. Fans were attacked during and after the match.

Post-match it was mob rule with bricks and stones as our fans had to make their way down a narrow exit in fear of their safety. It was just horrible and I saw decent people who I have known for years suffer injuries and shock. We took the matter further with the Isthmian League for what it was worth. Aldershot have never played Leighton Town again since that dark day in January 1993. That is probably the only saving grace from the whole episode. To add to the woe we also lost the match 1-0 but could have few complaints on that score.

# No Limit

1992

We never lost again that season in league action and it was really just a case of when promotion would be rubber-stamped. However, for the time being, league football took a back seat.

A tidy run in the Hampshire Senior Cup had seen higher opposition seen off with the likes of Newport (IOW), Gosport Borough and Waterlooville being defeated. It set up a semi-final against Conference neighbours Farnborough Town. It was decided to stage the match at the Rec, not that there would be any financial benefit for the club as the county association would net most of the gate receipts as it was a semi-final tie. Mind you, this match was huge and a real story. There had never been any real rivalry between the two towns within the borough of Rushmoor in football terms. Aldershot had always been the Football League outfit whilst 'Boro had progressed through the pyramid since their 1967 formation, reaching the Conference under the guidance of Ted Pearce in 1991 and finishing fifth in their first season behind champions Colchester United. However there was no doubt that this match was intriguing and would certainly capture the imagination of the local public. I have to be honest though I was staggered at the final level of interest. In truth our old friend Peter Hutchinson helped to stoke the fire. His article in the build-up to the match couldn't have been any more condescending to our football club. The bottom line was that the article belittled Aldershot, our fans and everything that we stood for. Yes we were playing at four levels below 'Boro' but despite their success in the Conference Farnborough had always struggled to attract the attendances their progress probably deserved. At the time of the match they were averaging 840 to our 2,000 or so.

Hutchinson hit right to the jugular though- *"Tuesday is Boro's training night, so they will simply switch from Cherrywood Road to the Recreation Ground"*- he started. *"A nice little run-out against Aldershot should give Boro ace David Leworthy the chance to boost his impressive tally of 41 goals"*. Then he hit the jackpot if he was aiming to rile us- *"Some cynics reckon soccer-starved Recreation Ground fans were so desperate following the death of the League club that they would turn out in force to watch Subbuteo...If 'Boro take it easy, they should rattle in four or five goals. But if Boro decide to turn on the style then Aldershot may find themselves on the receiving end of a seven or eight goals drubbing!"* The anger was evident all around. Steve Wignall was apoplectic. I was fuming and was straight on the phone to Penmark House, the home of the Aldershot News.

Hutchinson had played his part, although not deliberately, in building up the match and the Rec was buzzing two hours before kick-off. The High Street turnstiles had queues stretching beyond the railway bridge. Was this really a Diadora League Division 3 venue? By the time of kick-off there were 5,961 spectators inside the stadium. The final itself, the following month, attracted less than 1,000 spectators. The game was a treasure too.

There was a fear that Hutchinson may have cause to gloat when, after Leworthy and Aldershot-born Jamie Horton had given the visitors an early two-goal lead. However the match was a pure spectacle. We were actually on level terms for 23 minutes and I will never forget the reaction of the crowd when Chris Tomlinson levelled matters on 62 minutes. Leworthy did add to his 41 goals though and scored the eventual winner with five minutes remaining.

We had far from disgraced ourselves though and came out of the match with a huge amount of credit. The backlash surrounding the News article continued.

After the match I went for Hutchinson and had to be calmed down by our Youth Development Officer Paul Beves before I did something that I would regret.

As a bit of a laugh the Supporters Club organised a Subbuteo competition in the social club that summer and named it the "Peter Hutchinson Trophy". In fairness to Peter he took it in good stead and actually agreed to turn up and present the trophy to the winner. Pretty bold really as there would be plenty of disgruntled Shots fans in the tournament gunning for him. I thought I would turn up just to see how it was all going and ended up entering the competition. Imagine how I felt when I progressed through to the final and actually won it. There was I being presented with the "Peter Hutchinson Subbuteo Trophy" by the man himself. In a way though it broke the ice but there were still plenty of negatives to contend with. Peter had a knack of turning up after kick-off. He preferred the comforts of his local more than the Rec on a Saturday afternoon and he was more often than not inebriated. He would come over to me and I would give him the bullet points of what he had missed. Peter was an "old school" journalist and there are few of them remaining today. After a few years I decided that enough was enough. There was no point in keeping going to the Editor and complaining. I contacted Peter a couple of years later and said we should meet, just the two of us and discuss how the club and newspaper could work together. He agreed but he was to be on home territory, the Old Courthouse in Farnborough. He said to arrive at midday. A couple of hours I thought. Wrong! I didn't leave that pub until near on closing time. I don't recall how I got home but I remember that we must have had a competition to see who would slip off the bar stool the most. I may have endured the hangover of hangovers but it appeared to do the trick. We always had a mutual respect for each other afterwards and I got to know him well. When he left the News Group we often bumped into each other in Farnborough and reminisced. Peter passed away in 2011 aged just 71 and I attended his funeral. *"Have you come to make sure he's finally gone?"* joked Nick Cherrie. Actually I had come to pay my final respects to a man who eventually I came to like.

The remainder of the season was enjoyable. We gained promotion in Hertfordshire at Tring Town before winning the league at home to Thame United.

In between those Saturdays The Good Lady and I even managed to get engaged with the party, of course, in the social club! The season concluded with a carnival atmosphere in the final home match of the season versus Kingsbury Town and a 4-0 victory before a final day success up the road at Cove.

By the end of the campaign we had won the league by 18 points, made a profit of £29,996 with the playing and management expenditure at just £44,163. Fans had turned out in significant numbers at a level never previously seen in the third division of the Isthmian League. 30 home matches had seen a return of 111 goals added to 14 victories on the road.

Football returning to the town had significant effects elsewhere too. As a club we had a policy of community involvement. There had been the completion of a disabled facility and installation of a disabled toilet although I did have a chuckle regarding this, recalling an incident. There was a guy called George who was wheelchair-bound and ran the disabled section.

He was pretty switched on regarding funding opportunities. One day I needed to speak to him and was in Aldershot and knew where he lived. I decided to pop over but when I entered his house there he was up a ladder painting! I didn't know who was more shocked – him or me! I don't know what the extent of his disability was but he had always been in a wheelchair when I had previously been with him. It was all a bit of a surprise.

With a much improved relationship with local schools and community groups too it was a fact – Aldershot Town were very much "Alive and Kicking"! We even scooped the 1993 Rothmans Football Merit Award with the likes of Alex Ferguson, George Graham and, ironically, Teddy Sheringham who were also in receipt.

We didn't get everything right though and one matter I sincerely regret is not offering Tommy McAnearney a lifetime seat in the Directors Box. I never really knew Tommy that well but was in awe of him due to his considerable achievements as manager during my days as a youngster. The Scotsman had remained in Aldershot after his involvement at the club had ended in 1981 and was a postman. He often popped into our offices, mainly to speak to Rosemary Aggett and talk about good times from the past. I often thought about doing something for Tommy to honour the sterling job that he did but never took it further. I should have done. We had provided his coach John Anderson a similar distinction which was fully deserved. Tommy McAnearney deserved such an accolade too and I wasn't strong enough to provide a case for his defence. A mistake.

# What's Up

The start of the following season saw plenty of encouragement but it was going to be harder, that was for sure. Two clubs in particular had raised the stakes. Newbury Town and Chertsey Town appeared to have a never-ending supply of capital, far more than we could ever dream of as a club, which enabled them to attract some experienced former pros. It was obviously not going to last forever but for the short-term these two clubs would be difficult rivals.

The success of our first season and the increased demand and requirements of the club meant that a full-time position of responsibility was essential. Peter Bridgeman had stepped down as Company Secretary but, for the time being, retained the football aspect of the job.

The Board of Directors offered me the position with a remuneration of £196 per week and 15% net commission from the Shotsline. I accepted that I was never going to be a millionaire and there were no year in, year out annual increases either but it was a dream job in reality and I wanted to give it a go. The acceptance of my new role meant that I had to step down as Chairman of the Supporters Club and, indeed, the director representing the club on the Board. I passed this onto Barry Underwood and knew that the role was in more than capable hands. Representing the fans on the Board was always a difficult role.

In truth some of the directors never quite got it and it used to frustrate me even at the level of football we were at. It should have been so simple but there was often a case of "us and them" about it and it made it doubly difficult to get some common ground on occasions.

I remember having a row with one of the directors, Kevin Donegan, at a meeting and storming out and screeching my car in a backspin so they all knew how I felt at the time. On reflection it was pretty immature but I was 15/20 years younger than these guys. Kevin did call me the next day and apologise which was good of him but in the end it all became too tiresome and the fresh approach of Barry could only be of benefit to the club.

What did miff me afterwards is that after accepting the full-time position I received all kinds of dogs abuse from the fanzine "Talk of the Town" and even a letter from a "Name and Address supplied" in the local paper. I had written countless letters to the press over the years but was always brave enough to leave my own name and address to it.

One particular guy had the real hump with me even querying the fact that I had earned £5,298 during our first ever season. Never mind the fact that I was at the club most days during that first year. Another questioned my integrity on a large scale in the fanzine. Mind you I had made enough criticisms of Aldershot FC over many years and now the boot was on the other foot I just had to grin and bear it. Not pleasant at first but you soon learn to develop a thick skin if you are involved at a football club. You have to because you are constantly in the firing line. Somebody else always knows better.

On the pitch it was 'as you were' although after defeating Egham Town 3-2 in the opening match of the campaign I was a touch surprised at receiving a call on the Monday morning from a supporter. He told me, "We're not happy with what's going on at the club. It's going the same way as the previous club." The guy, who was never backwards in coming forwards for "freebies" for many years in the future, continued to tell me that we hadn't played well since Christmas.

I responded, stating that we had just won the league by 18 points and had lost just twice in 38 matches. The call taught me that despite the obvious progress the club was making there would always be a section of supporters dissatisfied and always looking for more. I thought the guy was being unreasonable and told him so. We slaughtered big spending Newbury Town 3-0 playing at Basingstoke Town's Camrose Ground whilst the Berkshire club's ground was being upgraded, in front of 1,310 spectators, mainly Shots fans. This was a Newbury side that included the likes of former Reading trio Martin Hicks, Steve Richardson and Stuart Beavon. They even had former England and Arsenal coach Don Howe coaching them. No follow-up call from the supporter after this polished performance.

We did suffer a setback in the Diadora League cup with a 4-0 home defeat versus Premier division Kingstonian in front of over 2,500 spectators. It was no disgrace to witness our first ever home defeat as the Surrey side were a decent outfit including the likes of experienced campaigners such as David Harlow, Phil Wingfield and Andy Russell. However it was the off-pitch drama that created all the headlines. "K's" were managed by the "Leatherhead Lip" Chris Kelly and he was true to his name with vitriolic abuse streaming our way before, during and after the match.

Kelly, nickname provided after his antics whilst at Leatherhead and their famous FA Cup run of 1974/75, accused our club and its officials of having an *"Attitude problem"*, criticising the way we operated off the pitch stating that *"It is easier to get into Fort Knox than Aldershot"*. This was another match waiting to be lit for the Aldershot News who couldn't wait to get started focussing more on the off-pitch matters than the actual match itself. There was even a contingent of our supporters who felt the best way to deal with the matter was to ban the newspaper altogether.

Despite understanding and recognising their frustrations I thought this was a step too far but it was an obvious problem.

By the time the "big" match with league leaders Chertsey Town came around in early December we went into the match still unbeaten. There was a capacity 2,150 attendance for the all-ticket affair at Alwyns Lane including 1,500 travelling Shots, many of whom had travelled by a chartered train from Aldershot Station-unheard of at this level. Chertsey were rich in cash at this time too and included the likes of Kenny Sansom and Ricky Hill in their squad in addition to former Shots players John Granville and Jason Tucker. This match was full-on too as we lost 3-2. However there was never any real doubt that we would gain a second successive promotion along with Newbury and Chertsey. The three teams were far too dominant. It was just left to see who would finish where in the top three.

The main "beef" I had in our second season as a club was the way other clubs would try to commercialise their home match with us at the expense of our own fans. Many's the time we would have to raise objections due to certain scenarios for the benefit of our fans. I can remember one such example at Egham Town. The Surrey club not only raised the price of admission prices and the match programme but they also took the liberty of providing Shots supporters with a separate bar. That all looked nice and cosy until we realised that our fans were being charged an extra 50p a pint! Our fans were decent too. Having experienced the demise of their club they were quick to show support to clubs facing a similar predicament. Nearly £900 was raised when Essex side Rainham Town visited the Rec and a year or two later a similar exercise was provided to help Dorking FC.

We weren't flavour of the month with all clubs though. Earlier that season I received a particularly frosty ride at a Suburban League AGM. I had to give a presentation to the members in order for us to be accepted into the established reserve team competition. The representative from Tring Town absolutely castigated our club, speaking against the application. "*Big Time Charlies*" he referred to us as. He wasn't moaning the season before when our fans packed the bars at Tring when we secured promotion and a few bob was earned. A guy from Ashford Town (Middlesex) called Alan Constable came to my rescue and I always remember that.

# Give it Away

Cup football became fever pitch from the turn of the year. We had another "ding dong" battle with Farnborough Town which attracted over 7,000 to the two matches. Although we lost to a late Andy Nunn own goal in the replay – boy does this guy still get ribbed about it over 20 years later – at least both clubs benefitted more this time financially as it was at the quarter-final stage.

The main emphasis was on the FA Vase. The rules in those days meant that we were ineligible for the FA Cup until 1994/95 whilst this was the first season we could enter the Vase. Promotion to the first division of the Isthmian League would also mean that it would be the only time too.

We were ticking along nicely in the competition having disposed of Gosport Borough (7-0), Thatcham Town (1-0), Herne Bay (2-1), Malden Vale (1-0) and Soham Town Rangers (5-0). All of a sudden we had reached the last 16 of the Wembley-bound competition. No Aldershot team had ever made it to the "twin towers" and there was going to be no better opportunity than this one. We were drawn at home to 1992 winners Wimborne Town in the fifth round and a team with some pedigree too. It was an incredible afternoon. Nearly 3,500 saw a special performance from Steve Wignall's men and a perfectly guided late header from Mark Frampton settle the issue and we were in the quarter-finals. I liked Mark. He was a Frimley boy and was in the year below me at school so that was a good start. A prolific goal scorer in local football he was at Aldershot at the wrong time because the Butler and Stairs partnership meant that it was nigh on impossible for him to break through.

We were paired with a side from Greater Manchester called Atherton Laburnum Rovers. We treated the match as a carnival and the East Bank was packed in an attendance of 4,246. Rovers were a physical side, set upon making life as difficult as possible for our players. They had a long-haired player called Stuart Humphries who was an expert in the field of wind-ups and he played up to the crowd at every opportunity and did so effectively.

Indeed they were so successful in doing so that Mark Butler suffered the fate of being the first player to be sent off since our formation. He was distraught. Mark scored our first ever goal, is the record goal scorer and owns a variety of honours and deservedly so. I always remind him too- *"Yes Mark, and the first to be sent off for us too!"* My own recollection of Atherton was that their Chairman Derek Halliwell came across as particularly unpleasant. However they succeeded in earning a goalless draw and a replay which nobody really fancied.

Information regarding the return game at Atherton was sketchy to say the least. They played at Crilly Park, somewhere between Bolton and Wigan. We were assured that their stadium had a stand and they would be able to accommodate our travelling supporters who wished to sit. The replay was held the following Saturday and we took over 1,000 fans to the north-west. Make no bones about it, this was a tough ask. Rovers were top of the North West Counties Division 1 by nine points and had won their previous nine home matches in the league.

It was an awful blustery afternoon and I travelled on the team coach, stopping overnight at Haydock Park, along with some nervous players, especially Tony Calvert who I recall placed a towel over his head to calm himself down. When we arrived there were a few discrepancies from what we had been told by our hosts. For one there was no stand that supporters could sit in. I had been told by Rovers officials and the police that we would have 200 seats available on the day. I don't know where they were supposed to come from. There weren't any seats save for some behind one goal that could not be used to watch a football match.

Some of our elderly fans who had travelled had to make do with watching the match from the team coach which had been made available to them. I provided a commentary on the Shotsline standing on the windswept roof of the dressing rooms. It was all so archaic but it was also intimidating too. Despite our huge support we were clearly the underdogs. The performance on the day was heroic. Our defensive contribution was superb and the match concluded at extra time with no goals. In those days second replays were the order of the day. No penalty shoot-outs and the destination of the replay would be decided by the toss of the coin. I was broadcasting live on the Shotsline as Steve Wignall, Dave Osgood and the manager and captain of our opponents were in the dressing room with the referee. Good old Roger Furnandiz from Doncaster. We won the toss and I went ballistic on Shotsline. It was all back to Aldershot on the Tuesday evening. There was no way Atherton would fancy that. We were in the box seat.

That was as good as it got though. Rovers won the match 2-0 and put in a professional performance on us. In truth we froze on the night with another 4,500 attendance and I cannot recall feeling as low as I did at the end of the match, not for another 19 years and a trip to South Yorkshire anyway. I just burst into tears and couldn't explain why. I was so desperate to see Aldershot grace the Wembley stage and this was going to be the only realistic opportunity for many, many years and we had blown it. I also felt for the players too. Most knew that this was their opportunity too and they knew the consequences. It may sound ungracious but the visiting players and officials were poisonous on the night and they didn't act in the manner befitting of their achievement. They more than intimidated our supporters and, sadly, some rose to the bait which was unhelpful. Whatever the circumstances they were in the semi-final versus Diss Town and we weren't. I did have a wry smile a few weeks later when they were knocked out by their Norfolk opponents.

There was no looking back in the league, however, and by the end of the season we had finished third in the table with a phenomenal 97 points. Both Newbury and Chertsey both managed 100 plus. All I remember from the end of the season was catching chickenpox on the May Bank Holiday at Lewes and taking six hours driving back from the south coast due to the traffic. Another decent season though.

# Parklife

1992

With two successive promotions the foundations of the club were in good health. Another profit had been made of just under £20,000 but there was a big step up into the Isthmian League division one. All of a sudden we were paired with the likes of Billericay Town, Maidenhead United, Basingstoke Town and Bognor Regis Town – established clubs at the level we were competing. However the biggest problem for Steve Wignall was that the Isthmian League committee had agreed to become an experimental league for allowing a kick-in to take the place of a throw-in – some FIFA initiative. This was all well and good but Steve had already assembled the squad by the time the notification came through. If he had been made aware of it earlier he would have signed a squad full of six-foot plus players capable of influencing the direct approach. Steve was fuming about this and it was another indication of the frustrations he experienced at the non-league level, having spent the bulk of his career in the professional game.

Despite some good results in the cup, an excellent 3-1 success at Newport AFC in Wales in an FA Trophy qualifier and an historic inaugural FA Cup victory at Bemerton Heath Harlequins (4-0) on the final Sunday in August and covered on BBC Football Focus, we stuttered somewhat in the league.

We reached the third qualifying round of the FA Trophy and were due to play at home to Northamptonshire side Rothwell Town who played in the Southern League Midland division. We drew the match 1-1 and had midfielder Danny Holmes sent off by referee Eddie Green. Steve and I traipsed over to The Crimea the following Monday to watch the video of the dismissal (we had no such luxuries in the club) to confirm whether it was justified or not.

It appeared harsh, very harsh. However that was the least of our worries. A phone call from the Football Association to our football secretary, Peter Bridgeman, explained that a protest had been lodged by Rothwell regarding the registration of our new signing Solomon Eriemo from Kingstonian. He had made his debut in the FA Trophy match. In those days seven days were required for clearance to play in FA Cup competitions. All the necessary paperwork had been completed and submitted from our end and, as far as we were concerned, Eriemo was able to play for us as a non-contract player at the time who had been registered with the league within the specified period to participate in the match. However as the Surrey club, whose Chief Executive by this stage was our old "friend" Chris Kelly, had not cancelled his contract when they confirmed that they would we were in a touch of hot water.

The replay was cancelled late on the Tuesday and I remember being in my office contacting all and sundry to let them know of the situation. It wasn't as though the Sky Television "Breaking News" ticker tape was available. There was no reason for anybody to think that the game would be in any doubt. Many fans turned up at Rothwell in addition to those at Redan Hill waiting for the supporters coaches. They were baffled and we had a lot of explaining to do to the fans. Working full-time by this stage upstairs within the main club building we used to have a buzzer to notify us of anybody making contact. I recall one such buzz and went down to meet the enquirer. An elderly fan, who I didn't really know that well at the time, just put an article relating to the Rothwell incident in front of me with the words- "*Explain THAT to me then*". We had a heated but fair discussion regarding the situation. The gentleman's name was Paul Muddell. I got to learn that this was Paul's way and that he was a terrific supporter of the club. I gradually warmed to him and he would do anything for the football club. He eventually became the Chairman of the Supporters Club before sadly passing away on Boxing Day 2007 after a match at Woking. We had one thing in common- our shared affection for Aldershot Town.

The FA disciplinary hearing ruled that we were guilty as charged and we were thrown out of the FA Trophy. We were learning that non-league football possessed some murky characters who would think nothing of turning you over if they could. As an organisation the FA exonerated us from any wrongdoing but still kicked us out of the competition. Explain that one!

I cheekily contacted the FA and spoke to Steve Clark in the Competitions department. I said to him that as the match versus Rothwell no longer counted due to the ineligibility of our player then the dismissal of Danny Holmes was also null and void.

He was having none of it but to me if the game doesn't stand, scorer Dave Hooker's goal doesn't stand then why does the dismissal stand.

I never understood Rothwell's thinking on the matter either. Why contact the FA the day of the replay to lodge the complaint? They would have been more intelligent to have waited until after the replay. The attendance at the replay would have been considerable and they lost earnings in all departments including social facilities. The irony is that when they played the next round fixture versus Gateshead the attendance was 422, the exact same crowd we had the same afternoon for a reserve team match at the Rec- a spooky coincidence.

We even had a continental occasion for a cup match too- well, Sylvans Sports in Guernsey in the Hampshire Senior Cup. This was some adventure too. The supporters travelled over on the ferry, a couple of hundred or so, and, with such an early start and a bar available throughout, were much the worse for wear by their arrival. I travelled over with the team on the Saturday morning on one of those propeller planes which you really didn't have confidence with. My brother had travelled the shortest distance, from Jersey, where he lived by then and it was some game. We eventually won the match 3-2 after extra time but had key players Butler and Osgood sent off. The Shotsline was buzzing from a live commentary until the battery ran out due to the extra time. Over 1,700 calls were made. Our supporters were not amused with the referee though and I can remember one of our fans getting carried away and running onto the pitch. I had to usher him off pretty quickly. Many years later standing behind the same fan, he absolutely slaughtered a supporter who jumped onto the perimeter of the pitch after we had scored a goal at the East Bank end. I should have reminded him of his Channel Islands experience. The evening was lively too as we were staying overnight. I ended up spending the Sunday morning in the local hospital on the island, coughing up blood after being continuously sick after a night out. It was nothing to do with those bottles of Fosters Ice- honest!

Not long after this the club lost the President of the Supporters Club, Bill Warren, 18-months after the loss of another stalwart in Les Chandler. A chirpy Cockney by birth Bill had been involved with Aldershot old and new for decades. He was the last of the "old school" committee members who had seen the organisation through tough times. These guys epitomised what representing Aldershot supporters was all about. Despite being over 80 Bill was always up at the crack of dawn and down at the ground where he was responsible for the refreshment huts as one of his duties. He was there every day and in those days they would open for every fixture, be it a first team match or a local schools cup match at the Rec. I learned so much from the likes of Bill and Les. They were always there to put me right if I was getting a touch carried away and they always had a story to tell. Their involvement was purely just for the love of the club and not for some egotistical or personal crusade that you find so much more these days, even in fan groups.

# Whatever

1992

Despite the cup success the league situation, for the first time since our formation, was proving inconsistent. We lost 4-1 at home to a lively Worthing side in the opening game of 1995 and then some fans started to turn as we narrowly lost at Barking on a quagmire of a pitch.

However in the background developments were at the initial stage that would see Steve Wignall leave the club to take charge of his former club Colchester United, for whom George Burley had left to become manager of Ipswich Town. It was a no-brainer really. Steve had the opportunity to return to the Football League at a club which he and his wife Anne had fond memories of.

I was sorry to see Steve go. I enjoyed working with him and learning much about his professional ethics. Many forget that, in addition to being a successful manager for our club, he was an inspirational centre half who made 199 appearances for the old club and was an integral part of the 1986/87 promotion squad. During the 102 league matches that he took charge of his team accumulated over 70% of the points available.

Some people have said to me that anybody could have achieved success managing Aldershot Town in our early days-absolute nonsense. The pressures faced were unique and Steve steered his team to overcome many hurdles to achieve what he did. He set the foundations of not just a football team but a club up to prosper and deserved his opportunity to progress his career.

The popular Paul Shrubb was put in caretaker charge and his claim to fame is that he is the only Aldershot Town manager to have 100% record as a manager after a 2-0 home success versus Berkhamsted Town. He should have been in charge the following week at Billericay Town. Despite the heavy rain that the country had succumbed to overnight our counterparts at the Essex club assured us that all was ok and the match would definitely be on. I recall travelling on the team coach. On arrival I went straight onto the pitch and my feet sunk into the grass. You could just about make out my knees. *"Why have we wasted our time?"* I said to their secretary. They had deliberately misled us to travel although there was no hope the match could have been played. This was a ploy that happened often over the years because the home club knew that if our fans arrived in numbers they would still benefit from the bar takings if not the admission fees.

The process for a new manager took place with the interviews held at Potters International Hotel. Make no mistake, it was a sought after job and we had some quality candidates at all levels of the game.

The successful candidate was 33-year-old Steve Wigley, a former winger of Nottingham Forest, Portsmouth and Birmingham City. Indeed Steve was still playing and had featured against the Shots for Bognor Regis Town earlier in the season. His character references, including Jim Smith and Alan Ball, were impressive and when we contacted them they spoke extremely highly of Steve.

When he returned for his second interview he had an abundance of contacts at his disposal. At the time he was a travelling salesman but was keen to return to the game full-time and he knew his stuff.

For me it was fortunate because at the interview process I was always the one who would meet and greet each candidate which enabled me to get to know them too. I also had the dubious honour of having to contact all the unsuccessful candidates personally by phone to let them know that they wouldn't be getting the job and to thank them for their time. Mind you it was always the Chairman who would make the call to the successful candidate.

Steve Wigley (left) signs on with former Secretary Peter Bridgeman

I can also categorically state too that whilst I was Company Secretary every managerial application was responded to. It's just plain manners to do so.

Steve's arrival did see the departure of a number of stalwarts from the original 1992/93 season over a period of time with Keith Baker being the first departure.

Keith was disappointed that Steve had not made contact with him and decided that it was time for him to go. His contribution to the club had been immense.

The team was ticking along fine under Steve's guidance until an April Tuesday evening visit of Tooting and Mitcham to the Rec. We were six points off the pace although we did have games in hand. This was one of them and victory would have put the pressure on the teams above us as we entered the business end of the season. The south London side were fighting a relegation battle. We were 3-0 down at the interval and, despite a late rally, lost the match 4-3. It was, indeed a setback but all I can recall was the post-match analysis of the match and Steve slaughtering his coaching staff in no uncertain terms. He launched into a verbal attack and it all surrounded Chris Hollins. The midfielder had played a number of matches earlier in the season under Steve Wignall but had since left the club. Still registered on Isthmian League forms and with the injury situation not great Steve was informed that Chris could do a job. He duly started the Tooting match and such was his performance Steve blasted his staff- "*If you're going to recommend a player to me in future make sure that he can f****** play the game.*" Chris never played for the club again but he certainly carved out a good career within the media working for the BBC. His claim to fame, however, was winning Strictly Come Dancing in 2009. I wonder if Steve had a wry smile if he was watching the programme?

A late rally saw maximum points collected from the final five matches. As we entered the last fixture of the season we were in with a shout. We had to defeat the now financially stricken Newbury Town who needed a point to stay up and rely on Chertsey Town not beating Basingstoke Town. We concluded our side of the bargain with ease. A 3-0 victory in front of 2,921 fans at the Rec was only spoiled by the dismissal of our captain Paul Chambers.

At one stage Chertsey were trailing at home to Ernie Howe's men. We had somebody at Alwyns Lane who was keeping me in touch with events and I was relaying matters via the Shotsline and to the supporters at the match. Our match finished a few minutes before the Chertsey game and I was providing a running commentary.

The Surrey side scored a late winner with Stuart Cash on the score sheet to win the match 2-1 and gain promotion alongside Boreham Wood and Worthing. There was an obvious air of disappointment at the final whistle. Many fans said that it was not a disaster for us and that we would be stronger for it the next season and gain promotion then. Wrong! It took another three years before we would be celebrating such a feat.

# Boom Boom Boom (Not!)

1992

We couldn't have started the following season off on a more negative note and it was a major lesson to learn regarding communications. We had previously told supporters that if we didn't gain promotion there would be no increase in admission prices. On the actual eve of the campaign it was realised that there would be a shortfall in our budget. The Board decided that there was no option but to increase the gate prices. I understood the philosophy, especially realising that to play at the Rec was becoming more expensive than we anticipated due to the aging stadium and additional costs that were required. It cost £125,000 just to use the facility in the first three seasons alone. I fought my corner along with Barry Underwood because we knew the outcry there would be from the terraces. As expected the fans went ballistic and I knew that I would bear the brunt of it as I was full-time at the club. Phone call after phone call followed. Conversations with people that I had known since I was at school and they weren't happy.

It didn't help that we started the season slowly and by the time we lost 3-2 at Staines Town in mid-September and had two players in Jimmy Sugrue and Tony Cleeve sent off the pressure was building. As is often the case when the football is poor supporters are microscopic in just about every element of their club. As the match ended at Wheatsheaf Lane I was walking from the stand to the dressing room when I was confronted by some fans. *"What do you do for this club, Brookland? "You're a disgrace."* I wasn't having that and the red mist descended. I responded and in the end had to be escorted away by club photographer Ian Morsman.

It annoyed me though but as previously stated you learn to develop thicker skin by the week if you are involved in football.

Around this time if we had lost at the weekend I knew what would happen when I arrived in the office on Monday morning. The ansaphone would be flashing and there would be message after message of abuse. A few years later one supporter who left messages and personal attacks sadly passed away. I was genuinely saddened to learn the news but not being close to the individual I didn't attend the funeral. I then faced criticism for not doing so. You can't win sometimes.

The honeymoon period was over though. An inconsistent season in the league left few memories although a visit to Whyteleafe is fondly recalled. A match seemingly going nowhere, it started to pour with rain. I lost my signal commentating on the Shotsline with us 1-0 up.

I left the main stand to find a suitable signal elsewhere, walking around the perimeter of the pitch. By the time I found it 10 minutes later we were leading 6-0. Yes five goals were scored in eight minutes in a truly bizarre afternoon in Surrey.

A fortnight later an FA Trophy match at Gloucester City saw a rare outing for The Good Lady. We arrived at 11am in the city but didn't get to the ground until 20 minutes into the game by which time we were 2-1 down. Every time we asked where the ground was we got directed to the rugby stadium. We also got lost down one specific road and found out it was Cromwell Street, the road where serial killers Fred and Rose West had lived. Kerb-crawling, passers-by may have thought we were sightseeing but we certainly were not and couldn't wait to get out of the road. The match was no better either and we made a swift exit from the competition, 5-1.

Kevin Donegan was voted off the Board at a shareholders meeting soon after and this certainly caused a rift within the Board which was never repaired. The removal of Kevin had been initiated by Terry and it all emanated from the fact that the club shop, of which Kevin was responsible for due to his own business within sportswear, made just £131 during the year. A hand vote (56 to 16) confirmed Kevin's removal and this was verified by a ballot. There was a public spat in the local paper who loved a touch more controversy. Kevin said *"Under Terry Owens I feel the club is doomed to failure. I'm calling for him to resign so a safer pair of hands can take over"*. After all the Boardroom uncertainty of the old club this was the last thing we needed as a club. What did occur is that for the first time in the short history a Vice Chairman was appointed in Karl Prentice. Karl was a Yorkshireman who hailed from Bradford and actually had trials for Bradford Park Avenue before they were replaced by Cambridge United in the Football League in 1970. Karl had moved south in 1976 and been a director since the outset. He had also been financially bruised by the old club as a creditor too, responsible for the production of the match day programme and one of those present at Barnet in March 1992 who had put his hands in his pockets to help fund the players getting home.

A home match versus Staines Town saw the return of that man Darren Anderson. Wearing the shirt of our Middlesex opponents he was true to form, getting sent off for violent conduct.

# They don't Care About us

1992

A fifth place finish in the league was achieved but we had managed to reach the final of the Isthmian League Cup, sponsored by Guardian Insurance in those days. The match, versus Kingstonian, should have been staged at Hayes Football Club. It soon became obvious to us that nobody really wanted to stage it and the Isthmian League were struggling after Hayes pulled out of being hosts. We were eventually informed that it would be held at the Rec.

The Isthmian League committee could be extremely stubborn when it wanted to be told us we had no choice in the matter. Picture this- we had no control over pricing, segregation, programmes and were only allowed 12 of our own officials into the Directors Box which would be catering for sponsors and league officials too. We couldn't even wear our traditional home strip and wore our white change kit. It was a recipe for disaster really. The Isthmian League wanted everything, warts and all. I remember working with Karl making sure we had extended arrangements in place for an additional party for the League secretary Nick Robinson in the South Stand bar. We eventually got hauled over the coals by the Isthmian League who said that we had underpaid them from the gate receipts, never mind all the additional costings that we accumulated in order to support them.

Prior to kick-off I was in the tea room adjacent to the dressing rooms when a rather perturbed referee came sauntering in. No introduction, nothing. He bulldozed me for the fact that there were only three seats in the match officials room when there should have been four as there was a fourth official on this occasion, unheard of at that level at the time. He was so rude and disrespectful and put my back up. His name was Steve Bennett, the guy who refereed that first ever away league match at Collier Row and who went on to become a top Premier League referee. His day didn't get any better once the match started either. We lost 4-1 but it was a total misrepresentation of the afternoon's activities with two goals scored in the final minute. Bennett didn't cover himself in glory on the day on the pitch either. He tried to report one of our officials after the match at the top of the tunnel entrance. His face was pure white and the official said to him quite respectfully, *"The fans think you lost control ref"*. He wanted to put our official on a charge and did, indeed, report him. We just pleaded innocence when the paperwork came through. *"What official? Could have been anybody. It wasn't our home match after all!"*

# A Design for Life

1992

**W**e signed the season off with two matches which, to me, were extremely important. I value community highly and believe it essential for football clubs to connect in this way. We were honoured to stage the 100th anniversary of the Aldershot Football Association with a representative side of the best local players featuring against us.

Whilst I was secretary it was imperative in my view to work with Eddie Spraggett and the Aldershot FA plus the Aldershot and Farnborough Schools FA and their hard-working President Charlie Mortimore who was "Mr Football" in the local area. We used to stage countless cup finals at the end of each season on the Rec and it meant the world to both organisations too. I did, however, used to hate it when we had late cancellations due to heavy rain and I would have to inform the waiting kids that the match was cancelled and see their obvious disappointment.

The Mark Francis Trophy was something that epitomised our club in the early days too. Mark was a young man who sadly passed away due to cancer.

He was an avid Shots fan and we used to stage an annual match in his memory at the Rec between the club staff and Supporters Club team. It meant so much to Mark's family and was important to Peter Bridgeman and me that we staged it. Mark's Dad Peter remains a regular to this day.

I had a rare break in the summer as The Good Lady and I got married and there was a good representation from the football club at the wedding. This was the nice side of football too. Our honeymoon was spent at Karl Prentice's luxury caravan in Poole. He and his then wife Lynne had taken the time to decorate it for our arrival too. In football you have fall outs all the time, it is that kind of environment, but you don't forget some of the gestures people make too and The Good Lady and I will never forget this one even if we did have a few rumblings for a short period later on down the line. Karl didn't have to give us his caravan but he did.

By this time my role had been expanded to incorporate Peter Bridgeman's duties. Peter was stepping down after four seasons' sterling service and the commitment he and his wife Lee gave to ensuring our football club was able to flourish should always be remembered. A volunteer, he did a terrific job.

# How Bizarre

1992

The opening day of the 1996/97 season was comical. Wigley's old club Bognor Regis Town, managed by Jack Pearce, were the opponents at the Rec. A real character, he was "Mr Bognor Regis" and had managed them in over 1000 matches even at that stage and went on for many more years in that position. The Sussex club had their keeper Dave Morgan sent off in the early stages for an apparent handling offence outside the penalty area and subsequently lost the game to a hotly disputed goal from Mark Butler late on.

At the final whistle Pearce, who became a respected FA Councillor of great longevity, lost his composure and went straight for referee Ralph Bone. I could see what was evolving and immediately ran onto the pitch to force him away from the officials. He was raging and had to be calmed down in our office downstairs before he went back into the away team dressing room. A Bognor fan had also made it onto the pitch to remonstrate with Bone and another letter from the FA was forthcoming about crowd control.

It was another season when a good result and performance would be spoiled by not following it up. A victory at Thame United on a Sunday in September was particularly pleasing for Steve though. In the match programme that man Bob Pratley was at it again. This time his manager's notes stated, *"Our last encounter with Aldershot back in February left a particularly bad taste in my mouth. Not so much the late strike and 1-0 defeat but the after match crap talked by the Shots' manager to the media in the interviews... Well Mr Wigley, I for one am delighted you missed out on promotion last season...I thought his comments were totally out of order- but it still takes all sorts! The pressure is on you Steve and it gets hot in the kitchen sometimes"*.

In fairness Steve was quoted as saying after Jimmy Sugrue's last minute piledriver the previous season earned a 1-0 victory, *"Thame played the most horrible football I've seen in a long time. I detested everything they did and I hope they are relegated because I don't want to play them again"*. It certainly stoked the fire. Heaven knows what Steve Wignall would have made of it had he still been the boss.

A home match in September versus Whyteleafe was memorable for another reason. Wearing the number 8 for Aldershot Town was none other than Neil Webb. The former Manchester United, Nottingham Forest and England midfielder was a personal friend of Steve's and, at that time, was keeping himself fit, looking to return to the game at a higher level. If he could help us out at the time then terrific. He stood out in the 5-2 victory versus Whyteleafe where striker Darren Adams netted a special goal. Neil was non contract at this stage but also featured in a 1-1 draw at Croydon a few weeks later. Kenny Sansom also played for the Surrey side. That match is best recalled for an altercation Steve had afterwards with a renowned supporter Quintin Drake.

Quintin has never been backwards in coming forwards to express his opinions on the players and, more so, match officials. Heaven forbid being a "lino" on the North Stand side when he is in full flow. After the match at Croydon Arena there he was, letting the players have it "hammer and tongs" by the tunnel. Steve wasn't having it and approached Quintin and dragged him into the dressing room to the amusement of everybody who witnessed it. He told Quintin to tell the players his thoughts face to face but for the first time before or since Quintin was suddenly lost for words.

Webb played again in an FA Trophy victory at Margate and I received a phone call from Karl Prentice on the way home from Kent informing me that Neil had agreed to sign a contract until the end of the season. I was staggered because I didn't think that there was a prayer of this happening. There was pressure from the Board for this deal to happen because they thought that the presence of such a recent international player would boost the gates.

My experiences over the years have told me that the only way gates will improve is if the team is winning, irrespective of who is playing for you. I also knew Steve was not over keen on Neil signing permanently. They were close friends but whilst it was all a touch razzmatazz at the time the cold realism was how would Neil do on the rock hard pitches at places such as Barton Rovers and Berkhamsted Town as the season progressed? Steve knew that it may not pan out as everybody hoped and that is ultimately what happened. Many's the time Neil would ping a ball 30/40 yards into space in the hope that a player would latch onto it but they weren't on the same wavelength sometimes. It is no coincidence that his best match in an Aldershot shirt was a friendly versus Crystal Palace later in the season when the pace of the game allowed him to run the show. I really liked Neil. You would never have known that he had experienced such a special football career because he never ever mentioned it. In fact the only time he did mention it was when the Board wanted him to sign his contract in front of the fans on the pitch prior to a home game. "*I never did that when I signed for Manchester United so I'm not doing it here*", he said.

The campaign was stuttering though, especially at home where we had suffered reverses to the likes of Canvey Island, Molesey and Marlow. The pressure was building on Steve around the club. This was the first experience I can recall of a bit of corporate bullying. In the days before wining and dining hospitality we used to have a gathering who paid an annual subscription and drank in the Arthur English Lounge prior to kick-off with a seat in the Directors Box. They were less than impressed with what was occurring on the pitch and it made life difficult as these were the very people Steve would come into contact with after each match and it could lead to difficult conversations. In the end he used to be out of the ground pretty sharpish after the match to avoid such dramas.

The first home match of 1997 is an occasion I will never forget. Promotion-chasing Chesham United were in town on a bitterly cold day in north east Hampshire. I received an early call from Dave Tomlinson which, of course, usually spelt trouble. Dave informed me that the pitch was rock hard and a real problem.

Now on this occasion I really wanted the match on primarily because my seven-year-old nephew, Matthew, was over from Jersey and the mascot for the day. However I always wanted to touch base with the opposition secretary as soon as possible to warn him of the potential problem. I hated leaving things to the last minute, especially when the problem was insurmountable. I contacted the match referee, Rob Styles, and explained the situation. He lived near Waterlooville and said that he would be up early. I arrived at the Rec and waited for the buzzer to announce the arrival of the referee. I came down to meet Rob and he informed me that he had parked in the Chairman's parking space. *"That's ok"*, I said. *"The Chairman is not attending the match today as he is away for the weekend"*. Rob responded, *"I've parked it there and whether he is here or not I'm not moving it"*. I thought to myself- What have we got here? We went onto the pitch to survey the scene and immediately Rob turned to me and said, *"Why have you wasted my time. There is nothing wrong with the pitch and I will now have to walk around the streets of Aldershot because I can't go home"*. I couldn't warm to this feller at all. He had hardly stepped onto the playing surface and, furthermore, hadn't checked the covers that we had stretching down the centre of the pitch.

I had heard plenty about Rob Styles and that he was one of the new up and coming officials destined for the top and that he often was the focus of attention, especially on the south coast where Steve had come across him on many an occasion. Although we had had him before I had not really noticed his presence previously. He went away and said he would be back after 1pm. When he arrived back I met him again and he looked at the pitch although this was not an official inspection. We rolled the covers off and the area underneath was rock solid.

There was no way the match should have been played and the expression in his face told me that he knew it too but he wasn't going to back down. The game was on! The pitch was one matter, the fog that came down was another overriding factor when the match started. Styles never allowed for the conditions at any time during the match and managed to book 10 and dismiss two players and totally spoilt a 2-2 draw. We had been issued only 16 cautions in our league campaign up to that point in 21 matches. We then had five in 90 minutes. Jimmy Sugrue was the Shots player dismissed and I can clearly remember it now. He was juggling the ball when a Chesham player was being treated for an injury and all of a sudden Styles ventured over and issued a second yellow. He explained afterwards that, in his view, Jimmy was *"Taking the mickey out of the opposition"*. Neil Webb was cautioned and said that Styles couldn't wait to get his name in the book, embarrassing him along the way by making a point of asking his name loudly with the other players in the vicinity.

Neil said afterwards that he had *"Never seen anything like it in 17 years of football"*. That said it all really. At the end of the match I was called into the referee's room. Lucky that because I was on my way there anyway. Styles informed me that he was reporting the club on three counts including two of steward misbehaviour and one crowd incident. When he finished his sermon I responded by informing him that we, as a club, would be reporting him for his totally inept performance that spoiled the afternoon for everybody concerned and where he failed in his duty to take into consideration the conditions at any stage of the game.

I added, *"By the way, you are welcome into the Boardroom once you are ready where we have a buffet lined up for you and you can meet the officials of both clubs."* I don't think he made it upstairs. We did indeed report Styles and I provided a detailed dossier of events.

We disputed his version of events and there was no punishment or sanctions against the club. Indeed, as with Bennett the previous year, he went on to be one of the top and most controversial referees in the country and took charge of the 2005 FA Cup final between Arsenal and Manchester United where the Gunners' Jose Antonio Reyes became just the second player in the history of the FA Cup Final to be dismissed. Many years later Styles refereed a Hampshire Senior Cup tie at Eastleigh. As I was waiting to interview our manager and players there were a group of kids autograph hunting. *"Who are you after lads"*? I asked, thinking that I could let our players know. *"The referee"* they responded. *"He's famous"*. It said it all really- just as Rob would have liked it.

We continued to hang on by a thread to a potential promotion position. A brace from our striker Roy Young at Molesey in late February put us in a reasonable position after recording a 2-0 victory. Our centre half Nick Burton made a superb save on the line with his hands, tipping the ball over the bar with the score still 1-0. Everybody saw it except the referee. After the match I asked Steve for his views on the referee as we always had to provide a mark. *"10"* he said- *"Fantastic decision"*. And that is why club marks on a match official mean nothing because you are swayed by emotion and specific events that occur in the game. The referee has no chance, especially if something goes against a club in the latter part of a match.

We missed out on promotion again but we still showed our caring side as a club. During the Easter Saturday match versus Abingdon Town their striker Steve Brierty was stretchered off and taken to Frimley Park Hospital.

He suffered a double break of his leg and was facing a lengthy lay-off not only from football but from work too where he was a self-employed decorator. Steve also had a young lad who was suffering from an illness. Barry Underwood and I went to visit Steve in hospital the evening of the match and at a future home match versus Worthing a collection from our supporters raised £650 for Steve. We used to get a fair bit of stick as a club but I don't think we could have been more caring and considerate if we tried at that time, behind the scenes.

Defeat at that Worthing match also saw a demonstration against the manager and Terry Owens went down to speak to those supporters to ensure that they could air their grievances face to face with a club official. Terry was of the opinion that a change of manager could be the way ahead but the remaining Board members, at the time, were adamant that Steve was still the man for the job. It is fair to say that the relationship between Terry and Steve was never the same again.

# Don't Speak

1992

Just prior to the end of the season the 1997 election campaign was in full flow. A number of our directors often attended Conservative Party luncheons and dinners, usually organised by Bob Potter at his hotel on the Farnborough Road. On this occasion the MP for Aldershot, Julian Critchley, was standing down. Not that it made a jot of difference to the football club. Critchley never came anywhere near the Rec. Such was his majority in the constituency there was never any need for him to do so. However this time there was a new boy on the scene, Gerald Howarth, and, as such, he needed senior Tory support to get his name on the map locally.

I have no interest in politicians. Show me a politician who is not interested in feathering their own nest and I will show you a liar. Not totally true in fairness as there have been some decent ones but as time progresses, not too many on the scene these days. Anyway on this occasion the Tories rolled out Margaret Thatcher for her first official engagement of the election campaign, at Potter's Hotel. After the luncheon her aides wanted a place of profile in Aldershot for media purposes to strengthen the awareness of the campaign and to benefit Howarth too. Aldershot Town Football Club was the chosen destination and the world's press was on call. We were visited by all sorts of official security to ensure that the setting was suitable and given the green light. I was then told that we needed to get some of our players to the Rec to do a training session on the pitch whilst Mrs Thatcher was present. I politely informed them that our players were part-time and there was no way they would be able to attend.

Furthermore knowing some of our players as I did I didn't think that an afternoon with Maggie Thatcher would be high on their agenda. Indeed it could prove detrimental to world peace. In the end we had to round up any Tom, Dick and Harry to add to the playing squad for the afternoon. Any mate that was available was "in the team". Steve took the session and I think Neil Webb was there too but so were a lot of pot-bellied individuals parading as players, borrowed from the Rushmoor Borough Council maintenance staff.

Those team shirts were fully stretched by the end of the day. Every news outlet you could think of was present too including foreign channels and also CNN. I am surprised nobody mentioned how unfit our team looked. God knows what Mrs Thatcher made of it all.

On the morning of the visit I said to our player John Humphrey, who also worked on the staff at the club during the day, that we would go to all the local book shops in the area and just buy up the Margaret Thatcher autobiographies and then we could get her to sign them when she arrived. The books could then be used at auctions in the future for the benefit of the club. They went missing a few months later and that annoyed me. I never did find out who nicked them.

In addition to the press attention it was also agreed that there would be a private gathering of club staff and sponsors with Mrs Thatcher. I was tasked to meet her on arrival and departure, along with Karl Prentice. As I said previously I have no real interest in politicians but couldn't help but be a bit intimidated on this occasion. When she arrived I didn't know what to say. Dressed in blue, she was extremely formidable. As she made an exit from the chauffeur driven vehicle I just stuttered out "V-V-Very pleased to meet you".

We took her up the stairs and when she was out of earshot of those present she tore into Gerald Howarth about some etiquette or other that he hadn't adhered to. I think it was to do with a rosette he was wearing or something as simple as that. Gerald is a pretty tough cookie too and has served Aldershot well as an MP but on this occasion he was pretty quick to back down.

I attended a gathering where the press officer for Mrs Thatcher briefed her about the history of Aldershot Town. Minutes later

Mrs Thatcher had the floor and the way she spoke about the club you would have thought that she was a season ticket holder or club historian. That's what politicians do, I suppose. Upon departure I took her down to her car and again got tongue tied. *"V-V-Very pleased to meet you"*, I eventually managed to say! How embarrassing.

What the visit of Margaret Thatcher did teach me was that politics and football just don't mix. Driving home, the main story on the local and national radio stations was discussing her first day campaigning for the election and it was on all the national news television channels too. The following day all I received was a succession of phone calls from angry supporters who told me in no uncertain terms how disgusted they were that their football club was publicly supporting the Conservative Party. Some said that they were ripping up their season tickets and never coming back. The fact that we had only one home match left didn't register with me until later.

Seriously though I have not seen or spoken to some of those fans since that day and wonder if they actually did fulfil their threats. We all support the same football club but don't all share the same views politically. It was a huge lesson to me but I am not so sure all those in the Boardroom agreed with me.

The Children from Chernobyl were a delight to
welcome to Aldershot in 1996

SMILING DUO! Aldershot secretary Graham Brookte (left) and director Karl Prentice with a selection of Recreation Ground programmes that were voted best in the division, second in the Diadora League, and fourth best in whole of England

We did win a few
programme awards
with Karl Prentice

Margaret Thatcher in town in 1997. Not to
universal approval! Rev Mike Pusey (2nd left)
Peter Bloomfield (3rd left) Aidan Whelan to left
of me in back row

# Bitter Sweet Symphony

S teve Wigley didn't make it to the start of the 1997/98 season although it was his choice entirely and I was actually on holiday when he departed. Prior to him leaving he had managed to end the involvement of one of the most popular characters in the club. Coach Paul Shrubb came to see Steve in the summer to discuss plans for the next season. I was in my office next door and had spoken to Steve just before Paul arrived Steve had told me that he was looking for a different kind of assistant and would be dispensing with Paul's services. I was dreading Paul's arrival because I knew how hurt he would be. This was a guy that had served the previous club for five seasons only to learn that his contract would not be renewed just after that promotion season glory of 1987. It was a touch of deja vu for Paul. When he left the building he was in tears as he said his goodbyes. Paul was diagnosed with Motor Neurone Disease a decade or so later and has dealt with his illness with bravery and dignity and when I am in his company he never, ever complains about it. I was honoured to help produce the match day programme for him when he was granted a testimonial versus Charlton Athletic in 2007.

A terrific bloke- he was made a Life Patron when he left the club in 1997.

Ian Morsman told me that he had taken a photo of Steve and his two lads during the pre-season and said to him. *"I think this is going to be a great season Steve."* He responded, *"It certainly will be"*. Three days later Steve had joined his former club Nottingham Forest within the Academy department. It all stemmed from a conversation he had with old City Ground team mate Paul Hart and upon weighing it all up he had no decision to make. A job where he would be given time to succeed at a massive club or one where he would have been balancing on a knife edge should the season not start well. He chose wisely in my view but the problem was I was on holiday at the time and couldn't have been further away- in Skegness of all places!

I only found out that Steve had gone when I rang the club on the Friday evening when, ironically, Nottingham Forest were at the Rec for a pre-season friendly. I spoke to Rosemary Aggett from a phone box and she said, *"You don't know, do you?"* *"Know what, Rosemary?"* *"Steve's gone!"* It took me 24 hours to locate Steve. I was in Glasgow by that time and produced an interview on the Shotsline with him. It all happened so quickly.

Steve often gets a rough ride regarding his tenure as manager. The fact is that during his time in charge we finished fourth, fifth and seventh and still won over 53% of our matches which is a decent return. This was before the days of the play-offs at this level and we would have comfortably extended our season in two of his campaigns. Look at Terry Brown and his time at AFC Wimbledon. He guided The Wombles to two of his three promotions via the play-offs.

Steve has gone on to have a successful career in football, most notably as a coach for the England Under-21s during Stuart Pearce's six-year reign. He was also involved in the full international set up when Pearce was caretaker manager before the arrival of Roy Hodgson. You don't achieve that unless you have something about you. Ironically he returned to Nottingham Forest in the summer of 2014 to once again be the coach under Stuart Pearce, just months after taking Fulham to the FA Youth Cup Final.

He did actually tell me a number of years later that his time as manager at Aldershot came too early though and he would have been better off starting as a coach. I do recall with fondness one session that he held. It was nothing to do with the first team. We hosted a group of children from the Chernobyl Children's Lifeline, all families that had been affected or suffering illnesses from the Chernobyl nuclear disaster in 1986. It was one of the most enjoyable weeks I had at the club. We invited all the children as mascots to a couple of matches whilst they were in England and asked for donations from supporters. You couldn't move in my office for the donations provided and our fans were so warm and affectionate to the youngsters. Steve provided coaching sessions to the kids none of whom none could speak English. It was a real eye opener to the talent that he obviously had in this domain because the expressions and enthusiasm of the youngsters was obvious for all to see and Steve made that happen. Great stuff.

The underlying question is, however, do I think Steve would have got us promoted to the Isthmian Premier division and I have to say that I don't think he would have at that time.

# Tubthumping (I Get Knocked Down, but Get Up Again)

This was a difficult period. Terry Owens had publicly stated that he would be stepping down as Chairman at the end of the season and now we were without a manager. Caretaker trio of Joe Roach, a former soldier with the Army FA, Mark Butler and reserve team manager Andy Meyer took charge whilst we looked to recruit the new man at the helm. What a fiasco it turned out to be. We were particularly studious in the process to identify the individual that we thought would take the club forward at interview stage where a short list of five was finalised.

The first up for interview stole the show. I met him at reception and he had it all. Chirpy, a swagger about him- cheek too but he could hold his own with the best of them and was never fazed at all, always assured of his own ability. His name-George Borg. A 39-year-old Cockney with a decent pedigree in non-league football, he had a fierce reputation too. For me the other candidates were wasting their time. George was the man we needed to get out of a division that the fans had had enough of. He had won the Isthmian Premier division in addition to finishing runners-up in the previous three seasons, plus had a bit of mileage in cup competitions too. At the end of the interviews it was unanimous that George was our man. The only problem- he was still contracted as manager of Enfield although permission for interview had been granted prior to George's attendance.

I recall contacting one on the unsuccessful candidates by telephone who had attended interview. He thought he had the job in the bag and was so disappointed when I told him the news. I couldn't divulge who our new man was at the time but this individual was adamant. *"You've given it to f****** George Borg, haven't you?"* he bleated.

We had called a press conference for the Friday morning to announce our new man and the directors and I were celebrating our new appointment at a restaurant in Farnborough when Terry Owens received a phone call from an Enfield director. The bottom line was simple- *"George is going nowhere"*. A joyous evening became splintered. I remember Karl Prentice walking off-fortunately for Karl he only lived over the road whilst the rest of us, all subdued, moped off to pastures a touch further away.

The bigger picture was that the press conference was still on for the next day. We cancelled it at short notice which added to the gossip. We had to cover it up with and it was embarrassing. *"Ladies and gentlemen, we would like to announce that the appointment of our next manager will not be revealed until Thursday 28th August 1997"*. Not quite what our media friends were expecting but George had made assurances that there was a clause in his contract and that he would have to serve a 14-day notice period. We knew George was the right man so were prepared to grin and bear this ridiculous ruling for the long-term gain.

During this period I was in regular contact with George and he even came to the club with his wife Kim and daughter Charlotte. He couldn't wait to get started and also attended a meeting of directors.

However come the time of the press conference George went AWOL and never let Terry or me know of his whereabouts. I was so annoyed because I knew that George fitted the bill perfectly for what we wanted but the overriding pressure at Enfield and from their Chairman Tony Lazarou appeared too much for him. Reluctantly we withdrew the offer but, embarrassingly, had to go public with this farcical state of affairs. Jack Pearce's Bognor Regis were in town at the weekend and our caretaker trio continued in charge. It was a traumatic time for the club though, with the uncertainty of the new managerial appointment, and this crept into performances on the pitch with league form erratic and a shock FA Cup exit on a grim day on the Isle of Wight at Newport.

Behind the scenes though I had still been in regular contact with George as had Terry Owens. It finally paid off because George sorted out what was required at Enfield and attended our home match versus Wembley on Tuesday 16th September; a match we entered already trailing a distance behind league leaders Grays Athletic and which attracted our lowest ever home attendance at the time of just 1,122. He was finally officially announced as the new manager of Aldershot Town prior to the Saturday home encounter versus Croydon. It was the start of a four-and-a-half-year period of fun, drama, controversy, success, heartache and a familiarisation for the secretary to become acquainted with many senior personnel within the Football Association's disciplinary department.

I received many calls from people within the game who all told me that we had made a huge mistake in the appointment and that George and the club would not go hand in hand. Indeed senior representatives within our own competition passed judgement that it would be a disaster and the reputation of the club would suffer as a consequence.

What I learned is that when you appoint a manager with the reputation of George Borg then you have to accept that there will be a certain amount of baggage that goes with it too. It is no good basking in the glories of the good days but not being prepared to deal with the difficulties that the bad would bring to the club and there were plenty of those. George Borg certainly kept me on my toes, that's for sure and it would be a memorable journey.

Indeed our first proper meeting was hilarious. George had requested an introduction with the coaching staff and chief scout-well only scout- in Eddie Larkham. Eddie had done a terrific job since 1992 and wrote some concise reports for the management regarding opposition.

He was a good bloke but had a speech impediment. Then Andy Meyer came in to supply his views and he had a similar speech deficiency. George came into my office and said that he needed to have a fry up. He told me that he was having difficulty understanding the Hampshire accent. "*You all speak a bit weird down here.*" he quipped.

Along with his new assistant Stuart Cash, who had denied us from a third successive promotion in 1995 with that late Chertsey Town goal versus Basingstoke Town, we went to the Panda Bar on the Ash Road. Imagine George's horror when I went and piled on a load of sugar onto my bacon and eggs, mistaking it for salt! "*You lot are a bit strange down here, aren't you?*" George added.

The transformation was astonishing though. From the doom and gloom of the opening few weeks of the season George and Stuart managed to connect immediately. The belief in the team had returned and you never quite knew what was around the corner.

George Borg signs on the dotted line in September 1997 with Terry Owens (centre)

Socially it was a good time to be involved too. Camaraderie with the fans and a close-knit community within the staff with functions and get-togethers where you could get to know everybody connected with the club. It cost peanuts and meant a great deal to those involved. The Shotsline call figures went through the roof too and we were averaging 2,200 calls per week making it the most successful line outside the Premier League. Everybody wanted to listen to George and his outspoken ways.

True to form, within a month of his arrival George received his first ban from the FA. He was not permitted in the dugout for the remainder of 1997 due to an altercation that occurred whilst in charge of Enfield versus Dulwich Hamlet. He made a nice seat his in the North Stand, just behind the dugout. He didn't fancy the surrounds of the Directors Box for a few matches.

We won at Staines Town 5-2 in November which was particularly pleasing for George who always received a frosty reception at the Middlesex club and a Hampshire Senior Cup tie against Wessex League Bournemouth "Poppies" gave me an insight and confirmation that I would be spending many occasions at hearings or writing letters of complaint during his tenure. George was incensed at some of the flying tackles during the game from the coastal side. He said at the time that the tackles *were more appropriate to the Hackney Marshes on a Sunday morning"*.

It was the visits to Essex that were a cause for concern though. There were a number of hostile venues and with George's reputation going before him the pressure was on. The bottom line was that many of these clubs didn't like Aldershot Town. The biggest problem was always Billericay Town. There was no love lost between the two clubs although George and the opposing manager John Kendall were ok with each other. There was tension at an FA Trophy encounter that was noticeable before and during the match and spilled into the bars. One of our fans, Gerry Fyfe, was attacked with an umbrella and suffered nasty cuts.

George actually saw the incident and was able to get our physio, Phil Sheddon, to treat Gerry before I drove his son to his Twickenham home and then Gerry to Frimley Park Hospital from the Essex ground.

What bugged the life out of me was that I was always having to defend our club and the reputation of the fans. The fact was that our fans travelled in large numbers to these matches and whilst they would generate a healthy income to the home club the expenditure to cope with larger gatherings and security wasn't so eminent. We were easy targets for blame and I didn't like it and would defend the club to the hilt. Even for the Billericay aftermath I had to attend an FA enquiry with Terry Owens at the then Lancaster Gate headquarters in central London; a venue I would become familiar with over the next four years. We had to explain our version of events as did our Essex counterparts. A rap on the knuckles and nothing else on this occasion.

A terrific win at Romford (who had merged with Collier Row a couple of years previously) just before Christmas at the old Sungate Stadium saw a fantastic 2-1 win with a depleted squad but is better remembered for new goalkeeper Gary Phillips getting sprayed with beer as the players headed for the dressing rooms. George introduced a post-match tradition when we won that was met with huge acclaim by the supporters. All the players would join hands and run at the celebrating fans and it was just another example of the togetherness throughout the club. George always said to me that he was involved in football to entertain and put smiles on people's faces. He was certainly achieving that at this time.

Mind you he wasn't best pleased in the previous away match, a night game at Berkhamsted Town. Delays on the M25 meant that we turned up late after being stuck in traffic for three hours. That was a fine for starters but when we got there the referee said that he wanted to start the match immediately. George wasn't best pleased. Imagine his thoughts 25 minutes later when we were 3-0 down to a side hovering around the relegation zone. We eventually lost 4-2 and this was followed by a 2-0 home reverse to Maidenhead United where all I can recall is George saying to his assistant- *"Anthony F****** Thirlby. Cashy- Why have we signed him? He's useless!"*

# Perfect Day(s)

1992

T here was no looking back from Christmas onwards. We entered the New Year top of the table and it was a fabulous period. From then to the end of the season George's team won 10 successive home matches where the attendances increased match by match. It seemed a long way from that 1,122 who attended the Wembley fixture just as George joined. Indeed the final home match versus Berkhamsted Town attracted a staggering 4,289 for an Isthmian League Division One match. Incredible! Karl and I shared the same views on "Kids for a Quid" schemes and this was the perfect time to initiate such a system. We operated it for the remainder of the 1997/98 home matches from Christmas and, with a winning team, it paid dividends. We also prepared coloured coded tickets for each local school involved to decipher where the interest in the club was strongest. Ash and Tongham were the usual areas.

There were some great days along the way too. A 3-1 win at home to Abingdon Town where the visitors had three sending offs in addition to their manager aiming the ball and kicking it into the stands towards our fans, earning himself a fine in the process and ourselves an apology from the Oxfordshire club. I particularly enjoyed an 8-1 drubbing of Leyton Pennant.

The match was played three days after the birth of my son Oliver and I enjoyed a rare afternoon on the East Bank with my dad and brother. Another future Shots fan born!

Promotion was gained after defeating Staines Town 2-0 at the Rec in front of over 3,500 fans, a week after another club attempted to try it on when Wokingham Town charged more than the price stated on the ticket stub for our league match at the Berkshire club. Terry Owens and I intervened upon arrival, after discussions with Town's legendary figure Roy Merryweather who was the general manager after many years previously in charge of the team.

That home match versus Berkhamsted Town was carnival time though. We won 3-0 but the game played second fiddle on the day. There was a terrific atmosphere with so many community groups present and a buzz around the place that spelt that the club was on the up.

After the years of turmoil and heartache of liquidation just six years previously the new club had carved out its own reputation within the locality as something to be proud of. We had achieved on the pitch with three promotions in six seasons but, importantly, had achieved off it too. The turnaround in eight months had been staggering. George, Stuart and Terry ventured into the East Bank to sing along with the fans on this carnival day.

The fans were happy in 1998 as promotion to the Isthmian Premier division was gained.

Pre George Borg the club had been stagnating at the start of the season and if we hadn't got it right with regards to the appointment we would have gone backwards in a big way and possibly never recovered. The appointment of George and Stuart at that time should never be underestimated. It was critical and we got it right. When they arrived we were eight points behind leaders Grays Athletic. By the end of the campaign we were 19 points in front of them. The crowd had come out in their numbers and by the end of the season we had averaged more through the turnstiles than Football League sides Doncaster Rovers, Chester, Rochdale and Hartlepool despite playing three divisions lower.

# Truly Madly Deeply

1992

Terry Owens had confirmed that he was standing down after six years in the Chair and that was a pivotal moment in the history of the club. It was also a difficult position for me too as I had worked closely with Terry and, of course, we always held the historic shares number one and two that formed the company. The truth was that Terry didn't want to go and was happy to withdraw the letter of resignation he handed in at the start of the season when Steve Wigley was still in charge but the remaining members of the Board felt that this would not be in the best interests of the club after the strength of Terry's initial actions. In fairness I believe that this was the correct decision after the original resignation had been originally produced. He remained on the Board and was replaced by Karl. The 43-year-old was somebody that I also had a good relationship with. I had worked closely with him especially with regards to the match day programme where we won a plethora of awards in the opening few years of the club. I compiled the programme and Karl edited it and printed it through his company Adline Group. Achievements we were proud of.

He had the best interests of the club at heart but he was a totally different character to Terry. He had a touch of Yorkshire directness about him that, sometimes, would provide a detrimental view from some supporters. You had to get to know Karl to understand him really. I would certainly do that over the next four years. His first signing was to bring his friend Bob Potter OBE back to the club as President. Fortunately I don't think Bob remembered our spat in 1984 although he certainly remembered a face better than a name. Despite the many conversations we have had over the years I doubt if I was standing with him at the bar he would know my name and it was a similar situation with the players. I could see the logic about him being appointed as President although the wealthy local businessman who had connections with the old club split the fan base. There was a core of supporters who expected more from Bob considering his alleged wealth. However whilst Bob wasn't one to "splash the cash" his experiences in the trade world added to his entertainments contacts were certainly beneficial to the club over a period of time.

My brother, David, also stepped down at this time too and his involvement had been huge. He set the foundations of the club up in his role as Financial Advisor and also provided monthly accounts which were crucial to the Board of Directors and how they operated the club.

I had also been sad to see the departure of Barry Underwood a few months before the end of the season. He was a terrific voice of the fans. Disciplined, articulate but capable and confident of airing his views in a dignified manner. Barry had just had enough of the pettiness that emanated within the Boardroom with regards to the Supporters Club and how it was viewed by some of the other Board members. The truth is that many of the Board believed that the Supporters Club rep was inferior to them. The monthly Board meetings we had were often intense and went into the early hours of the morning on many an occasion. Barry and I would leave once they finished but the other guys would usually crack open a can or two as though they didn't really want to go home. I usually couldn't wait to get out of the place but then I had been there for the whole day too.

Barry was a huge loss but adequately replaced by Ian Read who could start a row with a broom in a store cupboard if he disagreed with something and was a strong and principled replacement. Indeed Ian was a proper rep from the terraces too and not user friendly within the Boardroom. He and his now wife Carol were in charge of the "200 Club" which was a popular fundraiser for a few years. Ian used to collect the money and was extremely thorough in this. Many club officials and sponsors were part of the scheme. To collect their money Ian used to have to go to the Guest Lounge and Boardroom on a match day. *"You can't come in here with jeans on"* he was told when he first ventured upstairs. As a director he could have done what he pleased to be honest and it exacerbates my thoughts that the Supporters rep was not considered on equal terms at any stage. The guy who challenged Ian got pretty short shrift too. He never did change his jeans to trousers either.

On the pitch we also lost the final player connected to the 1992/93 season as Mark Butler made his exit. Mark was the record goal scorer with 155 goals and, at that time, record appearance holder with 303 matches.

His involvement was unique and his legacy too. He represented everything about what being involved in the club was all about. He wore that shirt with pride every second he was on the pitch because he knew what it meant to the fans as he had been one in his youth. I believe that he had more to offer the club at the time though and although Mark went on to serve Staines Town with distinction for a number of years after his departure I always believed that there should have been a role with him at Aldershot Town. But it wasn't to be. Mark went on to do a terrific job managing Ashford Town (Middlesex) on a shoestring as the club won a promotion followed by winning the Isthmian League Cup in 2006/07, then a highest-ever league placing- a staggering sixth position in the Isthmian Premier Division in 2007/08. He did eventually return to Aldershot in 2014 as the Commercial Manager.

George had a tremendous friendship and respect with Mary Sweet

# Deeper Underground

1992

That summer I took The Good Lady and four-month-old Oliver to Ireland via Scotland to visit my mother-in-law. In those days I was fortunate to drive a club car and it had the club badge emblazoned all over it. I thought nothing of it as we boarded the ferry at Cairnryan.

As we embarked the steward at the gate checked our tickets and then said *"Good luck with the car- you're going to need it"*. I paused and wondered what he was on about. Then it dawned on me. We were going to be driving on the fringes of Belfast through the centre of Londonderry to get to our destination of Buncrana in the north of the Republic. I froze. My car had the name of the home of the British Army all over it. I tell you now not a word was said during the journey and I was extremely fractious about the whole thing, especially the Londonderry part.

When we arrived at our destination I was told to put the car away from view. It was hidden for the duration of our stay. We had to do the same on the way back. It was at the height of the marching season and there had been a number of stand-offs in different parts of Northern Ireland. We actually had to drive through parts of Larne that had been affected and there were flags, tyres and debris all over the place on certain roads. We couldn't wait to board that ferry home and what a relief it was when we arrived on it!

# If You Tolerate This

1992

After another close season where we had to spend a small fortune on ground maintenance, turnstiles and, above all, repairing all the petty vandalism that was so common at the Rec in those days we were raring to go for the first season in the Isthmian League Premier division.

George had undertaken some good business in the transfer market during the summer including the acquisition of legendary non-league striker Gary Abbott, who reunited with his boss from their Enfield days. There were some murmurings about the fact that £8,000 had been spent on a 33-year-old from Slough Town. Indeed there was a fair bit of discontent.

It was a bit of kudos for Karl as the new Chairman to show support of his manager with the signing of a player that George felt was essential to his future plans. 120 goals in 156 matches later I believe the signing of Gary Abbott was the best bit of business ever conducted at Aldershot Town. The man was pure genius inside the penalty box and went down in Aldershot folklore.

The signing of Abbott was being completed as George and I travelled down to the Hampshire FA headquarters in Southampton along with Karl. The whole purpose of this was organised by myself and was due to the fact that our relationship with the county association had become severely strained.

This had heightened from the previous season, especially after comments made by George regarding officials within the county cup competition where George had thought that his side had been kicked off the park in a couple of matches without any protection from the referee. I knew the importance of a working relationship with the Hampshire FA and wanted to nip this in the bud before it all became too much. On arrival we were ushered into the committee room at Ashwood Gardens and the meeting commenced.

The County Secretary, Ray Barnes, was present in addition to the then President of the Hampshire FA. We were making progress or so I thought, then all of a sudden the President started to struggle with keeping his eyes open. His face was heading nearer and nearer to the Boardroom table before eventually he fell asleep, slumped across the table. George, Karl and I looked at each other whilst Barnes nonchalantly continued, ignoring the actions of his President. We couldn't take the meeting seriously after that and we gained nothing out of it but it was not for the want of trying! It was embarrassing for the Hampshire FA though and summed up the persona of county football associations at the time. Fortunately in that respect time has been a massive healer with the work that is now associated within the counties with healthy funding available from the FA too.

If ever a season would test the abilities of a secretary the 1998/99 season was it. George had a reputation as a bit of a cup fighter but this was verging on the ridiculous. During the course of the season in addition to the 42 league matches we played 23 cup games. The 52 goals scored at home in the league was also the highest from any team in senior football that season from our level of the pyramid and above. It was never-ending; a season that was to include everything about the game and life in general- good and bad. The Isthmian Premier division was a nightmare of a league too. Despite being the biggest club in the league name-wise we were a touch behind some of the seasoned clubs who had personnel who knew the system and knew the league. Despite having a seasoned pro in charge we were still playing catch up in some areas.

A former youth product of the old club, Colin Fielder, had been signed after a spell at Yeovil Town. He'd had a tremendous career in non- league football, making a name for himself at Farnborough Town before scoring the winner for Woking in the last minute of extra time in the FA Trophy Final at Wembley versus Kidderminster Harriers in 1995; he lived the dream of every football loving schoolboy in doing so too. Colin had to prove himself in pre-season to earn a contract but George liked what he saw and Colin obliged, netting the opening goal of the season a pearler in a 1-1 draw at Purfleet. This was followed up by a debut home hat-trick for Abbott in a 5-0 demolition of Hampton in front of 2,304 spectators on an August Tuesday evening. The first few games were a real insight into the division and some of the characters this level of the game provided. A goalless draw at Chesham United saw former Liverpool goalkeeper Bruce Grobbelaar between the sticks for the Buckinghamshire club who were managed by former England international and George's old sparring partner at Enfield, Graham Roberts. Those two in charge of any dressing room would frighten the life out of anybody.

This was the time when Grobbelaar was in the public eye for match fixing allegations which were later thrown out of court. He took the pounding he received from Shots fans in good stead including one quip as a fan asked him *"What time should I buy my Golden Goal Ticket for!?"*

An 8-0 demolition of Bishops Stortford, who were playing at Boreham Wood FC at the time, is remembered for our striker Joe Nartey netting five goals. All of a sudden a player who was just 22-years of age started having his head turned by agents and the like as rumours abounded of interest from professional clubs. I remember the match for another reason. As I was conducting my post match interviews, doubling up my duties as secretary, for the Shotsline Joe approached me with some real concern. He said to me in panic mode, *"I've got a big problem"* and he showed me to the dressing room, pointing at the benches. *"What is it Joe, tell me"*, I responded. *"My bible's gone missing from the dressing room"*. He was paranoid and I really felt for the lad. It was obviously a prank from one of the lads but Joe just wanted his bible back. A few words in the right direction and he was a happy man again as the book mysteriously turned up. Abbott was sent off at Bromley which saw a bill arrive from the Kent club for a damaged dressing room door. George followed up the tunnel after disagreeing with the referee and it all got a bit nasty.

Such was George's obvious frustrations with officials I took up an offer from Shots fan and converted referee Eamonn Smith, who was heavily involved with the Woking Referees Association, to attend a meeting with them. Eamonn was part of the crowd of Shots fans who I used to travel everywhere with in the eighties to away matches. Indeed he and fellow fan Peter Geoghegan were the two guys who charged over the train track at Scunthorpe to help during the Football League days of AFC. Eamonn took up the mantle of refereeing believing he could do a better job than some of those officials he was watching at Football League level in those days and, fair play to him, managed to progress all the way through to the Football League line. He was on the line at a fair few of our Isthmian League matches over the years and actually managed a middle in an FA Trophy match versus Havant and Waterlooville. A good referee but Eamonn had to keep his socks up. Why? He had the crest of the Aldershot Town badge tattooed to his lower leg! Anyway I took George and Stuart to Woking for the meeting and it was a real eye opener. There was plenty of hostility in the room at the start of the meeting. Many of the lads present would have come across George and his antics at some stage of their career or, at the very least, his name would have come up in conversation. Football League referee Lee Cable gave George the hardest time with some hard hitting but fair questions but by the end of it both parties were more than amicable with each other and there were a few laughs along the way.

# Believe

1992

A decent run in the FA Cup saw us qualify for the fourth qualifying round and, remarkably, we received a home draw with Conference neighbours Woking. There had never been any rivalry with the Surrey club at that stage. Indeed the two teams had not played each other in competitive guise in pre- or post- 92 format. That said, George was well known to Cards fans as he had endured some fierce battles with Woking during his time at Enfield and his relationship with the previous Cards boss Geoff Chapple was stretched to say the least. Future Reading and Leeds United boss Brian McDermott was by now in charge of Woking.

This was a big match for us though and the hours required to ensure that we staged it correctly were long, excessive, draining but, ultimately, rewarding. The attendance on the day was a remarkable 6,870; the highest Saturday crowd at the Rec for over 20 years and largest for an FA Cup qualifier for 30 or so years. Weather-wise it was an awful day and I was so pleased that we got it right. I remember being down at the High Street end checking the turnstile traffic and made a decision that enabled us to ease the flow of supporters gaining entry because I would rather have the fans inside the stadium than getting drenched outside. There is no point having frustrated supporters outside and, furthermore, once fans are inside the stadium the money they spend is of benefit to the club. It has always been a no-brainer to me and that is why I get frustrated when you see turnstiles shut and queues building all because a club wants to save a tenner on a turnstile operator. Every supporter was in the ground by five to three and, to me, that was a fantastic achievement with such a large gathering. We also had a healthy interest from the press that day which Nick Fryer was efficient and enthusiastic in dealing with. I was made up too because Bryon Butler was present. He was the commentator I remembered as a kid, along with Peter Jones, commentating on all the big matches on Radio 2. I particularly enjoyed our conversation.

You always knew when you had a big game on or, indeed, you were being scrutinised because of a misdemeanour somewhere. It was when the Football Association sent their Head of Security, Adrian Titcombe, to a match. The first time he came I instantly recognised him. I'd never previously met him but he was the guy who had led the teams out of the tunnel at Wembley for the FA Cup Final for more years than I cared to remember, dating back to when I was a kid. The fans of both clubs behaved impeccably and a goalless draw meant that we earned a replay at Kingfield three days later. We eventually lost 2-1, in a match refereed by Graham Poll, after extra time, but came out of the exercise with a great deal of credibility.

They start young at the Rec. 20 month old Oliver looks on as one of the 6870 attendance that saw an FA Cup qualifier v Woking in October 1999

It had been a long ordeal and I had worked closely with our opponents to ensure that all ran smoothly and have to say was chuffed to bits to see a letter from respected Woking secretary Phil Ledger to our Chairman complimenting me on my efforts. It meant a lot.

With the excessive cup exploits league form was a bit of a struggle at the time though and the team were not making any inroads on the championship. This was pre play-off days too. There was no pressure on George to win the league though. No expectation in the first season at Premier division level. However he was furious after a 4-0 reverse at former club Enfield. Abbott was then harshly dismissed in the final home match before Christmas versus Heybridge Swifts. What annoyed George even more was that referee Andy Harvey pulled up injured and had to be replaced by his senior assistant Andy Porter in the first half. Porter deemed the star striker guilty of leading with his elbow challenging for the ball. I spent ages going through the video footage and we sent it to Porter, who later became the Referees Development Officer for the London FA, but he was having none of it.

George was still going on about it that evening at the club Christmas party at the Lakeside Country Club but after a couple of drinks he was ok. It was just that he was so passionate about his players and the team.

By Christmas we were off the pace points-wise but there was plenty to play for and we had released our first ever single in time for the festive period! Called "Like a Phoenix", Karl Prentice was keen for the players to be involved on the backing vocals. They went over to a studio in Guildford. I can remember how proud Karl was when he prepared the packaging for the cassettes to sell them in the club shop. He came in with the finished product and was desperate for me to listen to the song. When he did I tried to keep a straight face. "*What do you think- great isn't it?*" he asked. "*If you say so Karl*". The truth is that it was absolute dross. I couldn't believe we were going to sell the song but we did and they wanted to play it on the tannoy. I don't think that lasted long but the chorus still grinds with me now. Once you start singing it -"*Like a Phoenix rising from the ashes we will be there again*" you can't get it out of your system. It was that bad that if it was released nowadays it would probably go straight to number one!

# Tender

1992

We were scoring goals for fun at home in the league after Christmas. The visits of Bishops Stortford and Walton and Hersham saw 12 goals scored within three days with Abbott and Nartey sharing 10 of those goals. It was another match versus Billericay Town that haunted me though. The relationships between the two clubs remained fragile. I was just hoping that this time around all would be smooth but it was not to be.

Fighting broke out in the East Bank between a small section of supporters and it really upset me. I went straight over there to try to stop it. After all kinds of accusations flying about at the previous match between the two clubs, this time around it was people claiming to represent themselves as a fan of our club that caused the problem. I remember one of our supporters shouting at me "*Resign Brookland*" as I tried to help calm the situation down. I never did quite get to grips with why he was blaming me but it hurt at the time and I was noticeably upset. We had to apologise to our Essex counterparts and that was embarrassing.

I did appreciate a touching letter from the then Billericay Chairman Rod Moore soon after. He was a tough cookie but on this occasion he showed a sensitive side to his nature and I appreciated that.

Cup football was taking hold and an excellent Ryman League Cup semi-final win at Bromley courtesy of goals from Abbott, Nartey and Steve McGrath saw a 3-1 victory and set us up for the second leg and a cup final appearance. This was followed up with a two-legged Hampshire Senior Cup semi-final victory versus Dr Martens League front runners Havant and Waterlooville which guaranteed a final versus Basingstoke Town to be played at Southampton's The Dell.

All was cushty really but George was expressing more and more concern with the impatience of a section of supporters, stating that a number of players were wanting to leave the club or, indeed, not join due to abuse, especially within the North Stand. Bold as ever he even tackled the issue in a match programme. Direct and to the point he said, "*At the end of the day my* notes may be tough and for those reading these notes you know who you are and whether you *have a loud mouth or not. You people are spoiling it for me, my players and staff plus the 80% of good supporters. You are sad people when get enjoyment from destroying young players who have a bright future*".

We had a big problem for the visit of Bromley in the second leg of the League Cup semi-final. Regular keeper Gary Phillips was injured and the Isthmian League were adamant that they would not allow us to register an emergency goalkeeper as cover.

This was primarily because we had a number of other keepers on our books. Those concerned were no longer connected with the club but we had retained their registrations. The league insisted on one such player, an American keeper called Eric Talbot. The problem was that, at the time, we couldn't locate him and thought he had actually returned to his homeland. The wild card was Paul Priddy, our 45-year-old goalkeeping coach, who was a former pro with over 100 appearances at Brentford and well respected on the circuit. However Paul hadn't played a match for 15 years or so after rupturing his spleen playing for Hampton. It was a massive ask but typical of Paul he didn't hesitate to offer his services. When it comes to nice guys at a football club Paul is up there at the top of the list for me. He is a totally respectful man who I looked up to and admired for his sincerity. He is a man who knows right from wrong and a hard grafter too. He never let us down on the night either. We lost the match 2-1 but progressed to another cup final on aggregate and Paul celebrated in emotional scenes with his family.

Ironically we actually fielded four different goalkeepers in matches around this stage with Luke Garrard, Phillips, Paul and then the returning Talbot who was eventually tracked down late in the evening prior to a league match at Boreham Wood. For his efforts Paul became the oldest player to feature for the club. Unless an eccentric future owner comes along and buys the club I believe his record is pretty safe.

The buzz around the club was brought to a sudden halt on the 13th April 1999 and a night that will never be forgotten at Slough Town, managed at this stage by Graham Roberts. The match at Wexham Park was an entertaining 2-2 draw. However there was a commotion going on in the stand. After enquiring about what was occurring I was told that Mary Sweet, the lady that had paid for my return trip from Hereford all those years before when I hitchhiked there, had been taken ill in the stands. It was serious and she wàs taken to the nearby hospital. As soon as the final whistle was blown George, Stuart Cash and I went straight over to the hospital to find out Mary's condition. We feared the worst and it was confirmed the next morning. We had lost our number one fan, aged 84. The lady that kept it all together. Mary was everything that epitomised Aldershot. The players were always referred to as "Her Boys". She loved the club and had started watching football in the town in 1926 when AFC was formed. Mary never had a bad word to say about anybody- never a cross word. She had formed a tremendous bond with George who had a talent in involving his players with the fans. They had a real friendship. George was devastated and couldn't keep his emotions in check because he was truly distraught at the loss. He broke down in a way I had never seen before because he genuinely cared about Mary. Indeed she had been an inspiration for him and there was only one thing for it now. Aldershot Town had never won a cup final and the message was pure and simple- "Do it for Mary".

Nick Fryer showed dedication that Mary would have been proud of a few days later. Prior to the visit of Harrow Borough to the Rec we hosted the Doncaster Rovers Supporters Club and played a match at Aldershot Park before the Yorkshire fans made the short trip to see their boys in action at Farnborough Town in the afternoon. Nick broke his arm in the match in the morning but declined to visit the hospital until after the Harrow game, desperate to preserve his record of never having missed a league match since our formation in 1992. It was good news for

Wally Clarke our social club manager too- the Rovers fans drank the bar dry!

Before the cup finals there was an evening where George felt particularly let down. We travelled to Sutton United on a Tuesday evening late in the season where the south London side needed a victory to win the title. I hadn't seen the Shots feature at Gander Green Lane since that embarrassing FA Cup defeat in 1987. That was bad but on this occasion we just disintegrated, losing 5-0 in the process. I drove George back to Aldershot after the match. By the end of the journey I wondered just how many players would be in consideration for the two cup finals because he was livid, believing that the players were just turning it on and off when they wanted to. In fairness the squad had to endure 10 matches in April due to their own success in cup competition added to early season postponements due to the inclement weather. At least they finished the league campaign on a high with a 3-1 success versus his old club Enfield.

# Right Here Right Now

1992

Before the "Cup Final Double" we had a fundraising dinner at the Lakeside with Jack Charlton and Rodney Marsh as the guest speakers. Charlton spoke well but Marsh was only on for less than 10 minutes. I was a bit concerned afterwards because everywhere I went he was following me around. I couldn't lose him no matter how I tried. He was like a leech. Then of course it clicked. He had been told that I was holding the purse strings and he wanted payment.

He wasn't cheap either and pretty poor value but I kept him waiting a tad longer, just moving around the room nonchalantly without any reason to do so.

The interest in the cup finals was huge. In total that season we had 65 competitive matches, averaged over 2,000 in the league and had that whopping near 7,000 versus Woking in the FA Cup.

The "Ryman" Isthmian League Cup Final was played at Slough Town on Bank Holiday Monday. It was that man Abbott who netted a brace as we defeated Boreham Wood 2-1 after extra time. *"Do it for Mary"* cried the fans- they certainly did that.

Two days later it was down to the Dell and the Hampshire Senior Cup Final versus Ernie Howe's Basingstoke Town. The scene was set for a special evening and the Shots fans travelled in numbers. The official attendance was 3,043 but the noise made that night made it appear far more with the Shots fans all gathered in the main stand at Southampton's famous old setting. Dealing with the Hampshire FA and the host club arranging this fixture proved more than a bit tricky though.

The usual attendance for the county cup final was far lower than the masses that turned out for this match and with heightened interest, more flexibility was required with regards to arrangements. This was never forthcoming and it put a barrier up between ourselves, the county association and more so Southampton FC who couldn't have been more unhelpful if they'd tried. They weren't prepared to accommodate our requests and failed to gauge what a huge night it was for our club at the time. The Hampshire Cup Final was a major part of our progression for a club still in its infancy and to reach the final meant everything to us. By the time kick-off started I was drained of energy, dealing with so many petty administrative problems that could and should have been prevented by the Premier League club. On the half hour we were down to 10 men when our midfielder Neil Champion was sent off after a challenge on 'Stoke's Toby Redwood. There was bedlam as Champion was dismissed and I thought at one stage George was going to take his players off such was the aftermath. Basingstoke's officials and management were particularly incensed with the challenge made. This discontent continued after the match. Redwood suffered a serious injury and although the animosity remained for a long time afterwards we, as a club, decided to arrange a collection for the player at a home match the following season.

I always thought that both players made a concentrated effort to win the ball and Redwood was unfortunate. Ironically a number of years later Redwood was sacked by Winchester City due to his disciplinary record which culminated in a reckless tackle versus Thatcham Town. The City Director of Football David Malone was quoted as saying, "*It was getting beyond a joke. Toby was starting to become a liability*".

The incident certainly hiked up the atmosphere inside The Dell but, with a minute remaining on the clock, you can imagine the scenes when Abbott headed home a typical left-sided cross from the majestic boot of winger Ian Hathaway. The Dell erupted.

Fans and management were on the pitch ecstatic. Abbott took off his shirt Ryan Giggs-esque and sprinted along the perimeter of the pitch saluting those fans. Seconds later and it was all over. It meant everything to the club to win in the manner that we did. We won few friends at The Dell on the evening and, indeed, the final the following season was moved to Basingstoke once we managed

Celebrations as Gary Abbott nets a last minute winner in the Hampshire Senior Cup Final at Southampton

John McGinty celebrates success with George Borg

to progress to it for a successive term. At this stage, though, George Borg's stock couldn't have got any higher. And Gary Abbott? 48 goals for the season- not bad for a 34-year-old! One journalist actually asked George if Abbott would be capable of featuring next season due to his age. George just raised his eyebrows to the sky. Mind you Abbott did only score 45 goals the following campaign!

Continuing the tradition of the previous season the 1999/2000 campaign is best remembered for more cup exploits. There was some big spending occurring at the time, notably from Essex side Canvey Island. I was on tenterhooks for the annual visit of Billericay Town to the Rec in August. We had all the "bigwigs" from the FA there again and we could not afford any further problems for this fixture. A defeat on the pitch was disappointing but, overall, we were commended off the pitch for the way we handled matters for this delicate occasion. Indeed only one individual let himself down and I was out at the High Street End with director Aidan Whelan making sure that everybody behaved themselves. This cretin was trying to board the visiting supporters coach to instigate a problem. I quickly got hold of him and told him to disappear pretty sharpish. Funnnily enough the same individual wrote a letter of complaint to the club about my actions stating that I had told him to F*** Off. I didn't but I should have done.

During the early stages of this season the club suffered three successive home matches where a supporter collapsed. We had excellent support services through our club doctor Richard Tiner and the St John's Ambulance. However it was suggested that we purchase a defibrillator that would improve the chances of saving a fan should similar incidents occur in the future. Shots supporters were often maligned but whenever a sympathetic cause was created they would rally. Nearly £5,000 was raised to purchase the equipment and for training purposes. John McGinty played a big part in this as did my old mate Cliff Jenkins, a confidante of mine for many years and another who we lost far too early.

# Why Does it Always Rain on Me?

1992

Cup football meant that the league campaign stuttered with interruptions including not completing a league match in October. Our fixture at home to Hampton and Richmond Borough was actually abandoned due to a waterlogged pitch as it bucketed down at the Rec. A number of years previously we had agreed a policy should a match be abandoned. This was in the days when tickets were not issued upon entrance through the turnstiles.

I rushed to get vouchers from the store cupboard and quickly briefed our stewards what we needed to do which was to ensure that every supporter leaving the ground was issued with a voucher that they could then use for the rearranged match. It was pouring down with rain and there were already big queues outside the main office for supporters wanting to purchase tickets for the following week's FA Cup first round tie versus Hednesford Town.

I was shattered when I returned to the main building but quite chuffed that the system had been effective and the fans had been looked after. Imagine my anger when at the top of the stairs Karl challenged me as to why I had just done what I had done. Upon explanation Karl and some of the directors weren't having it and told me that I was wrong in my actions. I just exploded- *"What should I have done then- let the fans pay for something that hasn't been completed. Stuff the job up your arse!"* I stormed out, oblivious to the queue of fans outside. I met The Good Lady in the local Safeway's in Farnborough. She wondered what I was doing back so early and I explained. I didn't speak to anybody on the Sunday and expected a frosty reception on arrival to work on the

Monday. Karl was excellent though. He was waiting for me and we had an honest conversation which benefitted both of us. As far as he was concerned that was the end of the matter and I respected that. Karl could fly off the handle too but never bore a grudge and just got on with matters. That said, I know that one director thought my time was up and other people had actually been sounded out for my job which was disappointing and always stuck with me, even though I never mentioned it. There are no secrets in a football club.

I was also fortunate to have a solid and loyal match day team around me on match days and they meant the world to me. It was the soul of the football club. One family epitomised what a football club is all about- the Pugh's, a local Aldershot-based family. David was the loyal Matchday Manager, his wife Carol provided the players' sandwiches whilst daughter Lisa looked after the mascot amongst a variety of other tasks. Denise Still has worked voluntarily at the club since 1974 on a match day. Her dad, Denis Lievesley, was a former player who worked at the club and the family tradition followed. All for nothing too. A football club does not function without these people and they are never appreciated in the way that they should be. The Club Chaplain, Reverend Mike Pusey, was also a guiding light to me throughout some dark days and a source of inspiration and belief which continues to this day. He was always there and has portrayed his role with great dignity and feeling.

The Hampton matter didn't disappear though and actually created a project in itself. The Ryman League informed us that the vouchers that we issued were not worth the paper they were written on. Their rules stated that the rearranged match would be played on cup terms with Hampton and Richmond receiving half of the gate receipts. The Middlesex club were laughing but I certainly wasn't.

Why should they benefit at all from the proceeds at the expense of our supporters? To me it was another draconian ruling that I wasn't aware of until it affected us. Yes, the Isthmian League would respond stating that we had the opportunity to change the rulings at AGMs but really does anybody read those law books chapter and verse? Actually some do but I wasn't so much the rules and regulations secretary where common sense would suffice.

The FA Cup then took control. Prior to the abandoned fixture versus Hampton and Richmond we had been drawn away at Jewsons Wessex League side Lymington and New Milton in the fourth qualifying round. Aware that the New Forest club played at a smaller stadium I arranged a visit to assist arrangements and went along with George. Yet again, upon my return, I was reprimanded for leaving the office unmanned for a period of time which wasn't doing a great deal for my morale at this stage. With our large backing apparent I was conscious of segregation issues and agreements were reached. Not for the first (or last) time on arrival everything that we agreed was not adhered to and this meant that many of our supporters were squashed into a smaller area than they should have been.

Fortunately there were no major issues, primarily because they had been used to this in the earlier Isthmian League days. We won 3-1 in front of over 1,500 spectators to set up a first round tie at home to Hednesford Town which we all witnessed in the Linnetts' Social Club. To be honest many Shots fans were disappointed with the draw. After reaching the first round for the first time since our formation everybody fancied a crack at a Football League side.

Hednesford earned a draw in a match that saw referee Grant Hegley take centre stage. The official managed to caution 10 players and dismiss midfielder Mark Bentley on the day.

As he came up the tunnel he was pure white. His body language suggested that he knew that he had not had the best of matches. George slaughtered him in the following match programme notes whilst I questioned Hegley's appointment and said that the match was *"Ruined by a referee that was quite noticeably out of his depth to officiate at the level that he did"*. My tolerance and understanding of officialdom changed many years later when I became Assistant Secretary of the Army FA with the role of Referees' Secretary! We contacted the FA and requested that Hegley was not given the replay – so who was the referee for the replay at Keys Park? Grant Hegley of course!

The replay was one of the most epic matches in Aldershot Town's history. I had to fight hammer and tongs on the morning with officials of our opponents to ensure that seating would be available for our elderly supporters making the trip. Fortunately, at a late stage, common sense prevailed. A murky Monday evening in Staffordshire yet over 700 Shots fans made the journey. We went behind just before half-time but never wilted against strong Conference opponents. The ever reliable Jason Chewins levelled matters midway through the first half and then that man Abbott slotted the ball home with just three minutes remaining, to wild scenes.

I was covering the match live on Shotsline and rarely recall showing such emotion. Indeed when Abbott netted I lost control and in celebration managed to rip my telephone from its socket. We were back online within seconds and all I remember from thereon in was screaming into the telephone- *"Grant Hegley- All is forgiven. Please, please, please just blow the final whistle"!* He duly did and we were on the road to Exeter City for the second round.

# You Drive Me Crazy

1992

If the Hednesford match was big then the visit to St James' Park was massive. The reason being was that it was the first time since the rebirth that Aldershot Town had drawn a Football League club. The tie became the most controversial fixture we would play during my tenure as Company Secretary. I still feel uneasy about the occasion even now because it could have been a tragedy.

When cup matches are arranged it is the responsibility of the secretaries to liaise and confirm. I duly spoke to Stuart Brailey, the secretary at Exeter City. *"How many fans will you be bringing"* he asked- *"2,000"*, I responded without hesitation. He certainly did hesitate and informed me quite flippantly that non-league clubs often said this kind of thing but the numbers never materialised. I told him that on this occasion it would and explained why. He wasn't having it and dismissed my comments. As the build-up to the match continued I became more and more concerned and expressed my thoughts to our police liaison officer and also spoke to representatives at the Devon and Cornwall Police. Brailey contacted me and said that should our numbers be in the region that we had estimated contingency plans were in place and he explained that additional seating areas would be made available. In addition Karl had also spoken with a director of Exeter that he met at our previous league match versus Enfield and reiterated that we would be taking a sizeable number.

I travelled on the team coach and we stayed overnight in Nigel Mansell's Woodbury Park Hotel on the Friday evening. We were all relaxed and looking forward to the match. When we arrived at St James' Park there was a buzz around the place already. There were hordes of Shots fans queuing at the turnstiles and then it dawned on me that our six official supporters coaches were still to arrive. Furthermore the contingency planning that Brailey had informed me about would not be possible because there were already Exeter fans sitting in that section.

As kick-off neared I could see that there were problems outside the stadium due to the queues as the coaches had, by now, arrived. I went out there to view it first hand and it was pandemonium. The fans were angry because, by now, Exeter had closed the turnstiles with no back-up plans to deal with the excess of fans who still required entry to the stadium and had travelled a long way to do so.

I rushed back to the main stand to speak to Karl and said that there was no way this game could start at 3pm. Karl went down to the dressing rooms with the City Chairman Ivor Doble but referee Clive Wilkes insisted that the match would start on time.

By kick-off time some fans had started climbing the perimeter walls and the terrace was now overcrowded. The match commenced but within two minutes there were supporters on the pitch and Wilkes was alerted to suspend it. Karl and I went straight onto the pitch and tried to help calm a heated situation. Whilst I was on the pitch I saw genuine Shots supporters who I had known for years in a real state of shock. Make no mistake, a serious situation had been averted but only just and due to no help from the authorities.

It is no coincidence that a number of proper fans lost their interest that day and some never returned or, indeed, with the same passion and affinity that they had previously. The stewarding and leadership from the security sources was non-existent. It took half an hour for the situation to calm and supporters either outside the stadium or, by now, on the pitch to be directed to other areas of the stadium to view the match. Ironically by the restart they were all spread amongst those in the main stand. If only Brailey and his cronies had listened they should have been there in the first place but congregated together.

When the match did restart few of us were interested. We lost 2-0 but none of us had any appetite for it. The day of celebration was now a day of farce. Exeter's previous home attendance had been 2,353 yet the final attendance for this fixture was 4151, proof of where the additional fans came from yet they tried to deny all responsibility stating that there were only 1,056 visiting fans. Do me a favour! Furthermore, in the obvious aftermath all kinds of accusations started flying. Brailey topped the bill.

He actually said, "*A lot of Aldershot fans turned up in the last 15 minutes before kick-off having been kicked out of the pubs in the town. It was the influx of last minute fans that created a bottleneck behind the turnstiles and caused the problem. There was plenty of room for Aldershot supporters. The whole thing was blown out of proportion*". Fortunately the local constabulary confirmed differently. Exeter looked a club in turmoil at the time. "*We'll see you in the Conference*" our fans taunted. They got their wish a few years later.

The Football Association opened an enquiry and Karl and I had to travel back down to Exeter just before Christmas for the hearing. Of course there was one person who sent his apologies due to illness – Stuart Brailey – which didn't impress me and probably those within the FA too.

The outcome exonerated our club and supporters from any blame for the situation and we received a letter from City Chief Executive Bernard Frowd OBE. He said, "*There should have been improved communication from inside the ground to those waiting outside the ground and there should have been better crowd management of the away terrace. Also we should have "persuaded" the match referee to have delayed the kick-off in order to get all your supporters in…*"*For our part and in order to close this episode and move forward in friendship for the future, any comments made or implied concerning the behaviour (inside or outside the ground) of Aldershot Town supporters are withdrawn. To those who did not enjoy their day, we apologise*".

It was a satisfactory conclusion to a woeful period for the club. However we wouldn't let the matter rest until that apology was received because we knew we were right. It couldn't have been achieved without the role played by our fans whose input was crucial to the dossier we provided to the FA.

This was also the season when Manchester United did not enter into the FA Cup due to playing in the World Club championship. That meant that there was a wild card on place to a second round loser.

On the day of the draw I was asked to go on the local radio station, BBC Southern Counties, along with a representative from Brighton and Hove Albion who were also hoping for some fortune too. Also on the line was television personality and psychic Uri Geller. As the draw was nearing he was encouraging the Brighton rep to think "Blue" and for me to think "Red" and for us both to be positive. It was all nonsense anyway as Darlington were pulled out of the hat for a reprieve. I was cut off the line instantly and then the presenter stated live on air that *"It was a bit rude of the Aldershot guy to hang up as soon as he knew they weren't the successful club"*. – Cheek.

There were few matches during this period that didn't involve one controversy or another. It drove us on I suppose because you were operating on adrenalin. A pre-Christmas match versus Dulwich Hamlet saw a 3:2 victory but also another episode that ended up with an official charge from the Isthmian League. It all centred round Dulwich's immensely talented but unpredictable Peter Garland. A former professional with Newcastle United, Tottenham Hotspur and Charlton Athletic Garland played to the crowd but not in a pleasant manner. He was continuously on the wind-up, intimidating and waiting for a reaction. His ability with the ball was unquestionable but he couldn't run. He looked more suited playing for the "Dog and Duck". As he was being substituted Garland produced a particularly unpleasant action towards Colin Fielder. A couple of months later in a column within our programme reputed journalist and Shots fan Guy Butchers called Garland "Odious". To be honest Guy could have been far more forthright with his views on the individual and the fact that his antics had been witnessed by many in the crowd of 1,696 meant Garland was bang to rights. Imagine my own thoughts when we received a letter from the Isthmian League charging Aldershot Town with bringing the league into disrepute. They actually informed us that we would have to release Guy from his voluntary duties on this one. I don't think so. They had no right to specify who we could and could not use. It was an ongoing saga.

The Christmas period saw the visit of Farnborough Town. George had been cute in the build-up to the match and I was in the office on Christmas Eve tying up the signing of former midfielder Otis Hutchings, who had featured in our championship side of 1997/98 and had played against us the previous week for Boreham Wood. It was a good coup for George who had a trait of signing players who had played for opponents the previous week. Some worked and some didn't. He wanted it kept under wraps because Otis was going straight into the side for the 'Boro' game. No mention to anybody. No problem with me as discretion was a big part of my game.

Christmas Eve was spent in the Plough and Horses pub in Farnborough. Karl was in there and no doubt a few Farnborough fans too. A few drinks in a fan came up to me and said "*Great news eh?*" "*Great news about what?*" I responded. "*Otis Hutchings signing for the club*".

I looked over at Karl and knew that there had been a slip of the tongue and knew he had been the perpetrator. He actually went beetroot colour knowing his error. "*Don't worry, I won't say anything*"- said the fan!

On the day, Owen Coll netted the only goal in front of 5,518 fans. Hutchings started the match and made a difference. It was actually the highest league attendance recorded at the Rec since the visit of Sunderland in 1988; an incredible attendance for two sides that were nearly 20 points behind leaders Dagenham and Redbridge in the sixth tier of English football.

The expectation levels were ridiculously high though in some sections of the supporter base. Many's the time George would have to contest his record in his programme notes. After a disappointing home defeat to Heybridge Swifts produced a negative reaction in some quarters he stated in his next notes, "*Some of our supporters expect miracles all the time. Again loudmouths made their comments heard after the match. Why don't you so called supporters grow up or do us all a favour and disappear?"* Always one to say it as he saw it George had a point considering during his two years at the club he had won a championship, two cups and, at that stage, his team were seventh in the table.

The problem being was that this was before play-offs were introduced at this level of football and some fans could not accept the fact that each season in the Premier division one club seemed to steamroller the league from an early stage which ended the competitive nature for promotion. There was also plenty of misrepresentation amongst fans of other clubs who thought we were the equivalent of a current day Manchester City or Chelsea or in more realistic terms, a "Fleetwood Town". The truth was that George was an extremely meticulous manager budget-wise who looked after every penny. Indeed if there was ever a case when the Board of Directors would suggest that he had "gone over budget" George would click open his briefcase, present the papers and ask *"Where Chairman, have I gone over budget?"* He knew to the penny where the funds had been spent. Indeed the overall playing budget for that promotion squad of 1997/98 was just £5,000 more than the previous season. Considering that a near additional £40,000 of revenue clicked through the turnstiles at the same time that was completely justifiable. Towards his latter days there were a few panic buys without doubt including Aldershot-born Adam Parker whom he spent £10,000 on days after Parker had been sent off for Hitchin Town playing against us. Lo and behold on his Shots debut seven days later Parker managed to be sent off again for his new club but at this stage he knew what was what.

A January visit to Gravesend and Northfleet resulted in another bizarre incident. At the end of the match, a 1-1 draw versus the Kent club, the players were exchanging post-match pleasantries (or maybe not) when our physio Alan McCreeney decked opposing midfielder Lee Spiller in the middle of the pitch.

I was sitting with our director, John Leppard and said to him, *"Did you just see what I saw?"* He nodded. All kinds of pandemonium started and I went straight onto the pitch to try to help the situation. We quickly got Alan out of the stadium to avert any further complications but he was heavily punished both internally and externally. Alan died many years later and I was sad to learn of his passing. He was a straight down the line Scouser who was always concerned more for other people's well-being. He would always try to educate George with regards to his antics around the dugout and what it was doing to his blood pressure. Not sure George listened much though.

# Go Let it Out

1992

Cup football had taken centre stage again and for the second season in a row we were drawn against Woking, this time in the FA Trophy. A draw at Kingfield ensured a replay at the Rec and another bumper 5,500 gate. The Cards won 1-0, however the match will always be remembered for an incident that occurred in the second half. It was a niggly affair throughout but turned when some "handbags" emanated from the North Stand side of the ground with a number of players.

From 30 or so yards recently introduced substitute Jimmy Sugrue ran over to be involved and waded into Woking's Dante Alighieri in the process. What on earth Jimmy was thinking about I don't know. He was immediately sent off but it was obvious that the matter would be heading towards Lancaster Gate.

After a significant period of time both clubs were charged with failing to control their players. We suspended Sugrue which was a shame because he was a lad that I liked. Despite his reputation that season he had only been cautioned once in the 21 matches that he had played up to that point. There is also sometimes a misconception regarding George, his teams and discipline. Yes there were often confrontational situations but this was a trend throughout the Isthmian League. Indeed our matches were always higher profile too. Yet by the time we submitted the response to the Football Association regarding the charge we had played 29 league matches and had not had a player dismissed in that time with just 32 cautions issued. At the same time our opposition had 55 bookings and six dismissals. From our point of view there is nothing more that we could have done. At the eventual hearing both Woking and ourselves were found guilty. If I had been Phil Ledger from Woking I would have been far from impressed upon learning that both clubs were being fined £1000.

That was a massive amount at our level too. I have to say that our annoyance with the verdict was somewhat lifted as we left Lancaster Gate. George, Stuart Cash and I had represented the club and as we departed Stuart went to his car only to learn that it had been impounded and he would need to go to Brent Council to get it lifted at a cost of a few hundred pounds. The laughable part of this was that Stuart's full-time occupation was…a bailiff"!

George Borg in good spirits with referee Joe Ross. He was never short of a word or two with officials.

Despite a resolute effort to catch runaway leaders Dagenham and Redbridge the early season gap was too big a task.

Gary Abbott did, however, set a club and Isthmian League record by scoring in 11 successive league matches; an outstanding achievement in which we won eight matches in a row. Gary lived in the south London/Kent area and often had difficulty with his car. During one of the matches during his inspired run he broke down. A call came into the club- Would we square away a cab fare from Dartford? *"Of course we will Gary- just make sure you get here before three!"*

A 2-1 win at Dulwich Hamlet is not remembered so much for the goals of Mark Bentley and, of course, Abbott so much as for the antics of home keeper Les Cleevely. The Dulwich captain was a colourful character it was fair to say but what originally appeared to be "friendly banter" with the majority of Shots fans in the 1,241 crowd during the first half started to spill over. At half time Cleevely had to be seriously restrained from attacking the Shots fans behind the goal. He made a real spectacle of himself and whether he would come out for the second half was debated. Eventually he did and all was calm to the end of the match when he started again, trying to locate a specific fan. He took an age to calm down but it appeared that he had come to his senses only to enter the bar a few minutes later to start another commotion. In one of George's more surprising moves later on in his tenure he appointed Cleevely onto the coaching staff. It didn't last long.

# Fool Again

Then came Farnborough Town. We were due to visit Cherrywood Road on Easter Monday. To be honest there was little on the game. 'Boro were struggling to attract 300 to matches at this stage. However our neighbours were now owned and managed by Graham Westley.

I knew little about the west Londoner prior to the build-up to this match but was aware that he was ambitious to push the club forward and that he had this bizarre 10-year plan to take the club to the Premier League which proved more than a touch hilarious with Shots fans. Indeed even when we beat them over the Christmas period there was little to suggest any future problems with the guy.

However a war of words broke out in the Aldershot News between Westley, Karl and George. Karl went to town in a match day programme article after Farnborough had publicised the fact that they were to increase admission prices for our encounter. He went as far as questioning Westley's intentions with the club after recent rumours linking Farnborough to a possible move to Twickenham, nearer to Westley's roots. "*Could this be the reason his new 'Boro' logo is in the shape of a rugby ball- maybe FTFC stands for Farnborough and Twickenham Football Club*" said Karl. George followed by asking our fans to boycott the match and "*Take the wife shopping*".

At the time I found it all a touch humorous but then it started to get out of control. The home side had started to advertise ticket sales and arrangements and we had to inform our fans not to make any purchases until we were satisfied with arrangements.

I contacted Farnborough Secretary Vince Williams, a good friend of mine – our career paths have followed bizarre parallels. We used to work for an insurance brokers in Farnborough called

Leslie & Godwin in our teens but we were both hugely active within the respective Supporters Clubs before I became Secretary of Aldershot Town and Vince likewise at Farnborough Town a few years later. Vince lost his father Peter in 2007 where he was a patient at the Phyllis Tuckwell Hospice six years after I lost my dad at the Hospice. We also found out that our dads spent the majority of their working life at Heathrow Airport working for British Airways. Vince joined the RAF FA in Oxfordshire full-time in 2006 after leaving Farnborough Town.

A year later I started working as Deputy Secretary for the Army FA in Aldershot.

*I lost count of th*e amount of times Vince and I would look on in bemusement at the antics going on at our respective clubs, especially during the Borg/Westley eras. It would always be left to Vince and me to try to keep the peace and calm delicate situations down.

On this occasion I suggested that a meeting be arranged to try to rectify the situation. I felt sorry for Vince because he had not been involved in any of the arrangements for this match as he wasn't full-time at that stage. The arrangements had been left to the General Manager, Shiobhan Kenny, who was extremely pleasant but obviously working for Westley.

Vince wasn't at the meeting. In attendance were Hampshire Police, the Hants County Council Safety representative and, importantly, Rushmoor Borough Council. I was the only attendee from our club. Westley chaired it. I wasn't introduced to him and had never met him before. He didn't know me and I didn't know him. He opened the meeting stating that he was a busy man and had far better things to do than attend such a meeting that wasn't at the request of his club. He turned to me and said, *"And next time I expect your club to send the organ grinder and not the monkey"*. He was referring to the absence of George and Karl but I was livid. How dare this man be so patronising and talk to me like that? I kept my counsel, just, and politely informed those present that I had called this meeting in an attempt to deflect the bad press that had emanated from the situation and with the aim of both clubs coming out of it with some credibility.

I looked at the police representative and then looked Westley straight on and said that if there was one more assertion cast on our club or me directly I would be leaving the room and they could sort their own mess out.

He chaired the meeting like a spoilt brat and challenged every item we discussed. He told me that we would have to travel by coach to help save on the parking passes.

I responded, *"Why would all our players, the majority who live nearer London, drive past Cherrywood Road, assemble at the Rec and then travel back by coach costing us a few hundred quid in the process"?* I thought that a reasonable assertion. He didn't. *"Well, we won't be allowing your players in by car"*. The man was just being ridiculous. He questioned complimentary ticket distribution (we would be restricted in his view, despite us providing 40 to their players earlier in the season) and seating tickets (our fans wouldn't be given any seats). He was well over the top but after the involvement of the authorities every request I asked for was granted much to his chagrin. To this day I have never spoken to Westley and he probably wouldn't recognise me if I walked past him. He has gone on and done well within the game but my experience in dealing with him was unpleasant and unhelpful. He is obviously a man who likes the sound of his own voice and expects to get his own way. I could never warm to such an individual though. As it happened the match was a woeful goalless draw witnessed by just 1,524 supporters.

I recall it only for having a fierce argument with an over-protective steward as I attempted to get into the dugout to try to calm George down after striker Wayne Andrews was sent off.

After receiving another Isthmian League charge after an article I wrote in the final programme of the season it was only right that the season ended in controversy. Alan Turvey and co gave us a "rap on the knuckles" and no more after a lengthy but constructive meeting with his committee where I vented the obvious frustrations of a gruelling season that had consisted of 63 matches.

A runners-up spot was a solid achievement from George and his team and this was enhanced with a record 9-1 victory in the Hampshire Senior Cup final versus Andover. Abbott netted five,

Bentley three and future "So Solid Crew" member "Junior" Harvey was on the score sheet. It was his final match in a Shots shirt but not the last time we would come across him. However it was activity off the pitch in the build-up to the final that hit the headlines. As soon as we were confirmed as finalists the Hampshire FA stated that the final would be held at The Camrose, Basingstoke. This was a touch bizarre as it was always played at one of the Football League venues and, usually, at Southampton.

The bottom line was that after the previous season's final we weren't wanted at The Dell although we were never officially told that. It was pretty obvious though.

I attended a meeting at Basingstoke with the Hampshire FA and Andover hierarchy and boy did they lynch me. "*Your club has cost us playing our biggest match on the biggest stage due to your fans and we aren't happy about that*". We didn't really build a rapport with Andover.

I felt that their accusations were unfounded especially as they had no official knowledge of what had happened the previous year, although the fact that they mentioned it told its own story really. I didn't feel sorry for them when the ninth goal went in.

Farnborough and Westley had the last laugh the following season (2000/01) when they won the Premier Division at a canter although so they should have with the funds and players they had at their disposal. This increased the pressure on George but we had our own situation to deal with when after winning four (which became five) successive league matches before Christmas plus taking the club to the FA Cup first round and a sell-out tie at home to Brighton and Hove Albion, he was offered a new contract. Everything was duly signed, sealed and delivered. It was agreed not to release the news until the New Year. In that period we lost the Boxing Day encounter at Farnborough Town followed by an embarrassing display on and off the pitch at Maidenhead United and a further defeat at home to St Albans City. We only won once in eight attempts after the deal was agreed. There was never an opportune time to make the announcement and when the news finally leaked out I believe that a lot of respect was lost between the Boardroom and the fans. Added to the fact that the pressure was now increasing on the boss.

# Affirmation

1992

We had some fun when we visited Slough Town in the early part of the season. The Berkshire club had Junior Harvey training with them.

I was informed by George an hour before kick-off that they wished to play him that night and that his name was to be included on the team sheet. Slough needed to know if Junior had signed for us on non-contract terms in the summer. I had been on holiday when the Isthmian League forms were signed in pre-season and my loyal voluntary assistant Steve Cottingham had taken the registrations. That said the forms were my responsibility and I was pretty certain that Harvey had not signed. Anyway one matter was a dot on the card, the phone call required to the league Administration Secretary Clive Moyse would be a waste of time. Clive was a great support and advisor to me but he never answered his phone on a match day. This was pre online of course. I entered into the fray just as the team sheets needed to be exchanged.

George spoke to Rebels boss Steve Browne and Paul Melin, the referee and said that he couldn't be sure that Harvey was registered with us and it was their call whether to play him or not. As the club signing the player it was their duty to find out the registration clarification but they were unable to do so. George also planted the seed in Browne's mind that should the registration not be correct they would be playing him illegally and would have to accept the consequences. Browne withdrew Harvey who had to be restrained in the stands from approaching George who he deemed had been playing mind games with him. For what it's worth Harvey did not register with us and could have played. It totally threw Slough and we won the match through an Abbott goal. The matter didn't rest there though as Slough, through their secretary Roy Merryweather, wouldn't let the matter drop. They reported us and actually requested that the match be replayed. We ended up at another hearing, this time on local ground at the Lakeside Country Club and the top brass of the league were there including Alan Turvey.

With George's reputation with the league hierarchy and our own regular summonses I thought we might be on a sticky wicket and at one stage we were. Then George spoke and he said of how he wanted to help Browne who was a rookie manager at the time and due to their friendship from their days at Barking. "*Steve's an old mate of mine*" said George. "*Mate, I'm not your f****** mate.*" replied Browne who totally lost it in front of the Commission. There was no charge to answer for from that moment onwards.

The spiritual home- The Rec!

# Trouble

1992

By the time Dover Athletic visited the Rec for an FA Cup fourth qualifying round tie in October the place was buzzing. Due to the inclement weather the tie had been put back three days which meant that we knew that Brighton and Hove Albion would be the opponents on home soil for the victors. Abbott scored again and the dream was a reality. It would be the biggest match to be played in our short history.

Before the nitty-gritty of the Albion match we faced Newport (IOW) in the Hampshire Senior Cup, three days before on a windswept rain-sodden evening. George wasn't there, stating that the reserves and youth would be playing due to the Hampshire FA's decision not to postpone the match due to our impending FA Cup tie. We lost 5-0 and I got home in the early hours of the morning and I am sure I saw that old President who fell asleep at our meeting at Ashwood Gardens a couple of years previously.

Such was the interest in the Brighton match that BBC Match of the Day confirmed that we would be one of the highlighted ties-a nice tidy five-figure sum for starters! Who would have thought eight years previously that we would be on the national stage in such a capacity? It was a privilege to work with the commentator, the late Tony Gubba, for such an occasion. I really enjoyed that.

The pre-match arrangements for this encounter took hold like no other before had ever done. We had to make sure we got it right. Learning from that Oxford experience of 1987 the prices were not increased and were actually still cheaper than they were for that ill-remembered occasion 13 years previously.

Martyn Perry, the Albion Chief Executive, and Chairman Dick Knight came to the club for a meeting and all was good. Their only concern was the entry at the Redan Hill end for their

2,500 travelling supporters. Mind you they had little room for manoeuvre considering they were staging home matches at the Withdean Stadium at that time.

Organising it was a huge ask and out of all the directors Karl had really played his part and proved a great support to me. Terry Owens turned up on the day to deal with the television cameras. Then again he was always good at that!

It was a 7,500 sell out and I remember selling the last ticket with a sense of pride. I also recall Rosemary contacting me on a Sunday afternoon when she was selling tickets to state there was some confusion as a number of tickets that should have been reserved for season ticket holders in the South Stand had been sold in error. This was due to a block being put by for sponsors who were attending a function in the Social Club. I went straight over to the club and Rosemary and I contacted all season ticket holders in that area to ensure that we corrected the situation and that they had replacement tickets as close to their usual seat as possible. Only Stoke City achieved a higher attendance in the first round of the FA Cup that weekend and ours was higher than Reading, Swindon Town and Wigan Athletic to name but a few.

I love this photo with my Dad and the FA Cup as Brighton/Hove Albion came to the Rec in 2000 for the highest ATFC crowd- a 7500 sell out and Match of the Day cameras too

The only disappointment itself was that on the day Mickey Adams' high-riding side won 6-2. In fairness the result somewhat flattered them. At one stage we were level due to a Gary Abbott penalty. I always questioned referee Paul Rejer's decision late on in the first half to award a penalty to the Albion after Bobby Zamora tumbled over our keeper Andy Pape's hand. Effectively it gave the visitors the platform and they killed us off thereafter although the usually reliable Pape didn't cover himself in glory in the second half.

The following weekend we had, arguably, a bigger match; a league encounter with the leaders Canvey Island. Wayne Andrews netted the only goal to put us in a three-way tie with Farnborough Town and the Essex club. Whenever they came to the Rec Canvey came mob-handed. They were like a mafia organisation but we always did our best to accommodate them.

They were doing well in the FA Cup too at this time and the BBC wished to do a feature on them at our game. I even gave Jeff King, their manager and money man, and their Chairman my office in order to conduct an interview. All was nice and dandy until minutes before kick-off when the Islanders entourage was bigger than normal. We couldn't sit all of them in our Directors Box and I informed their Chairman. He took umbrage immediately and got nasty. "*You will sit them all down.*" he snapped. He got my back up and I became a bit of a jobsworth which is unlike me but I didn't like his tone. I stood my ground with him and he took all of his people away with him. None of them sat in the box. Upon leaving the scene he said to me. "*Don't you bother coming to Canvey Island later in the season. If you do and I see you at the turnstiles I'll do your kneecaps.*" I thought that was a bit strong but was a touch nervous visiting Park View later in the campaign. Oddly enough he was on the turnstiles but he never said a word. In fact I don't even think he recognised me- just a part of their day to day life. Funny enough the following season I received the same threat from a representative of Purfleet Football Club all because I wouldn't agree to a rearranged fixture date to suit their liking. As the match was at our place I held the trump card but he didn't like it. Must be an Essex thing!

As we headed into 2001 the club was brimming with funds, primarily earned through the FA Cup run and a healthy home average attendance due to our impressive league form. However all that was to change on New Year's Day and the tone was set for a desperate second half of the season, mainly due to the weather ensuring the cancellation of so many matches and, unbelievably we were denied the opportunity of actually completing our fixture list by the Isthmian League itself.

We were due to entertain Harrow Borough on New Year's Day and anticipated a 2,500 crowd. On New Year's Eve I had the floodlights on and knew we had a problem with the pitch. I rang

193

Karl up on New Year's Day morning while on the pitch with Dave Tomlinson. *"No chance"* I told him. Karl told me that the match had to be played. I responded by asking him to come down and have a look for himself and knew that he wouldn't- hangover and all! The cancellation cost us thousands of pounds. When it was eventually played the attendance was just 1,226 and that included 572 season ticket holders. The loss of earnings was horrendous and as quickly as we had made a few bob to be stored in the bank it quickly evaporated. By the end of the financial year we had lost a six-figure sum which was not clever for a club at our level.

A horrible incident at Maidenhead United followed involving our supporters which led to George calling them "vultures" continued the trend and, to be honest, the atmosphere was changing and the place was not so pleasant to be around.

We were due to play on a Tuesday evening at Chesham United in February. I went into Farnborough town centre during the lunchtime period to catch up with The Good Lady and three-year-old Oliver. As we were leaving I lifted Oliver up to put him in the car and my back seized up. I couldn't move and the car park came to a standstill as the ambulance was required; I was lodged between other parked cars and couldn't move. The Good Lady had to call George and Stuart to come and move my car once I had been embarrassingly lifted into the ambulance. However on arrival at Frimley Park Hospital I was more concerned with the fact of who was going to do the "Shotsline" that evening. The Good Lady had to keep leaving the hospital and make calls to ensure that everything was covered. Then the news came through that the match was in doubt and although I couldn't move I was becoming increasingly worked up because I couldn't get a message on the Shotsline to say that there would be a pitch inspection. Then, as happened, the match was postponed. These were still pre-Twitter and Facebook days, of course.

Shotsline was the third most popular phoneline in 2001. At its height it netted more than the budget for the first ever playing squad in 1992!

A Tuesday evening at Basingstoke Town saw an even more comical experience for me. We sold tickets in advance for the visit to The Camrose and I agreed with Richard Trodd, the 'Stoke secretary, that I would return the unsold tickets and monies that afternoon so they could be prepared on the turnstiles. As I parked up and entered the portakabin at the front of the stadium I handed over the envelope but it felt light. I looked into it and half the money was missing- hundreds of pounds in fact. I froze and rushed outside to see all the notes floating around the car park. As I had left my car I hadn't secured the envelope and the money flew into the sky behind me. Ernie Howe, the Basingstoke manager, was extremely helpful and he came out and we gathered the notes together. I eventually worked out that I was only £20 down and went back out and finally found the last two notes struck to a tree under the bushes adjacent to the entrance. It could have been a disaster trying to explain myself out of that one.

By the last week of the season we were still due to play four matches and the Isthmian League refused to extend the season beyond 5th May. Indeed the final month of the campaign saw 13 competitive matches played. One of the scheduled fixtures, Hendon, was postponed on the Sunday afternoon and moved to the Friday evening.

On the Tuesday (1st) we were scheduled to play Billericay Town at home. Attractive opposition and the final match at the Rec where a decent crowd would have sufficed but as had happened so often that season a heavy rainfall caused the match to be cancelled. We now had a dilemma. We were already scheduled to visit Grays Athletic on the Thursday, Hendon (Friday) and end the season at Heybridge Swifts on the Saturday. When would we play Billericay?

We offered the Sunday but this was blocked by the league. At one stage it was deemed that we would have to play Heybridge Swifts on the Saturday afternoon and bring the kick-off forward to 1pm, then venture around the M25 in time for an evening kick-off at the Rec.

It was totally ludicrous. The league would not budge, stating that they could not change a ruling made at a previous EGM and ourselves, Billericay, Sutton United and Harrow Borough never completed our final match whilst Hendon only played 40 games that season. Fortunately none of the void matches affected promotion and relegation but not playing that final match cost us at least £25,000 and there was nowhere to turn to retrieve that money.

I had had enough by this stage and this was compounded in May when I lost my Dad after a brave fight against cancer. He was well-known at the football club and was a volunteer after retiring and, until his illness, had come in most mornings to help around the stadium. We were desperate for our own Club Chaplain, Rev Mike Pusey, to take the service and we managed to track him down with hours to spare before having to find an alternative as Mike had been on holiday in the West Country. We were truly humbled when such a large presence from football club directors, staff and supporters attended his funeral. It meant everything to me and my family.

# Have a Nice Day

1992

I made a big error the following pre-season. We had the opportunity for a friendly versus old traditional rivals Reading on what would have been my dad's birthday too. I was asked my take on the fact that there used to be history between the two clubs and should we entertain such a game. I thought that it would be ok. Whilst we had had to start again in the ninth tier of the pyramid in 1992 the Royals, courtesy of the backing of Sir John Madejski, had left their decrepit Elm Park and moved into the impressive Madejski Stadium and were making great strides to push themselves eventually to the Premier League.

Whilst the younger generation of both clubs would wonder what all the fuss was about older supporters who remember the days when the rivalry was intense will always state that Reading will always be that team. Ask any player from the sixties and seventies and it was the matches versus "The Biscuitmen" that they recall vividly and there were plenty of them too in league and cup action.

What an error of judgement it was to agree to staging it though. On the morning of the match Karl and I were putting up netting in the East Bank to ensure that segregation was enhanced. Mid-morning I peered out to the High Street end and noticed a large group of men who were in their forties and fifties. They weren't there to wash the laundry that's for sure and I recognised many of them from years gone by. They were the kind of blokes that when I was a youngster you just knew that they were not to be messed with. Many had not been to the Rec for years. That afternoon the town centre became a battlefield and there were further problems inside the stadium between the two sets of supporters in the East Bank. That netting lasted five minutes.

I walked up to the East Bank with Aidan Whelan. A supporter came straight up to me and said, "*What f****** idiot arranged this match then*"? I didn't have the heart to tell him that he was looking at that "idiot". The two clubs have never met since.

The police were on the premises as soon as I arrived on the Monday morning and politely suggested that perhaps we would review our pre-season strategy for future seasons as we had agreed to host Reading, Brighton and Hove Albion and Southampton within seven days of each other.

We started the season well, winning seven of our opening eight matches. The signing of Frenchman Ivan Mballa didn't have a huge impact on this progression though. George told me that he wanted to sign Ivan and asked me to deal with the paperwork. Was this a complicated state of affairs?

I sympathise with those secretaries who these days have to have a degree in the League of Nations to do their job. Ivan needed to provide all kinds of paperwork including his passport. We weren't getting anywhere though and eventually I said that we needed a translator. I had a CSE Grade 4 in French. I didn't think it was going to pay dividends on this occasion and Ivan couldn't speak any English at all. We found somebody suitable and after completing his registration forms Ivan came on as a substitute in the early season home victory versus Braintree Town never to return again. His impact was minimal shall we say.

Purfleet were the opponents on Tuesday 11th September 2001 and preparations were going well. I was sat in my office at the time when I received a phone call. "*Have you got your television on*"? I hadn't but was told to do so pretty quickly. I couldn't believe my eyes, witnessing the dramatic scenes in New York as the Twin Towers of the World Trade Centre came crashing down in front of the eyes of the world. As the afternoon progressed a discussion commenced as to whether the match should be played or not but the directive was that it should be. However it very nearly wasn't. When the referee Phil Crossley arrived he inspected the pitch and came to see me with Dave Tomlinson. He informed me that the measurements for the goal at the High Street end were incorrect and if they weren't amended then the match would be postponed.

It was a laughable scene really as Dave and his ground staff had to dig across the goal line in order for the distance to be at the appropriate level with about 20 people, mainly officials from Purfleet, clamouring to have a view. As Phil came out to give his final verdict we were all sweating. Fortunately Dave and his team had got their measurements correct and the game was on. We won 4-1 with John Nutter netting a pearler but I often wonder whether it should have been played due to the events across the Atlantic.

The visit of Billericay Town in September gave my family the opportunity to remember my dad – my brother and I sponsored the match. Our children were the mascots. Three-year-old Oliver was mesmerised by the referee Steve Chittenden who gave him a red and yellow card plus whistle before the match with one instruction- *'Don't blow it while the match is on'*. The message didn't quite deliver.

As soon as the match started there was Oliver whistling in the Directors Box to his heart's content shouting *"Red card"!*

We were also hosting Chelsea Reserves during this season and it was putting untold pressure on the pitch. It was great to see the likes of Gianfranco Zola and co gracing the Rec and get the four and five thousand attendances but I used to sweat every time a match was scheduled and the weather started to intervene. I would

Oliver and his cousins Matthew and Victoria as Mascots in memory of my Dad in September 2001

be on the pitch with Dave Tomlinson who would say *"No chance"*. I would call Karl who would reply *"It has to be played no matter what"*. Great fun!

I also tried to involve George within the community whenever I could. On one occasion we were having difficulties with one of our junior teams. One youngster who resided in Ash appeared to be being picked on and we had been notified about his situation. I said to George that it would be a nice touch to pop over and meet the lad and start to give him a confidence boost and to stress that the matter would be resolved and the perpetrators would be sorted. After an hour with the lad and his Mum and a signed shirt in the process we investigated to find out the background of the problem. *"What did you go to see that lad for? He's the cause of the whole situation and the one that is causing the problems for all the other lads!"* we were told.

# Fallin'

1992

By mid-season George was gone. Despite a chink of light and a two-match FA Cup first round battle with Bristol Rovers the seed had been sown after league form started to flounder.

He had also been affected after an incident that occurred at Harrow Borough when a former player, Mark Pye, confronted him on the pitch after the match and attacked him. George, never one to shirk confrontation, had come out second best on this occasion, was left prostrate on the pitch and required hospital treatment for, shall we say, a serious groin injury. He actually had to miss our next match where he had to endure my commentary on the Shotsline to find out what was going on. Pye, who didn't like the way his time at the club had ended, was sacked by the Middlesex club who were aghast at what had happened but it was an unpleasant experience for all concerned. The incident made the national papers too.

After announcing that the longest-serving player and club legend Jason Chewins was to be transfer listed it all became too much for George. The difficulty for Jason was that George was also a left back during his career and maybe scrutinised that role a touch more vigilantly. It all stemmed from a league match versus Croydon. George took Jason off at half-time and told him that he wouldn't play for the club again.

Jason then turned up on the Tuesday evening, ironically for a cup game versus the same opposition. He brought his training kit in the knowledge that he wouldn't be playing. When George named the starting line-up Jason was included and it was all a bit of a shock.

By the end of the match he was even wearing the captain's armband as per George's instructions. The transfer listing wasn't a popular move but it was all bluff and mind games really. But when the East Bank started chanting *"Jason Chewins' Red and Blue Army"* you sort of knew that George's days were numbered. This was triggered even further when George went on the attack in a radio interview against some supporters. We tried a damage-limitation exercise at Gravesend and Northfleet on New Year's Day at an aborted fixture with me interviewing Jason to say it had all been a misunderstanding but the writing was on the wall. A Boxing Day draw at home to Basingstoke Town hadn't helped matters and a 3-1 home reverse to Canvey Island three days later wasn't helpful for George either when the administrators of the supporters message board Shotsweb posted a message stating that it was time for George and Stuart Cash to go before kick-off.

# Gotta Get Thru This

1992

The Board actually agreed the decision in early January but it lingered on for weeks and took its toll on me in a big way. I became the middleman as the relationship between Karl and George broke down. I would get a directive from the Board and inform George by telephone. He would respond and say that he wanted the instruction to be sent by recorded delivery. I duly did this most days and was spending more and more time at the post office than in the club office. I was even sent to George's house in Essex to try to agree a severance payment with him but it dragged on longer.

I wanted to ensure that everything was in order when he did leave and we even conducted a leaving interview on Shotsline and a message to the fans in the next home programme versus Bedford Town.

Severance payments for managers who have spent the majority of their career in the non-league game are totally different to those in the pro game as I was to learn later down the line. It is that individual's livelihood and, more often than not, their only income with them having little or no savings. Totally different to a manager who may have spent a considerable period of his career in the Premier League earning a tidy sum where the financial aspect would not have come into play in such a way. If they are not working within the game then, more often than not, they have to find an alternative source of income or fall back on the trade they had before they entered football management.

The eventual departure of George was the correct decision for both parties in my view despite the arduous way that it was allowed to drift on for nearly a month or so. We had some terrific times under his helm but towards the latter part it was obvious that he was losing his way, which happens regularly for managers. Sometimes the harder they try the less likely they are to succeed and this was becoming the case for George.

However for the majority of his tenure it was fun. There was rarely a dull moment and he looked after his staff behind the scenes. George and I had an excellent understanding and I knew what made him tick and when he needed a helping hand or just somebody to talk to. He involved me.

I used to love the post-match inquests we would have in his office after conducting the interviews along with his coaching staff; real eye-opening stuff and a pleasure to be involved in.

I never cast my opinion on players and their performances to any manager in my various roles within the club. I never felt that was my domain and, to be honest, never believed I was qualified to do so.

When George joined the Shots in September 1997 we were experiencing our most difficult period since inception in 1992. You never quite knew what was around the corner when George was about. When he first came to the club he galvanised the place with a unique bond connecting himself, playing staff and the fans. The post-match running bow to supporters, his close affinity with Mary Sweet and her band of friends showed a touch of the camaraderie that was lost after we later reached the Football League. Indeed George was the manager who insisted that every player must become a member of the Supershots Lottery and then "200" Club and that every player must turn up to club functions. There were no excuses. In the early days of his tenure as manager he had it right.

Don't get me wrong though, he was ruthless too and upset people, not that he was bothered by it. If he didn't want a player in his squad he knew how to get rid and there are many players who will bear the scars of this and many still hold a resentment. Many a late night I spent cancelling an agreement or contract after a player had held a meeting with George. He didn't portray himself in the "toe the line" manner and that's a fact and that could be to the detriment of the image of the club in the public domain.

As secretary, and later in charge of the media my loyalty was always to the manager whilst they were in pole position. I felt that was my duty. There were some times in the latter days when he overstepped the mark and I found it difficult showing support. His treatment of a youth product who made the first team called Toby Sumner was less than inspiring and I am sure that if Toby's Dad was in the same room as me now he would not wish to speak to me. I would understand that but that was the loyalty to the manager and club. George also had issues with Ian Hathaway, fining him for being overweight but it had no chance of getting through the Isthmian League Commission. It all eventually came to a head with his treatment of Lee Holsgrove, another local product and a decent lad. George made Lee's life extremely difficult and I had to intervene on this one after speaking to Lee and his father John, a former professional with Wolverhampton Wanderers and Sheffield Wednesday.

It was towards the end of George's reign and I just said to him "Enough is enough".

There was also the time when George was instructed by the Board that he needed to trim down his coaching staff. He had a decision to make between Colin Fielder and Stuart Cash. He was uncomfortable making the decision but chose Stuart purely because he had been with him since day one. The manner in which Colin was informed, by letter, was not the correct way to dispense with his services though. Not for a local lad who had progressed through the district schools teams and had served both clubs admirably and deserved a better explanation.

Colin would still resent George to this day for the way the situation was handled. However I also take responsibility for this because I should have advised George to deal with the situation in a more sensitive manner. What I do know is that George now bitterly regrets how he dealt with this.

The best example of how to speed up a departure of a player was when an experienced campaigner who had obviously seen better days was deemed injured and producing certificates for absence. George produced an itinerary for the said player to attend training with the youth team on a Sunday morning and meetings with the physio at 8am most days; all kinds of demands to unsettle him. The player concerned wouldn't relent though and adhered to every request despite living a long distance from the ground. George went that extra mile and hired a private detective. He claimed that he had evidence of the player moonlighting during match time. He sacked the player for breaching his contract and an appeals hearing was called by the player which he was entitled to do. When the player appeared he was adamant that he had done nothing wrong. When it looked as though he may actually be reinstated George produced a video from his brief case and said to the player *"You don't want me to embarrass you and show the Commission this do you"*? The player immediately backed down and accepted his dismissal for misconduct. The video was never shown. I said to George afterwards- *"What was in that video"*? He responded- *"Oh just an episode of the Teletubbies for my daughter"*!

He also knew how to stretch the boundaries to the limit with regard to officialdom and relationships with other clubs. A few of our England cricketers could take a lesson or two from George regarding sledging that's for sure. He was a master at it. His antics ensured that he was always a thorn in the side of authority too. No pal of the Isthmian League hierarchy and the FA – well that was another matter. The amount of times I travelled to Lancaster Gate followed by Soho Square to represent George I have lost count of but I was certainly on first name terms with the members of the disciplinary staff there. Believe me it was an education.

That is George though. When you employ a manager with his reputation you have to accept the good with the bad. You have to expect the unexpected. You cannot take all the plaudits when things are on the up but not be prepared to deal with the rough edges too when they come into play.

The 1997/98 season was one of the best seasons in our history. George and Stuart Cash turned it around in formidable style upon their arrival from Enfield.

The following season saw us score more goals at home than any team in the country from our level of the pyramid upwards added to that special double cup winning week in May 1999.

Additional cup runs and placings in the league which, these days would have earned a stab at the play-offs, and it wasn't too bad really. Gary Abbott, The Dell, Hednesford Town, Christmas 1999 versus Farnborough Town in front of 5,500, a full house v Brighton and Hove Albion, Exeter!

Life was never dull and perhaps we took some of those occasions for granted at the time but they were special and continued the footprint of the club.

Unfortunately the final season of George's tenure became arduous. In the public domain it all got too much for him. Desperate to achieve that promotion to the Conference it just wasn't happening and he said things that I know he regrets but as soon as they were vocalised his time at Aldershot Town was up. It was all a shame really because up to that point he had had an excellent relationship with Karl as Chairman but it was all soured and became more fractious after George's departure with all kinds of accusations flying. Indeed I know that if I had still been the secretary at the time none of George's ill-judged comments that were printed in the Non-League Paper regarding allegations of an "under the table" payment to secure the services of Mark Bentley would have happened. Why? Because I could read George like a book and I know that frustration got the better of him because the club had not made a payment on time that George was due as part of his severance. I should know because I arranged it and gave George my word that it would all be paid on the specified dates. Unfortunately I had left my position as secretary by the time one of the payments was due and all hell was obviously let loose. George went to the papers, the club was the centre of an enquiry and it was all a bit of a mess. The club suffered but so did George too. I don't know the full extent of what happened thereafter but George and Karl's relationship was also severed permanently. George eventually fell out with Stuart Cash too. This all stemmed from Stuart taking the Caretaker Manager role upon his departure. When we went to Billericay Town in early March I was missing due to attending a wedding. I started to receive calls during the after dinner speeches and couldn't wait for it to finish to find out what was going on. I couldn't believe what I was hearing. Our players Mark Graham and Ollie Adedeji had been sent off for fighting each other. By this time George was on the coaching staff at Billericay and I just thought to myself *"What role has he played in this?"*

After many years I caught up with George again after our Football League match at Dagenham and Redbridge in October 2012. Primarily Oliver wanted to meet him and I made the arrangements. There he was in fine form with all the old stories coming out and a great night had by all. A grandfather now, balancing working in the UK with a coaching job during the summer months in the USA he told me he was much calmer and enjoying life. He was even mentoring referees! There was nothing to suggest a return to the dugout after his last job at Braintree Town ended in 2007.

He did eventually return to manage Enfield Town in December 2013 and he led a team that were rock bottom and certainties for the drop on arrival to a miraculous last day survival.

Then he departed the club early into the 2014/15 season amidst more controversy.

I once thought that if George could calm down regarding one or two of his antics then he could progress much higher up the chain. Nowadays I ponder and believe all of that is nonsense. If you take those antics out of him then you knock the stuffing out of the man. It is the rebel in George Borg that makes him tick. The devious nature of his demeanour is what drives him on.

There are many players and club officials in the game who would want nothing to do with George but there are many players too who have followed him around who thrive on his management style. Yes I probably went a touch greyer as secretary in those days but do you know what, it was fun and I wouldn't swap those experiences for the world. For me some of the days under George were the best and most exciting in our history.

# Whenever Wherever

1992

Within two months I was gone as the full-time secretary too. My choice as I had had enough but I also knew that with the precarious position the club was in financially that there would be efforts to make my job part-time and that was never going to happen. I also felt that some of the Board felt that it was time for me to move on too. I was not being involved in a number of areas of which I previously had input. This included involvement in the process for the application of a new manager and a new share issue. I felt as though it was all "cloak and dagger" and that my views were not for consideration. I had also submitted a document of how I thought the club could professionalise its image moving forwards. It never even got considered. I have retained the proposals to this day and they should have been taken seriously.

I was really disappointed when I left about some of the things that occurred. Terry Owens was stepping down as a director at about the same time and we both left to standing ovations receiving presentations from the Supporters Club at half-time. I know that didn't go down well universally too. The bottom line is that all I received from the football club for my years of service was a blown-up framed photograph of an old "staff and officials" team that included half of the people on there that were the real reason why I was leaving. I didn't even get a mention in the Chairmans programme notes on the day versus Heybridge Swifts. The Board always thought I was close to Terry and that wasn't popular either because there was a rift between Terry and some board members and had been for a while. I was often in the middle of it.

I believed I was professional to the end and, indeed, two days before my exit represented the club at an Isthmian League hearing after the club had sacked Ollie Adedeji and Mark Graham for that spat at Billericay Town. The two players had appealed. Both appeals at the hearing were dismissed and we reserved the right to a transfer fee for both players. A job well done I thought especially as it was difficult to speak on behalf of the club against two players that I actually liked.

It was also fitting that my last match day duty was to present a cheque to the Phyllis Tuckwell Hospice from the football club for £2,550 as part of our FA Cup "pool" to charities. This meant a great deal to me as the Hospice was where we lost my Dad and it was where I would eventually end up working.

# How you Remind Me

1992

Although I had stepped down from a full-time position I never really left the club despite wanting to. I ended up working with Philip Torjussen from Telefonix, the sponsor of the Shotsline, for a brief period. He said to me that the Shotsline wasn't being updated and that as sponsor this needed to be rectified pretty quickly.

Part of the deal of me working with him was that I would resume my duties on the line. He arranged a meeting with Karl Prentice and I had no choice in the matter.

There is no doubt that I fell out with Karl for a period of time. We rectified this sometime in the future but I was so disappointed with his comments in the paper stating that the secretary job was a "part-time" role and he actually took on some of the duties for the remainder of the season. I felt that it belittled me. I know that after I departed, the club were being fined for all kinds of administrative matters that they weren't dealing with. It confirmed my old adage- a good secretary may not earn you money but will save you much, much more! This was eventually confirmed when the club decided that they needed the services of an experienced administrator and appointed Graham Hortop who had been Chief Executive or Secretary at clubs including Millwall, Charlton Athletic and Fulham. I would have loved the opportunity to have worked with such a professional in my early days because I could have learnt so much.

Graham and I forged an excellent relationship and we spoke at length regularly over the next few years as he departed and returned. His experience wasn't taken seriously enough either. Why? Same old adage that he didn't make money but, boy, did he save the club some with his contacts and knowledge.

In the main though Karl and I had a strong relationship although I felt that I could have been supported more in those final months, but I also accept that we were all suffering a touch from the pressure that had emanated from the departure of George and the fact that the fans were not happy that another season in the Isthmian League was looming. Karl came in for a bit of stick a few years later regarding an incident involving chucking supporters out of the Social Club who had brought a KFC meal in to eat. Those supporters have never let him forget that and the situation could have been handled more diplomatically.

Karl was, however, a great advocate of promoting the next generation of supporters including cheaper tickets for juniors including the "Kids for a Quid" scheme. In this area, in addition to the excellent marketing initiatives that he created, he doesn't get the credit he deserves. He wasn't afraid to make decisions too. Some right, some wrong but I would rather have that than pussyfoot about getting nowhere fast.

Karl has shown how much the club means to him because, despite being stung on occasions himself over the years and eventually being forced out of office in 2007 in unpleasant circumstances, he stood by the club and continued to attend most home matches. There are few who have been in official positions who have shown this commitment once they are no longer involved. He also had plenty of front. On the opening league home match of the 2002/03 season he called me in the morning and asked me what I was doing that afternoon. I thought that maybe he was inviting me belatedly as a guest in lieu of my services to the club. *"Fancy doing the tannoy?"* he asked!

# By the Way

1992

Stuart Cash was the caretaker manager when I stood down and I was delighted that he was kept on by the incoming manager Terry Brown. I was the only person Terry knew when he was appointed. We had completed a loan signing of Lee Holsgrove at a McDonalds in Farnborough Gate over a cup of coffee when he was in charge of Hayes, a club which he led from the brink of the Isthmian Premier division relegation zone to third in the Conference during his nine-year tenure. Instantly I knew he would be a great appointment and he certainly turned out to be. It was Karl's best move whilst in the chair that's for sure and I know that he played a big part in the appointment, impressed with Terry's pure enthusiasm at interview added to the fact that he wanted the job so much. Another quirky Londoner, Terry possessed an instantly likeable nature about him and was a terrific coup on the public relations front. Nobody had a bad word to say about the former Hayes and Slough Town striker. He wasn't a name Shots fans were familiar with, indeed we hadn't even played Hayes in a friendly, but they would soon grow accustomed to his sheer will to succeed.

For me though after being at the hub of the club for 10 years I was now on the periphery. Yes I was still doing the Shotsline but that was all. Not involved in the decision making process and that took some getting used to. You learn plenty about life in these kind of situations though. Often was the case where I would be in a certain vicinity and I knew just by the body language some people were thinking *"What's he doing here"*?

Through my initiative and Karl's support we set up my new full-time employers, Phyllis Tuckwell Hospice, as the official charity of the club and this went superbly well. Through the kindness of supporters, players (past and current) and sponsors over £100,000 was raised through football club initiatives for the charity in a five-year spell. Colin Fielder and main sponsor Ian Dawkins ran the London Marathon whilst newly-signed goalkeeper Nikki Bull was absolutely fantastic for the cause. I even managed to persuade Terry Brown to enter a five-mile run "Logan's Run" with Ian McDonald. At the launch a presentation was made by staunch Shots fan Nick Jolly, who became another active fundraising supporter of the Hospice, in memory of his father Ray.

This was made on the pitch at half-time at the February match versus Boreham Wood.

Due to my familiarity with the local community and support bases I submitted a plan to the Board of Directors of how I felt they could actively involve the community to a wider degree and attract a new fan base. It was never taken any further and the report back to me from one director's comments? – "Well Graham's not with us anymore so why do we need to bother to discuss this"?

The opening match of the season was a supposed "Celebration" match to mark 10 years of the club. Chelsea were the opponents and they sent their first team which, at the time, was part of the agreement for their reserves playing at the Rec. This changed soon after. For me though this was the kind of match where those players and officials who had played their part in that 10-year period should have been invited back – but nothing. This was a taste of the future too.

I had said in a parting shot a few months earlier- "Never forget where you came from". I don't think this was taken seriously enough internally.

# Time for Heroes

1992

On the pitch Terry Brown was flying but he was also under pressure to succeed too under strict expectations from Karl and the Board. The club needed to reach the national stage after four seasons in the Premier division. Terry bolstered the squad with experience throughout and, especially for the run-in, the introduction of experienced centre half Ray Warburton, perhaps the most exquisite defender ever to wear the red and blue.

The funny factor is that although we won the league at a canter it was not a season where famous matches roll off the tongue. Terry's squad just did their job steadily and effectively. From Christmas onwards only one defeat was suffered in 21 matches, ironically at Terry's previous club Hayes which particularly hurt him.

The main contenders were Canvey Island and we needed to travel there on a Tuesday evening in April safe in the knowledge that promotion would all but be secured if we won that match. Defeat and the pressure would just be on a touch for the run-in. It seemed as though the whole of Aldershot turned up on the Essex Island that night. As we arrived there were Shots fans massed outside the pubs and all in a good mood.

There must have been approaching 2,000 visiting fans packed into the stadium to see Roscoe D'Sane's penalty separate the two sides. A hat-trick from a teenage Aaron McLean, who went on to play at Peterborough United and Hull City, ensured a 5-1 success versus St Albans City in the following match. Easter Monday saw "job done" with a 1-1 draw at Sutton United. "*Bye bye to the Ryman League*" sung the Shots fans gathered on the pitch to the saluting players afterwards. It gave me a period to reflect.

I didn't actually feel a big part of the celebrations at this stage as I was not at the sharp end but had a sense of pride knowing that this was now four promotions achieved in 10 years; a monumental achievement. Aldershot were back on the national stage. Even Nikki Bull scored a penalty in the celebration 6-2 victory in the final home match of the season versus Hendon. It was definitely party time. I spared a thought for Terry afterwards. Accustomed to his bottle of "bud" I knew that he would have a skin full after that match and he had committed to that Logan's Run the following morning. True to their word Terry and Stuart Cash didn't let me down!

Terry Brown and Ian McDonald helping to raise funds for the Phyllis Tuckwell Hospice

# Something Beautiful

1992

Being a fan of the club at this time was a pure dream. For the first time since the demise in 1992 Aldershot were back on the national stage. It meant everything to be playing the likes of Halifax Town, Chester, Shrewsbury Town and Exeter City, the latter I noted that the name of Brailey no longer existed as secretary!

The season couldn't have opened any better either, with a home match versus Accrington Stanley, the last club before Aldershot to be kicked out of the Football League during the season, way back in 1962. The match was live on Sky on a Sunday afternoon and attracted 3,680 spectators. It must have been big- even The Good Lady attended.

Tim Sills and Roscoe D'Sane netted the goals and we were up and running. Terry and his men couldn't put a foot wrong. I always rib Terry about a match at home to Northwich Victoria. We were cruising 4-0 when he made three late substitutions. Within seven minutes the match was on a knife edge at 4-3. It was one nervous manager I interviewed afterwards as we hung on for the win. But that was what the Conference was all about in the early stages for Aldershot. You score three, we'll score four! There were some particularly satisfying victories at home with Woking, Farnborough Town, Halifax Town and Exeter City all beaten; perhaps the win versus the Devon club was the most poignant considering the FA Cup events of 1999.

The return match versus Accrington Stanley at the Crown Ground is not remembered so much for the 4-2 defeat but for a bizarre flare-up in the dugouts. I was sitting to the right of them and the match had been tetchy. All of a sudden everybody piled in to try to witness a fracas that involved Terry and Stanley boss

John Coleman; the latter was eventually taken to task at the FA but it was fun to watch. It was a proper barney.

The "derby" at Farnborough Town in January didn't go to plan. We were mullered 4-0 at Cherrywood Road and deserved nothing out of the match. The Good Lady usually waits until a few hours afterwards before asking *"What was the score today?"* If at all. On this occasion as soon as I walked through the door she said, *"What went wrong there then?"*

A visit to Woking on Easter Saturday was also strange. We went 2-0 up early on and were in full control. Still with a goal advantage deep into injury time we conceded a bizarre goal. Referee Bob Desmond blew up for an infringement as the ball was in play and gave us a free kick. The ball entered the net but the referee reversed his original decision, even though he had originally blown, and appeared to give the goal. The bench went ballistic as did the fans. Terry was raging afterwards, *"No doubt the referee will be heading to the Premiership with a performance like that because he spotted something 4,000 people couldn't see"*.

An Easter Monday home defeat by Hereford United suddenly put the dreams of reaching a play-off place in jeopardy. We went into the final match of the campaign at home to Tamworth knowing that we needed a draw to extend the season which would be a magnificent achievement for a part-time team. Lee Charles became the hero, slotting home from close range to level against the midlands side. The celebrations at the end were as if we had won the league. To be honest it felt as though we had.

# Dry Your Eyes

W e managed to draw at home to Hereford in the first leg of the play-offs. They had finished runners-up to champions Chester City by one point but 21 points ahead of ourselves. That man Graham Turner was in charge of the Bulls by this stage.

I believe that Hereford thought they would cruise the second leg at a packed Edgar Street. They had scored over 100 goals that season too. They were clearly the better side but referee Andrew Woolmer's early dismissal of defender Andrew Tretton for a foul on Aaron McLean upset their rhythm and incensed the home crowd. We managed to hold on for a goalless draw to force the contest into a penalty shoot-out. Nikki Bull performed heroics and it was the 1,000 or so visiting fans who lost all composure when Will Antwi guided the all-important kick home. The boss and Stuart Cash came wading onto the pitch with funny hats. It was a day to party that's for sure and we duly did with the team in a pub on the outskirts of the town. I will always remember how bitter the home boss was in his post-match interviews. 21 points between ourselves and Hereford this time around but also in 1987 Turner's Wolverhampton Wanderers had finished nine points above us in the play-offs and lost out then too. I don't think Graham Turner thinks highly of Aldershot.

Stuart Cash and Terry Brown celebrate reaching the Play Off Final at Hereford.

Keeping the community aspect intact, the day before the trip to Edgar Street I was delighted to organise a cha-rity football match in aid of the Hospice

Over £100,000 was raised for the Phyllis Tuckwell Hospice over five years through initiatives involving the club and supporters. This event raised over £6000 as Shots and Farnborough Town Legends played at Cherrywood Road in May 2004. Steve Wignall, former Boro boss Alan Taylor and my good friend Vince Williams

commemorating 25 years, between Farnborough and Aldershot Town Legends teams. The majority of those players from the first season were in attendance including Steve Wignall with his wife Ann. It raised £6,000 and set the tone for the following day's visit to the Welsh borders.

One dream that I have never yet experienced is to see Aldershot play at Wembley. It was sod's law that Wembley was being rebuilt at this stage. Similar to 1986/87 when we were involved in the play-offs as a two-legged affair before they were introduced at Wembley, this time around Stoke City's Britannia Stadium was the venue.

Bearing in mind that opponents Shrewsbury Town were just up the road it was always going to be a tough ask but the 6,500 Shots fans in the 19,216 attendance more than made their mark on the day. To be honest there were few expectations from the fans who counted the fact that we had reached this stage of the season as a bit of a bonus.

There was a buzz around the club too. I said to Karl *"Make sure you remember those that got us to this stage but are no longer involved officially"*. I felt so strongly about this and laboured the point to Karl. He didn't disappoint and kept to his word though and I respected that.

There was a huge amount of pride as I looked out over the stadium with Terry Owens and my brother who had flown over from Jersey and hired a car from Gatwick Airport. To see our fans in such good spirits and knowing how far the club had progressed and knowing what our involvement had been at the outset was extremely satisfying.

The "day to day" operation was administered by others now but, on this occasion, the club had remembered where it had come from. Even on arrival I recall bumping into our first-ever captain Dave Osgood and the first-ever Youth Development Officer Paul Beves, all keen themselves to see history be created.

We were so close to achieving the miracle too. We were centimetres from seeing the name of Aldershot back in the Football League 12 years after it was made extinct. If Lee Charles had managed to head home Adam Miller's cross in extra time the whole script could have been so different. After a 1-1 draw we lost the penalty shoot-out tamely 3-0. It wasn't to be and in the players bar afterwards there was plenty of disappointed faces reflecting on what might have been. I told Karl and Terry Brown to be proud of the achievement. They wanted more though. They wanted to take Aldershot Town to the Football League.

I always wondered what would have happened had we won that match because I feel as a club we were nowhere near being in a position to be in the Football League. There is no doubt that it is a step up in a massive way with regards to rules, regulations and administration and I wasn't convinced that we were up to it at that stage.

One disappointment from the play-off final was that record appearance holder Jason Chewins never got the opportunity to bow out. I think it was lined up that, if the circumstances had been right, he would have come on as a substitute but this was not possible due to injuries. Terry was keen to adapt a younger squad and Jason didn't figure in those plans. After all the negotiations were done I sat down with Jason and conducted a pretty emotional interview with him.

I was pleased to serve on Jason's testimonial committee and he went out in style with a match versus Portsmouth, the town of his birthplace, before eventually emigrating to New Zealand.

A firm favourite with the Shots faithful, quiet and unassuming, he wore his heart on his sleeve and continues to play at a decent level in the southern hemisphere into his forties.

# Vertigo

1992

During the summer of 2004 the club went full-time on the pitch. The costing of this would be in the region of a minimum of £250,000. It was a bold decision to do this but I also feel this was the start of a change in how the club operated both internally and externally. However, despite the euphoria, the club was never going to exceed the previous season's average of over 3,300 on a regular basis. Indeed as soon as the performances declined the attendances would decline rapidly too. That was a fact of life. That was a fact of Aldershot. Yes it was a necessary decision to make to be competitive but financially the pressure would heighten as would the expectations. I also started to notice more pressure surrounding those internally running the club. I particularly felt for the Secretary, Andy Morgan, who had replaced Graham Hortop. Andy was in the firing line for all kinds of matters that were out of his control. As a former secretary I sympathised with his plight. I felt that Andy may have also felt threatened thinking that I might have fancied his job. The problem is that it couldn't have been further from the truth.

I would never have returned to that role if it had been the only job in town despite being offered it back to me on many occasions over the years.

By this time I had extended my "Shotsline" role to incorporate articles in the match day programme again after being approached by Karl whose company continued to print it. It made sense as I remained the link between management and players and had developed many contacts with the current and the past too.

Terry's men reached the play-offs again the next season albeit this time finishing the season pretty strongly. They actually started stronger than the previous campaign before a 5-0 reverse halted proceedings at home to Carlisle United courtesy of five goals from striker Magno Viera. We also played Wycombe Wanderers for the first time in the LDV Vans Trophy; Conference clubs had been admitted into the competition for this season. Former Arsenal skipper Tony Adams was in charge of the Buckinghamshire side and I remember vividly how uneasy he appeared during the post-match interviews on the pitch. So uncomfortable and he rambled on at length that I think few journalists actually understood what he was talking about. He didn't last too long at the helm at Adams Park.

Stuart Cash decided to leave to take up the manager's position at St Albans City. It was a role that lasted all but a few days before Stuart realised that he would not be able to commit. It probably worked out well for Stuart as he teamed up with Terry Brown again a couple of years later to take AFC Wimbledon through three divisions to reach the Football League in just nine years. I cannot emphasise enough what an asset Stuart was to the club over his seven-year tenure. He knew how to deal with people, sympathise, empathise but also knew the difference between right and wrong. We had also worked extremely well together and he is a man I have huge respect for.

Martin Kuhl had progressed to the first team arena by now. Martin had had an extensive and respected career in the professional game making over 500 appearances for club such as Portsmouth, Birmingham City, Derby County and Bristol City, where he played with another local lad come good and future Shots player, Darren

Terry Brown (right) and Stuart Cash (left) lifted the club into the Conference and a penalty shoot out away from the Football League

Barnard. He first came onto the scene when I was secretary. We had played Carshalton Athletic just before Christmas 2000 where Martin had featured for the visitors. He had a running spat with George in the dugout, not unusual to be fair. However George contacted Martin and wanted to add him to the squad. I am not sure what was in George's mindset on this one but Martin kept coming along to the club. Upon arrival he would buzz up to the main office and I would answer and he would say that he was here to meet George as arranged. I would then contact George who was never in the office at the same time. Eventually they did meet but Martin is convinced that George had the last laugh because he hardly played him but just kept him on the bench!

The FA Cup started to become interesting after we progressed into the second round. There was an air of excitement as the draw was made on the Sunday. However I was unable to get a signal on my phone and had to dash to a pay phone to make the all-important call to see who we had drawn- Bournemouth, Bristol City, Swindon Town, Brentford ? No, none of them. It was Hartlepool away, the team with the best home record in League One. We couldn't have travelled any further or had a more difficult tie. Still, 400 Shots fans travelled to the Victoria Park, a venue I hadn't visited for over 15 years. A near 600-mile round trip and we got thumped 5-1 on the windiest afternoon you could imagine.

Another long journey was to be experienced between Christmas and New Year too. The Conference, in their wisdom, had programmed our away match at Carlisle United to be played on 28th December. Undeterred a group of us flew to this match (no, not on expenses either!) via car to Stansted Airport and a hired vehicle from Newcastle to the Cumbrian town. At least a Mark Watson goal secured an unlikely point. I always felt a touch uneasy at Brunton Park. Carlisle is a big club with expectant supporters and there was never a welcome feel to the place. We were to experience this tenfold later in the season.

By the turn of the year we were now wedged in mid table after recording just two wins in 12 matches and the pressure was on if were to emulate the previous season.

A fruitless trip to Morecambe was aborted just four miles from Christie Park as Nick Fryer and I were in Lancaster when we received the news of a waterlogged pitch. 550 miles all told and we just turned around and headed back home without stopping;

another Tuesday evening on the Lancashire coast to look forward to. These were the days when Shotsline was still beneficial to supporters and it was so important to get the message on immediately. I hated keeping the fans waiting.

Only one defeat in the final 11 matches including an Easter Sunday 4-0 thumping of Woking at the Rec in front of the Sky cameras ensured that the play-offs were reached again and we were paired with Carlisle United in the semi-finals.

# Somewhere Else

1992

Actually the Cumbrians were the opponents for the largest attendance at the Rec for an FA Cup fourth round qualifying match in 1970 which attracted a staggering 19,138 fans. I was too young, of course, but my Dad and brother were there. Fans up the pylons- it must have been a special night.

This time around there was another near full house but with the reduced capacities that have been common over the recent years. 6,617 fans saw a Nick Crittenden goal give us the edge after the first leg. For some strange reason the second leg was arranged for a Friday evening at Brunton Park despite the fact that the match wasn't to be featured live on Sky. When we arrived you could sense the tension all around. Carlisle had only been in the Conference for a season and their fans didn't particularly want to be hanging about any longer than the one term. They started intensely and we were 2-0 down at half-time and heading for the exit door.

With the match deep into injury time one of those moments that defines your football club occurred. A deep centre from the right was played into the danger zone and met by the head of substitute striker Jamie Slabber. Jamie hadn't set the place alight in his previous four appearances since his arrival but he connected perfectly to see the ball glide over home keeper Matty Glennon into the net. The moment is always remembered for BBC Southern Counties commentator Tony Sharp's *"Slabberrrrrrrrrr!!!"* as the goal was scored. At 1-2 we sent the match into extra time and survived the additional 30 minutes. Just prior to the goal the Carlisle supporters were all edging to the perimeter of the pitch waiting to celebrate. They were stunned and so were we.

I was watching the match with the Shots fans on this evening. As we took a 3-1 lead in the penalty shoot-out it was just a matter of time before we were celebrating a second successive play-off final. All we needed to do was score or rely on another miss. Simple eh? Maybe not. 3-1 became 3-2 and then back on level terms. At one stage the hordes of home fans ran onto the pitch believing they had won the match, but they still required their side to convert one final kick. They intimidated our players in a way I had never seen before and Nikki Bull was actually attacked. If he had gone down who knows what would have happened. My feeling of elation was now turning to anger and the stewards in the visiting section were not helping the situation. Once the field of play was cleared the final kick was converted and the celebrations started again.

I ended up having an argument with the stewards who would not allow me round to get to our dressing room to conduct the post-match interviews and a few choice words were said before the police became involved. Quite frankly I couldn't have cared less by now. Not only was I annoyed at proceedings I actually thought the physical safety of our fans was seriously threatened and I didn't think the plans were in place to deal with this. One thing is for sure, if I had still been an official in the decision making process at this stage I would have taken the matter further. Not to get the match replayed or anything like that but the scenes before that final kick were unacceptable and Carlisle should have been punished for it. As a club if we did make a complaint we should have informed fans of the outcome and if we didn't then we should have. An ugly evening had by all. I have never interviewed such a dejected manager and players post match. There was only one fixture that would supercede that in the future.

# Bad Day (s)

1992

If ever there was ever a nondescript season at Aldershot Town it was 2005/06. I was honoured to be asked to write the programme for Charlie Mortimore's pre-season testimonial versus Farnborough Town, the club where he was the President. I spent a fascinating evening around Charlie's house going through his scrapbooks. This man netted 278 goals in nearly 450 appearances between 1949 and 1968 for Aldershot, Woking and including one for Portsmouth. Few people could have links with all the three local senior clubs and command the same respect at each club; Colin Fielder is the other player that comes to mind.

Furthermore Charlie had been the mainstay of local schools' football since 1949 when he joined Cove Senior School as a teacher.

I got to know him well when I was secretary a few years previously when the local schools cup finals were staged at the Rec and Charlie was really a one man band in organising the games. During his time in charge of the Aldershot and Farnborough District School teams he oversaw 100s of young lads who made their way to a decent standard in the game, many into the pro game. As a match though the testimonial should never have been played. Terry didn't have a squad with many of his play-off squad of the past two seasons having moved onto pastures new or on the treatment table. A pre-season friendly at home to a Charlton Athletic reserve side backfired. The Addicks' arrived in town with Alan Curbishley and their full first team on show and defeated a depleted Shots side 8-0.

The first match of the season, at home to Tamworth, even saw Terry publicly state that "We *may be out of the blocks slower than normal*" and he was correct with that assumption. We lost that match 2-0 and four of our opening five matches. By the end of the month we were actually bottom of the table but recovered to finish comfortably in 13th position.

I had been asked to increase my role again at this stage by Karl with the introduction of a new website.

The official website had been operated through the supporter-based Shotsweb site for a period of time but difficulties had obviously emanated between the Board and the administrators on the site and it was deemed that the said site would prefer a return to being independent. I do believe that club officials get too carried away with message boards. My advice was that message boards should be monitored in order to ensure that if there was a problem relating to a non-footballing matter it would be noticed, due to being consistently brought up on the board. Thereafter the club could act on it but I always advised not to use the message board in answer to any queries raised but to channel any responses via the official site. What used to happen was that club officials would get embroiled on a topic but then get dragged into other areas where they would be less comfortable and it opened up a can of worms. Emotions take over on message boards after matches, especially where the team has not performed. I used to tell players and management not to get engrossed in the message boards but I think it is a nature of habit.

Karl contacted me and said we were launching in a few days and asked whether I would take charge of the site. I was given the contact details of the web hosts and couldn't believe it. They told me that they had been given no information at all from the club and that the website itself was an empty shell. I pleaded with Karl and said that there was no way the website could go live when he wanted it to as he would get laughed out of office by the fans. Karl had always referred to the site as "The Tool" and it stuck all the time he was Chairman with a section of supporters. It bugged me a bit because I ran "The Tool" and eventually it became a pretty decent site considering what happened later on when the club had no option but transfer to a Football League Interactive site that couldn't have been more "user unfriendly" if it tried.

We eventually did launch the new site after so much work behind the scenes and then, after a few months, the "Premium" site hosts Spider Networks, separate to the main website, went bust with all the subscription money disappearing at the same time into a black hole that the football club could never recover. It was a logistical nightmare to repair the damage and I felt left in the lurch to be honest. It took a long time to restore the reputation but the host company, Digital Ink, took control of both sites eventually and I have to say did a terrific job.

Football clubs are about people though. During the Christmas period of the 2005/06 season Richard Aggett passed away after a brave battle with cancer. Richard's wife Rosemary is, quite simply, the bravest lady I have ever known. She battled back from two serious illnesses in my time as secretary at the club and whenever she knew she was going to be away from the office for a few weeks due to her illness and treatments she had everything all organised and structured. She went way above the call of duty and was a loyal club person. Believe me, every club needs a Rosemary Aggett and we were extremely fortunate. A few weeks before Richard's passing Rosemary ended her 30- years plus full-time association with the club to tend to her ill husband. When you talk about a man of integrity Richard was that man. A former servant of the British Army he also served Aldershot Football Club for many years in a variety of roles.

Always impeccably dressed whenever he turned up to collect Rosemary from the office, I quickly used to make sure my shirt was tucked in and had a look at my shoes to ensure that they looked shiny. He was an Ambassador on a match day and was always the first face a manager would see climbing those stairs to meet the hierarchy and guests. If it had been a defeat he was always supportive of the boss at the time. He and Norman Penny, a former Paratrooper, put me on the straight and narrow many years before when I was that outspoken youth, just letting me know the damage that could be caused sometimes by idle gossip and how it can affect people's livelihoods. The club was well represented at the funeral and I was proud, and a touch nervous, to be asked to speak at the service by Rosemary.

On the pitch New Year's Eve is remembered for a visit to Forest Green Rovers. We were getting hammered 4-1 deep into injury time when the floodlights failed. With supporters desperate to return home to bring in the New Year electricians were frantically trying to get the lights back on. *"For crying out loud we're 4-1 down"*, said Terry. *"They can have the game. We're not going to score three in a minute are we?"* he said to the referee, eager to return home in good time for his New Year's drink! Rules being rules though the ref wanted to get the match restarted. After half an hour or so the lights did return and, ironically, we actually scored in those few remaining seconds.

Overall though this was a season to forget. The average attendance dropped by 500 fans per match and the pressure was on in the Boardroom. I can remember sitting in a hotel in York prior to a Sunday match at York City with director John Leppard and he was quite vocal stating, *"Tomorrow that team that you see wearing the Shots shirt will be the most expensive in our history."* The fact that it was 14th in the table at the time just proved that it was a difficult period. The danger was that Aldershot fans only come out when the team is doing well.

The attendances were now starting to drift below 2,000 and when champions elect Accrington Stanley demolished us 4-1 in early March less than 1,700 attended.

In typical fashion the season ended as it began, in farce. Head groundsman Dave Tomlinson was retiring after 44 years of service. I had said to Karl that we needed to make sure we honoured this in the right way. We got some photos together and Karl was to assemble them onto a presentation montage with suitable inscription. We were due to make the presentation just before kick-off at the final home match of the season versus Woking. I went up to make sure all was organised about 30 minutes beforehand. Karl showed me what he had done. *"Great, isn't it? Dave will really like this"*, he said proudly. I looked at it in disbelief. *"Look how you've spelt Tomlinson,"* I responded. *"THOMLINSON"* I couldn't believe it. Whilst Karl was trying to chip away at the "H" to make it look presentable I rushed down to see Terry Brown with an idea.

In respect of Dave I said that it would be good to have the teams line up side by side as a Guard of Honour with Dave being announced to the crowd through the middle with the players all applauding. Terry was all for it so we went to see the referee to inform him. Dave really appreciated the gesture but probably doesn't know the real reasons behind it until he reads this!

# Naive

The 2006/07 season would be, in my view, Terry's last season in charge should it not go as planned. He had always said that he would leave if he thought the time was right and if the fans were not onside. As it happened he did leave but for none of the above reasons. In early 2007 his wife Sue was diagnosed with leukaemia and he decided to step down. The season had started full of high expectations with some quality signings including the likes of experienced pros such as former Wimbledon, Glasgow Rangers and Brentford player Marcus Gayle and Ricky Newman, formerly of Millwall and Reading. There was even an effort to sign former Nottingham Forest striker Jason Lee that was aborted by the player himself after agreeing terms, meeting with club officials and having a medical. It had all been announced that he was on his way to the Rec. I received a bombshell phone call from Aidan Whelan a few weeks later when I was at Oliver's sports day. Lee had done a "U turn" and decided to sign for Notts County instead. I had to draft up a carefully worded press release to get the club out of some murky waters on this one.

The new players were all introduced to the fans at a pre-season "Party in the Park" event that was a total disaster, primarily due to admission prices totally out of line with the unknown acts that were present. It was all built up to be something special- *"This is the strongest ever squad we have assembled here at Aldershot Town. It's all about getting confidence and getting a good start to the season- if we can do this and injury free then there should be no stopping us in my opinion"* said Karl in pre-season. No pressure then! But in fairness the optimism was all around the club. There was a belief that this could be the season-the conclusion of that dream to see the name of Aldershot back in the Football League. Many friends put a few bob on the Shots that season on my recommendation. I felt a touch guilty really. Only a touch though!

Coming home from holiday we left Great Yarmouth at 7am in the morning to ensure we got to the Rec in time for the opening match of the season versus Gravesend and Northfleet. 2 0 down we eventually won 3-2 which was just as well because Oliver and I didn't get to the game until 3.10pm due to horrendous traffic.

In truth though it was another tough season that never really got going. The September 4-0 victory versus Stevenage Borough was as good a performance as I have ever seen from the Shots but this was followed by an insipid 3-1 reverse at home to lowly Northwich Victoria four days later. It sort of summed up the season.

There were many who thought that we were invincible after that Stevenage match and that it was only going to be a matter of time before promotion was achieved. Two players, Dean Smith and Louie Soares, actually signed new contracts on the pitch prior to the visit of Northwich. Not so sure that was necessary at Conference level and I don't think the boss did either. Smith's form deteriorated in rapid proportions after his new deal was confirmed.

A live match on Sky at local rivals Woking proved to be a total disaster. The referee was not happy with the Aldershot kit for the evening and after some dispute with Woking boss Glenn Cockerill it was deemed that the alternative kit on offer was also unsuitable. After some lengthy debate of which I was unaware of at the time we were forced to wear a spare Woking kit. Imagine being the main sponsor of the club, Tim Elliott of EBB and briefly a Director of the O'Connell regime in the mid-1980s. There he was all ready and waiting to see his brand exposed on the international stage only to see his team parading in the home team's throwaway kit. It was an embarrassment internally and there were many repercussions. It got no better on the pitch as we lost 2-0 on a night to forget at Kingfield.

The FA Cup provided some respite before that "draw" curse raised its ugly head again. For the first time in our history we reached the third round. Dreams of Manchester United and Liverpool were soon expunged as we drew League One Blackpool at Bloomfield Road. We were 2-0 down in four minutes and eventually lost 4-2.

Over 1000 Shots fans at Blackpool for the FA Cup.

# Shine

1992

Iused to meet Terry every Thursday morning at the Aldershot Military Stadium, adjacent to where the players trained. We would sit and chat in his car before conducting the pre-match interview. Week by week I started to detect a manager becoming more and more frustrated and tired. The disappointment of not challenging for the title on the pitch was enhanced by noticeable turbulence in the Boardroom by now. The signs were ominous.

By the end of the year Karl was replaced as Chairman by John McGinty. John, by this time, was 68-years-old and ran a successful local removals business.

He was one of the directors Terry and I chose in the summer of 1992 and became hugely popular but to be honest he was the last person I thought would become Chairman from my own experiences of him within the Boardroom. He galvanised the position extremely well and became a firm favourite with the supporters but it was obvious that the pressures were increasing from within. This was also the start of a merry-go-round of new directors or senior employees that the club never really recovered from. Different personnel with different ideas but none who really had a background within the game. My old adage "Know your club" wasn't really being taken seriously.

However then it came as a bolt from the blue. We played Rushden and Diamonds, then managed by Graham Westley, at home in February and Martin Kuhl told me that Terry wasn't at the match and the reasons why. I was stunned as was Martin.

It was a truly difficult day because the message wasn't to be broadcast into the public domain. I sent Terry a message that evening amongst dozens from concerned friends. Despite my reservations about Westley due to my own personal dealings with him I know that he offered huge support to Terry and that should be applauded.

Terry continued for a period of time but his demeanour suggested, quite rightly, that his focus was elsewhere. Then we sat down on the Thursday prior to a Friday evening match at Gravesend and Northfleet. "*I'm calling it a day after tomorrow's match*". He told me. Not surprised at the news I said to him "*Why don't you wait until after Tuesday's match at home to Weymouth? We can announce the news after Gravesend but it will give the fans the opportunity to give you the send-off you deserve.*" He liked the idea and met John McGinty and then Chief Executive Doug Wilson at the Holiday Inn in Farnborough on the Saturday morning; I was also in attendance to conduct the interviews with Terry after they had concluded business.

The announcement was made and his farewell match versus Weymouth on Tuesday 27th March 2007 was the most emotional I, and many of those present, have ever felt at a football match. If only all managers could bid farewell in the manner that Terry did, witnessing sheer adulation and affection. The gate was up a few hundred to what it would have been for a nondescript Tuesday evening match with nothing to play for. A Guard of Honour paraded as Terry made his way onto the pitch to a standing ovation and it never stopped all evening. A Rhys Day goal ensured that we won the match and afterwards the playing squad lined up in front of the North Stand where Terry embraced each one individually. He then did a lap of honour to the crowd who, as one, had stayed behind to salute the departing boss before he bowed to his knees to the East Bank. It was pure "Roy of the Rovers" stuff. I had never seen anything like it in football before and neither had some of the senior players and staff such as Marcus Gayle and Martin Kuhl. It was special. Emotional, I struggled to keep my composure interviewing Terry afterwards and for the first time he was struggling to get the words out too. "A bottle of bud" was the tonic he needed and he certainly sunk one or two afterwards.

The biggest battle lay ahead for Terry and his wife Sue. He never, ever moaned about his own circumstances at any stage always adding that there is always somebody worse off in the world.

I was delighted that Sue made a recovery and both were guests of John McGinty and the club at a later date when he was in charge of AFC Wimbledon, a club where he earned three promotions to take the Wombles to the Football League just nine years after their formation.

I felt for Terry. I always thought that he would be the man to take the club into the Football League. Indeed I always told him that he did things the wrong way around. He was too successful in his early days steering the club to the Isthmian League championship in the first season followed by being a penalty kick away from winning the play-offs as a part-time team the following year. This was then followed by further play-off involvement. He never quite mirrored that thereafter but as an ambassador for your football club there is no better man and that is why he left to such huge acclaim. He returned with his AFC Wimbledon team in September 2011 and received a standing ovation from all quarters of the Rec. The build-up to his return alongside the management team of Stuart Cash, Paul Priddy, Simon Bassey and even chief scout Paul Shrubb had been huge. Our manager at the time, Dean Holdsworth, said *"It's like being at your ex-wife's wedding"*.

Interview with Terry Brown on his last day.

Terry Brown bows to the East Bank after his emotional departure.

# Dream Catch Me

1992

ay 2007 saw the arrival of Gary Waddock as the new permanent manager. Wow! We were now employing internationals as manager. Gary made 21 appearances for the Republic of Ireland although his accent is distinctly of north-west London origin. He was also a proper legend from QPR for whom he had played for in the 1982 FA Cup Final versus Tottenham Hotspur and, as respected journalist and Rangers fanatic Tony Incenzo states, "*QPR's most popular player of the eighties*". He had also managed there too. A manager with no non-league experience, it was certainly a massive gamble by John McGinty and the Board but John was always certain that it was the correct choice. He grew the strongest Chairman/Manager relationship I have witnessed in my time in football and that was so important.

One player who also expressed happiness was Nikki Bull. He had played under Gary as a youth player at QPR and had always spoke extremely highly of him. It was a match made in heaven that's for sure.

Similar to the arrival of Terry Brown, Gary kept the caretaker manager on the staff as his assistant. Martin Kuhl was that man and, behind the scenes, he was a massive influence on Gary. A firm reputation as a player, Martin's not the kind who you idle into a long conversation with but he is loyal, knows his football and we always got on well. He had seen the previous season out with an impressive style of quiet but efficient leadership. A visit to Dagenham and Redbridge saw the east London club secure promotion to the Football League in April.

Watching the sheer delight in manager John Still's face and what it meant to him I thought to myself- "*I want to experience a*

Gary Waddock (right) signs on the dotted line with Martin Kuhl (left) as John McGinty looks on.

*bit of that"*. Little was I to know that "The Ginger Mourinho" would produce in such a special way.

This was even more significant because it was a tricky period for the football club behind the scenes. Despite John being at the helm things were not settled and a continuation of end of year losses since the club had turned full-time was catching up.

The financial position was precarious. It may have been a special season on the pitch but "behind the scenes" was a shambles.

The bottom line was that because the team started to do so well under Gary Waddock it papered over the cracks that were appearing and which would, eventually, become a permanent disfigurement beyond repair. This was when a succession of new directors and Chief Executives started making the rounds and, to be honest, I didn't know if I was coming or going at times. Every new official or employee wanted a piece of me to learn about the club. One director, Paul Foy, from the main sponsors Ezylet, offered me the position as Director of Communications and Public Relations and to become a permanent fixture within the hierarchy after an impressive discussion and presentation he gave at his offices in the town. From sponsoring the club to then becoming a director he became an influential part of the set-up only to disappear as quickly as he arrived though and another false dawn and promise in the process. He was also the advocate of removing the ruling that no shareholder could own more than 20% of the shares. This was a strict regulation that had been put into place when the club was formed in 1992. However the financial situation was such that Foy made an appeal at an EGM that the only way the club could move forward was to remove this stipulation. I have to say that he convinced me even if his manner was a touch brash. I should have started to read the writing on the wall at this stage but, as you do when your team is flourishing on the pitch, you put it to the back of your mind. Another chapter in the club's history that I never quite got to grips with. One minute this guy looked as though he was going to be the saviour, taking the club forward, building a terrific bond with fellow Irishman John McGinty and the next minute he was gone along with the main sponsorship and, of course, the Director of Communications and Public Relations role! I've lost count of the times a new employee or official would say to me- "*I've fallen in love with the club*" only to go missing once their involvement with it had reached a conclusion.

Little was expected in terms of a play-off challenge from Gary. Stabilising the playing squad was the priority. I don't think Gary had a similar view though. He always had a belief that he could steer the club into the Football League and he didn't disappoint.

On the pitch the first home match of the season was a disaster. We lost 3-0 on a Tuesday evening to Torquay United where former striker Tim Sills netted for the visitors.

Walking Gary from the dressing rooms to take him to the press box for the post-match fun I didn't quite know what to say to him. I just said, "*Do you know last time we lost 3-0 at home in our first match of the season we*

Interviewing Gary Waddock- the manager who realised the fans dream of returning the name of Aldershot to the Football League

went on to win the league?*" He acknowledged the statement but I think deep down he was thinking- "*What is he on about?*"

I still used the Directors Box for the media requirements for the website responsibilities during this season. I can recall a woman shouting at the top of her voice at an early fixture- "*You want to pull your finger out Waddock*". I thought this was a bit strong. Blimey the bloke's only just taken on the job and we did win the opening match of the campaign at Kidderminster Harriers! It was only afterwards that I learned that the lady in question was actually Gary's wife. It made me laugh and you need to have some fun at a football club. It is so important.

A new "main job" move during this period was fruitful too. Joining the Army Football Association ensured that the players training headquarters was located at the Aldershot Military Stadium, the home of Army football. Handy to say the least! I was also able to link with the club by arranging the big Army Inter Service matches to be played at the Rec each season which was a welcome boost too. It also hosted the German Armed Forces for the first ever match between the two military services since the Second World War and, poignantly, the 100th anniversary of the Christmas Truce where the two forces participated in an emotional and international occasion in December 2014.

Ironically a week after I had joined, the club arranged a match in honour of the Army for the visit of Ebbsfleet United. It saluted the return of the Grenadier Guards and 4 GS Med Regiment who were returning from Afghanistan. It was a fine gesture and loads of fans kept coming up to me to say thanks for arranging it. I couldn't take the credit for this one although the timing was nice. It was all down to John McGinty and his sincere affection for the Armed Forces.

Gary had set his side up to win matches with a basic philosophy. If you score three then we will score four! I started to believe that this had the ingredients to be just a touch more than your average season after away victories at Forest Green Rovers and Oxford United; both 3-2 wins in September. At Forest Green we played delightful football and the victory sent out a message especially as defender Anthony Straker had been sent off. Lewis Chalmers scored a late winner at the Kassam Stadium after we had let a two-goal lead slip. There was just something not only about the style and swagger but that steely determination to win. There was work to do but the foundations were certainly in place. Whatever was happening off the pitch if the team is doing well then that is all the fans are interested in.

# Apologize

1992

The league campaign was interrupted by an FA Cup first round tie at Crawley Town. Glaswegian Steve Evans was in charge of the Sussex club who had beaten us at the Rec earlier in the season in the league. Evans hadn't stopped harping on about the referee that afternoon, all surrounding the dismissal of his player Jean Paul Pittman.

He said in the programme notes for the cup tie, "*We overcame a match referee who seemed to favour the home team all afternoon…The match referee is important today, and let's hope he too has a good game. I understand he is a good quality official from my sources in the game up north, so let's all hope that is the case*". What Evans didn't realise is that the official for both matches was the same person, Graham Scott. I wonder what his view of proceedings were reading the programme prior to the match.

I cannot stand Evans or his assistant Paul Raynor. In my view and experience Evans is an immensely unpleasant character who I have seen close at hand, behind the scenes, with his nastiness and vitriol. The opening two matches had seen the benches simmering and it all reached boiling point during the replay at the Rec which we won 1-0 courtesy of a goal from Louie Soares. Sick to the back teeth of the antics and continuous rantings on the touchline from the visiting bench Martin Kuhl actually knocked Raynor to the floor. The crowd loved it and the referee had to send Martin to the stand but even he had a smile on his face upon doing it. You ask referees up and down the country. They cannot stand Evans or his counterpart. Even those managers who try to be friendly, few actually like him. That said, I cannot knock his managerial record. He has done pretty well over the years wherever he has been.

I was embarrassed at Cambridge United on the day of the FA Cup first round and it was to do with the programme. The club had decided to dispense with the services of Adline Group, the providers of the programme since 1987. It was obviously a political decision as Adline was the company of Karl Prentice whose position on the Board was obviously precarious. I was really uncomfortable about the whole situation because Karl and I had worked closely on the programme for years and I didn't like the way that he had been treated by the club, especially considering his years of service. In a matter of weeks Karl was eventually ousted from the Board along with Aidan Whelan. I had worked closely with them during some difficult periods in the past and was sorry that they were on their way.

I believe Karl, as Terry Owens did previously, found it difficult to adjust from being a Chairman back to a director. The football club also cost him on a personal and professional level too. Aidan had always kept in the background but had been responsible for some important initiatives including within the youth section. He actually came through the old AFC youth system in the seventies as a player. He went on to have a spell as Chief Executive up the road at Farnborough. Whatever happened there he was, in the main, effective during his time as a director at Aldershot. I used to say to him to keep a record of everything he had achieved for the club because one day he may need to use it. That day eventually came and he hadn't kept that "list of achievements" and it didn't work in his favour.

At times Karl and Aidan were too close and too powerful for their own good and, sometimes, didn't have a full understanding on building relationships with volunteers and I think that eventually rebounded on them. It rubbed some people up the wrong way. Mind you it should also be remembered that they too were volunteers. With Karl gone Bob Potter tendered his resignation as President and I believe that was detrimental to the club too. I remain convinced that Karl's relationship with Bob was so strong that, unlike the Aldershot FC situation, the latter would have been a vital asset when the financial woes became public knowledge later down the line. We will never know for sure.

Due to the change of printer for the programme I didn't want the club to suffer as a consequence and agreed to step in as programme editor. I totally revamped the programme and arranged a meeting with contributors. However after compiling the first edition my computer crashed and I lost the lot.

Livid, after six hours of fruitless conversations with the computer suppliers I thought to myself that this wasn't going to work. I contacted my old mate Guy Butchers who agreed to step in and I met with the newly appointed Chief Executive Bob Bowden and John McGinty in a corner of the Boardroom at the Abbey Stadium to let them know of my decision. We had won a number of programme awards during the new club's existence, especially in the Isthmian League days. It is easy to criticise putting together a football programme, especially for those matches at short notice. Believe me it is not easy as every programme editor up and down the country can vouch for. You are always reliant on your contributors and if they let you down or do not provide copy by the deadline it then puts you as the individual under immense pressure.

The Conference was making a name for itself too mainly due to its sponsorship with Setanta, an Irish television company. They were covering the matches live although it took them some while to make their introduction at the Rec. Indeed I believe that when the first phase of matches destined for live coverage were announced at the start of the season few expected Aldershot Town to be involved as one of the pacesetters. However once November arrived we had made it onto the "big" screen. The problem was, however, that the flexible approach to dates from the television company seriously affected attendances. We went from a 3,000 plus figure versus Rushden and Diamonds to lose over a 1,000 fans for the next home match, the first ever Setanta match at the Rec versus Grays Athletic on a Thursday evening in November. Then it was a Sunday night at Salisbury City in December and a 4-0 success.

By Christmas time it looked as though it was going to be a two-horse race for the privilege of automatic promotion to the Football League- ourselves and Torquay United.

After losing just once in 16 league matches there was a slight dip in form in January. A home defeat versus Forest Green Rovers when Mark Beesley netted in the first minute was followed by a 2-0 reverse at York City; no disgrace either as The Minstermen had been unbeaten in 12 too.

I laughed at one of the northern hacks' post-match questions to Gary at York. "*Gary, This must be a difficult period for you after suffering two successive defeats. Questions will be asked about whether your team has the capability and mental attitude to win the Conference League. You must be concerned about some of the other teams around you and whether you are capable of turning this run of form around. Are you starting to feel the pressure now?*" "*No- move on*"- was Gary's brief response with a stare into the reporter's eyes as if to state "*What are you talking about?*"

He said to me as we left Bootham Crescent , or the "Kit Kat Crescent as it was called then, "*I see all the doom and gloom merchants are back on the scene. We will be fine*". He wasn't wrong either. We won the following Tuesday evening at home to Oxford United and never really looked back.

# Call the Shots

S etanta were regulars at this stage. The first Monday evening
in March saw us travel to the only real contenders for the
title race, Torquay United. The Devon side were a real
threat. Managed by former Shots player Paul Buckle they really
needed to defeat us to keep themselves in the chase.

Gary had missed the previous week's Setanta Shield match at
Crawley Town in order to travel down to watch the Gulls entertain
Altrincham. It certainly paid dividends. We took a magnificent
following to Plainmoor with many fans anticipating that this
could be an important evening. To be honest, I would have
accepted a point and sat nervously in the Press Box. Danny
Hylton set the match up nicely with an early goal which he didn't
really know how to celebrate. The match was level on 90 minutes.
In the fourth minute of injury time a hopeful ball across the
halfway line into the left-hand channel was chased down by
substitute Junior Mendes. The ball fell to Scott Davies who was
just outside the penalty box and did he hit it!

*"There is to be late drama."* commentator Steve Bower said
on a clip that Shots supporters will have played over and over
again. I have to say that I went absolutely mental. I was sitting on
the end seat of a squashed press box and jumped onto it and
started celebrating. All the locals turned round to look at this
idiot. Who cares? I thought. We'd waited 16 years and we now
had 95% of the jigsaw completed. Gary knew too but it was all
kept under the radar. We hadn't won anything yet but it was
certainly in our own hands now.

Playing back the Setanta highlights upon returning home
from Plainmoor Gary's reaction to Davies' goal was simple.
*"F****** get in there"* you could lip read. Few would disagree

with that. Nikki Bull, who had been outstanding in the match and had been presented with the Man of the Match award, summed it up eloquently on Setanta afterwards speaking to presenter Rebecca Lowe. He said, *"You look at the people behind the goal and this is for them. They had their club taken away from them through no fault of their own. People have dedicated their lives to bring this club back up from nothing. The boys in our squad have got to realise how much it means for these supporters to go up. It is up to us to get over that finishing line now"*. What the victory did confirm though is that we had extended our lead to 11 points at the top of the table.

Nikki Bull (left) provided an emotional post match interview after Scott Davies' late winner at Torquay.

We did come a cropper in the FA Trophy semi-finals versus Ebbsfleet United which was a major disappointment because that lifelong dream of Wembley was scuppered again. Although a taste of silverware was experienced in the final of the Setanta Shield.

The match was played at the Rec after we won the toss for venue and Rushden and Diamonds were defeated after a terrific 3-3 draw and an immaculate penalty shootout which saw us home in front of over 3,500 fans. What this match did was give the fans the taste of winning some silverware and what we were on the verge of achieving.

There were a couple of aborted attempts at securing the title, at Ebbsfleet United and at home to Burton Albion, despite winning the latter match so it was all set for another live Setanta match and familiar journey down the A303 in midweek.

Fate dictated that it would be a return to Exeter City's St James' Park on the Tuesday evening (15th April 2008) needing a point. And I had a bit of a problem. This had a rare clash with the "day job". We had the Army FA Referees Day planned for Aldershot. Soldiers travelling from all over the world for their annual get together. I had to be there as it was my responsibility to organise it.

In addition my Chairman, a tremendously knowledgeable football man Lieutenant Colonel Tony Rock, had asked if he could travel to Exeter for the match in my car with our guest speaker, former Premier League Referee Alan Wilkie. I told them that we had to be gone by 3.30pm; the seminar over ran as Alan continued talking for England... Scotland, Ireland and Wales too!

3.30 became four then 4.30. I said to Tony that we had to wrap this up quickly otherwise we wouldn't get there on time. When we got in the car Alan then said that he needed to get back to the barracks to change. The barracks weren't in Aldershot but in Minley, 15 minutes away.

I started to panic now. What could be our moment, the day I had dreamed of since 1992, the greatest night in our history and I had visions of being halfway down the A303 and missing out. We eventually left Minley at 5.15pm. The journey wasn't for the faint hearted and we arrived at St James' Park with five minutes to spare before kick-off. I decided to sit with the fans for this match. Forget press boxes and anything else for this one. I wanted to be with the people who had played their part to get us to this momentous occasion. We went 1-0 down courtesy of a goal from the late Adam Stansfield on 39 minutes but three minutes later Scott Donnelly levelled. The second half took an eternity and Nikki Bull made a double save with just a few minutes remaining which was out of this world, right in front of where the Shots supporters were massed. We had to hold on. If we didn't Torquay were playing at Rushden and Diamonds two days later and I had visions of them failing to win that match and us winning the Conference when we were not playing. What an anticlimax that would have been.

Then came that moment. Referee Chris Sarginson blew his full time whistle and it started to sink in. The name of Aldershot was back in the Football League. The emotion was evident all around. The realisation of what we had achieved was enormous. From those dark days travelling to an auctioneers in Southampton to retrieve part of the old club's furnishings; to opening the doors of the Recreation Ground in the summer of 1992 where the only remaining items were manky old carpets. To not having a team, structure, nothing.

No money until the fans paid their part by becoming shareholders to ensure that the capital was raised to get the club functioning. Then the five promotions.

It was a wonderful story and to have played a part in that filled me with pride. I turned around and looked at fellow supporters in the stand. Nick Fryer was in the row behind me with his wife Bernadette and I could see in his face what it meant. I was delighted to see Barry Underwood along with his wife Sheila, who used to help out in the office on a voluntary basis, there. Despite his shoddy treatment towards the end he had made the effort and we all embraced. So many supporters came up to offer their hands in appreciation. It meant so much to everybody concerned. I was soon on the pitch interviewing player after player and then caught up with Gary and Martin Kuhl- the conductors of the script. There is a photograph of Gary and John McGinty embracing each other on the pitch that should go down in Aldershot folklore. It was a natural embrace from two people who had the utmost respect and affection for each other. As I was on the pitch my phone rang. Who else but that man Terry Brown offering his own congratulations. This was a man who had set the infrastructure of the playing squad as 16 of the players involved during the league campaign had played under him. Some would be bitter about that thinking that *"It could have been me"* but not Terry, honest and loyal in consideration of the club. Even Terry Owens made it onto the pitch and why not. It was great to see him there. If anybody deserved the adulation it was Terry. I made a point of phoning a few people over the next few days too including Steve Wignall and George Borg. I said to them both, *"Never underestimate the role that you played in this achievement"*.

It was just a fantastic time to be involved in the football club, the likes that will probably not be experienced again. We were on the pitch for over an hour and full marks to Exeter for the way they allowed us to celebrate. This was a different Exeter City to that of 1999 and was now run by a Supporters

Trust and they were terrific. They actually gained promotion via the play-offs that season too and I wonder if witnessing the scenes of that night at their ground gave them that additional spur that they needed.

I will never forget the return journey either. My one disappointment was that I had to leave the celebrations to drive home; the following day was the biggest in the Army FA calendar- our own Cup Final; one of the oldest football cup competitions in the world which actually started in 1888/89. Many supporters stayed overnight in Devon whilst the players and some fans remained in the bars at St James' Park until the early hours. It must have been some bar bill!

On my way home I was buzzing of course until Alan Wilkie told me that we would struggle in the Football League. "*You only have two players who are good enough. Your goalkeeper and central defender*" he told me. To be honest I couldn't give a hoot if he was right or not. This was about "now" and not the future. To savour the moment. On the way home my phone was busy but the call that did it for me was from my brother.

He had been on business in South Africa but rang to tell me how proud he was of me and what a huge achievement this was and one that I should remember for ever, considering the dedication and part I had played over many years. I was holding back the tears of emotion driving up the A303. That meant the world to me.

# Always where
# I Need to be

1992

W e had confirmed our promotion but now it was all about sharing it with the fans at the Rec. Our final home match of the season was versus Weymouth on a Tuesday evening. It was party time for us but not for the Dorset club. They needed a point to avoid going to the last day of the season in a relegation battle.

John McGinty contacted me and said that the casket of rum that was originally presented by the then Clapton Chairman Mike Fogg at that opening match in August 1992 remained in the Boardroom. The instruction was always that it could only be opened when we made it to the Football League. John said he was going to track down Mike and he duly did. I then arranged for former players of both clubs (old and new) to be invited alongside people who had put their own stamp on the club during their time there.

The chaos that was prevalent behind the scenes was apparent on this occasion too. We had over 30 former players invited and it was only a few hours before kick-off when I was told that we had nowhere to put them because of the demand for space. I wasn't best pleased because I knew that some of the "dignitaries" that would be present were only there because of the occasion and not for what they had contributed towards the success story. Eventually we found the old hospitality box in the South Stand to put the "Class of 92" in with other former players and management scattered around the Directors Box and North Stand. The Directors Box itself was over-subscribed in a big way. It was standing room only at the back but, to be honest, who cared?

Just before the interval I went down to the edge of the pitch because I was compering the half-time introductions. I forgot that Weymouth were scrapping for their lives. They were managed by former Chelsea and Arsenal midfielder John Hollins, whose son Chris had played for us a few years previously. I entered (just) the away team technical area and Hollins was less than pleased. In fairness I understood his annoyance as I shouldn't have stepped inside. I apologised but he kept going on about it. *"How many times do you want me to apologise?"* I responded to him as, by now, the stewards were intervening and it was all getting fraught. Fortunately the half-time whistle brought proceedings to a halt. We managed to introduce everybody onto the pitch which was an effort in itself before the final announcement. Mike Fogg appeared and opened the casket of rum in front of the near 6,000 attendance for a special moment.

It felt as though the journey was completed. The goalless draw was immaterial to us. Good news for Weymouth as they avoided relegation that night but the presentation of the Conference Trophy to our fans afterwards was what it was all about. The celebrations went on long into the early hours and I made sure that a "toast" was provided in memory of "absent friends".

That one was for my dad and for many supporters no longer with us but for whom this would have meant everything to.

John Leppard made me laugh that night too. The bar was heaving for hours until time was called and the bar finally closed. All forlorn John, unable to get another drink, turned to me and said, *"The evening's been spoilt now. Ruined".* I responded, *"Steady on John. It is three in the morning!"*

I was also delighted that my old mentor Norman Penny was able to attend. Norman served in a variety of roles for decades. He was another pure Aldershot man and when he had to work away from the

Oliver and I with the Conference Trophy in 2008

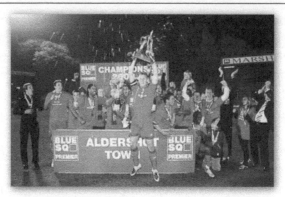

Aldershot are back in the Football League

To me it was essential that former players of both
clubs were invited back to share the joy of
promotion to the Football League in 2008

John McGinty with former
Clapton Chairman Mike Fogg in
April 2008 opening the casket of
rum 16 years after it was presented

My brother David (left) and Terry
Owens celebrating as the Football
League dream is completed

club in the early years to make ends meet his heart was always at the Rec. The Weymouth match was his last ever visit to the Rec. He knew it would be too. We sadly lost Norman a few months later but what an inspiration he was for me.

The club organised a "bus procession" around town to be held after the season had ended. Terry Owens sponsored it and certainly made sure he was on the bus. At the conclusion of the tour a reception was held in the Sponsors Lounge. I was in and

My mentor Norman Penny taught me so much

out pretty rapidly to be honest. It stood for everything that I didn't; dignitaries who had played no part in our rise through the divisions being given the grand treatment whilst supporters who should have been involved not being given the opportunity.

What really annoyed me was that there were people, mainly councillors, present that day who had actively opposed us in public in 1992 when we formed the club. It didn't fit well with me but it didn't spoil my season. To me the camaraderie of this playing squad matched the first ever season of 1992/93.

Only 24 players were used in league action and that showed the togetherness that Gary and Martin had forged. Gary always told me about his views on loan signings. *"Only if they are better than what we have got."* he used to say because he hated disruption in the dressing room. That season Scott Davies was the only player signed on loan and that was for a whole season too.

I did say to John McGinty at the end of the season that he should stand down and take the honorary role of President and relieve himself of the day to day pressures the Chairman endured but he wanted to be Chairman of a Football League club and I understood that.

# Five Years Time

1992

Once the club reached the Football League though I detected that the mentality changed. It became too corporate. Don't get me wrong, it was a necessity to widen the opportunities in this area because entry to the Football League ensured a heavy financial burden due to the required work needed to meet Football League criteria. It was a heavy cost too with the club losing not far short of £500,000 in its first season in the Football League but I felt that the corporate concentration was to the detriment of the regular supporter. I believe that the regular fan was taken for granted with the attitude that "*Don't worry, they'll come to the match come what may*".

As time progressed that wasn't the case although the introductory season of the Football League was always likely to see decent attendances both at home and away with many venues not visited by Shots fans for over 20 years in addition to a fair few new stadiums too.

At the Rec though down went all the memorabilia in the bars and sponsors lounges dating back to 1926 and the heritage of what football in Aldershot was all about. This included a framed montage that I had presented to the club covering that last ever AFC match at Cardiff City in March 1992. In addition to the match programme and ticket stub it included an array of photos of the players in the dressing room after the match, totally dejected, along with photos of the supporters in the stands at Ninian Park. It was presented for a reason – to ensure that we never, ever forgot that day and how it had all come to that. The trouble is that as time moves on people with the strong connections disappear one by one. Of course by this time I was not a Board member or full-time member of staff so didn't have that influence within the walls to change things as I once had. I certainly made my views known but these fell on deaf ears. By the opening day of the inaugural Football League campaign the club had 10 directors and another new Chief Executive. Word kept getting back to me that there were some members on the Board not interested in *"1992 and all that"*. That is the point though. You have to have an understanding of what it was all about. There weren't enough around the table who had experienced that pain that the supporters had felt at the time. Some say *"History is history"*. I say *"History should never be forgotten"*.

By the end of the first season in the Football League the Board had been split into two. An "Investment Board" which included directors who had made investments into the club including Polish businessman Kris Machala, who was based in nearby Camberley and an "Operations Board" who were due to assist in the day to day running of the club.

I never did get my head around this but one fact that was missed by many but significant to me was that, for the first time since the club was formed, there was no Supporters representative on the main Board of Directors, a stipulation I had set up in 1992 with Terry Owens. I was disappointed with this and the fact that it had been allowed to happen.

New photographs were added in the bars of the previous season's promotion which was fine but not to overload it with just one season. There had been football in Aldershot for over 80 years! As time progressed it got even worse as photos of former players were taken down and replaced with photos of sponsors playing in charity matches at the Rec; as if any proper Shots fan was seriously interested in this. You cannot replace history and it is important to cherish it, not to discard it. This was just one factor as it was my belief that now the name of Aldershot was back in the Football League some believed we were bigger than we actually were. Added to this was the fact that, although he continued on bravely and with no mention of his condition, Chairman John McGinty was battling cancer and was not able to run the club in the way that he would have wished no matter how hard he tried.

I thought the world of John and we never had cross words until that summer and it was something I regretted. It was all surrounding Nikki Bull. At one stage in the summer it was looking highly likely that Nikki was on his way and Torquay United looked a likely destination. They were, of course, still in the Conference.

I remember saying to Nikki, "*How will you feel on the first day of the season when we are embarking on our historic first ever Football League match and you will be playing in goal against Histon!*" – No disrespect to Histon but after Nikki had been an integral part of getting us to the Football League he needed to be a big part of our future. I became involved in the saga as John had blocked any new agreement, stating that the deadline for Nikki has passed and there was no way he would be playing for the club again. John had even gone public on the fact too. This just couldn't happen and I kept talking to John reminding him that Nikki had only just become a father too and how this would have had an effect on him. Gary Waddock, who was abroad on holiday but obviously wanted his keeper to remain in post, kept in frequent touch. After many discussions and phone calls Nikki and the club came to a deal. This was good news and I said to John that I would prepare a real "feel good" statement that we could release to the general public and announce at the right time. I remember coming out of the cinema with Oliver in Basingstoke that day, turning on my phone and then the bleeps started. John had already made the announcement. Two lines on the bottom of another announcement was hardly making it the "good news" story that it was supposed to be, more of an afterthought. I was furious and John and I had a blazing row in the middle of Basingstoke's Festival Place Shopping Centre. I always remember as he ended the conversation saying to me "*You've spoilt it now*" and he hung up. I felt really bad and rang him up that evening and apologised. It was the only time we ever had an argument and I hated it really because John was just not the kind of person you wanted to fall out with. His passion for the club was obvious but he needed support and guidance from those around him.

# Take a Bow

1992

The return of the name Aldershot to the Football League was fittingly at Accrington Stanley continuing the historical links between the two clubs. It was a day of joy at the Crown Ground as over 500 fellow Shots fans made the journey to Lancashire to witness that man Scott Donnelly net the only goal of the game to celebrate a special occasion. It felt right and whether the club was ready off the pitch it certainly was on it. This was followed by an introduction in the League Cup at Coventry City's Ricoh Arena. If ever there was a time to realise that we were back this was it. A fabulous stadium and a traditional football club. We held our own for 58 minutes before succumbing 3-1.

AFC Bournemouth were the visitors for the historic first league match at home in a 1-1 draw. Regular visitors to the Rec whilst I was growing up in the 70s and early 80s, it was a perfect fit. I wrote in my programme notes at the time, *"The Football League sounds great but you only have to look close at hand at clubs that have suffered severely due to a failure of being able to balance their finances. So yes it's great to be here. Make no mistake about that but only if we make the most of the opportunity and are able to cope financially. I'm not here to sound negative but realistic about the situation. There is plenty of work to do".* I never realised how symbolic those comments would be but a few years later.

On the pitch I loved the first season in the Football League. To be fair there was never any pressure on the team from the first match due to the fact that Rotherham United and AFC Bournemouth started the campaign on -17 points for administration-related issues whilst Luton Town started on -30. We were safe before a ball had been kicked. I loved the fact that we were playing clubs such as Notts County, Brentford, Gillingham and Bradford City on a level playing field and getting results against them all.

Watching hundreds of our fans at the away matches, albeit from the press boxes with requirements of new age media and technology, instead of the half-full minibus loads we used to have for journeys to places such as Rochdale, Crewe Alexandra and Hartlepool United in the eighties. There were some great matches. You never tired of watching Gary Waddock's side. A fantastic 4-4 draw at GIllingham saw a bizarre circumstance of events whilst even a 5-1 defeat at Chesterfield on a dreary Wednesday evening in October posed no alarms.

One match at Exeter City, yes St James' Park again, saw a debate ensue in the press box. City levelled with just over 10 minutes remaining. It was an own goal from our defender Andy Sandell that did the damage. The Aldershot News reporter Charlie Oliver and I thought it was Sandell that scored. However the home press guys were adamant that the goal was scored by Ben Harding. There was a bit of a difference in the physique of these players. We were told that the BBC Devon guys were on the ball and to ask them. "*Dave Winfield*" they responded. No nearer forward then. All of a sudden City Director of Football and one of the most respected defenders of his generation, Steve Perryman, stepped in. "*He's bound to know*" I thought.

We asked the legend of 866 appearances for Tottenham Hotspur for his view. "*The centre half with the fuzzy hair wearing number 6*" he said. Mmm, the player Perryman was referring to is in fact one of my favourite of the new club's existence, defender Anthony Charles, but he certainly wasn't the player in question either. Anthony's black for a start. To add to the woes we also lost the match 3-2 to a late goal.

A visit to Darlington's 25,000 capacity Northern Echo Arena had a touch of hilarity too. I couldn't believe I was being escorted by a Commissionaire via a lift to enter the press box. When we finally arrived I was the only person sitting in the "scribes" part of the box as the radio commentators were in another part of the stand. It was surreal because three quarters of the stadium was closed too. By kick-off time the stadium was less than 10% full. Sadly Darlington was another club to fall by the wayside due to crippling financial debts.

The second half of the season was much tougher than the opening exchanges and we did dip from contention in the play-offs before finally finishing 15th after winning just two of the final 11 matches. Attendances were averaging over the 3,000 mark but they had dipped significantly in the final third of the campaign which was a concern. There was, however, much to be enthused with Gary developing a tidy squad where most of the players had hugely benefitted from a season in the Football League.

Funnily enough we were being written off before a ball had been kicked for our second Football League campaign. Indeed "442" magazine had said we were certs for relegation and would finish 23rd. I told Gary Waddock this and he laughed. I also told him that Oliver was in a predicament. His school trip was planned for France at the end of May. The date clashed with the date of the League 2 play-off final. I had told Oliver this and said that if a commitment was made to go to France then he would have to go come what may. He chose not to go just in case we got to Wembley even though it was nine months away. "*No pressure then*" said Gary laughing.

The pre-season actually provided a decent victory at home to a strong Tottenham Hotspur XI although I recall the match for something that occurred afterwards. I was in the middle of a post-match interview with one of our players in the tunnel when Oliver came to approach me in the background. "*Harry Redknapp's just walked past. I want to have my photo with him*", he said. Unprofessionally I halted the interview with the player and ran with Oliver to catch Harry before he got into his car and left the stadium. I managed to do so and Harry was more than obliging for the pic. I duly took it, thanked him and we went on our way. Imagine my horror when I looked at my phone and noticed that it hadn't taken. I told Oliver. He wasn't happy. "*You've got to go back and ask him again*" he said. I couldn't let my 11-year-old son down. I chased back up to the car park and

Harry was heading the other way. I flagged him down and he wound his window down. After explaining the situation he got back out of the car ready for another pic. As much as I tried the phone wouldn't work. Five times I tried before I managed to video them together. Harry Redknapp was first class and it is something that Oliver treasures.

# Not Fair

A nother change in the Boardroom saw a guy called Tony Taylor become Vice Chairman. It soon became apparent that John McGinty's health was deteriorating too. By now John confided in me at every opportunity regarding club activities. We trusted each other because we only wanted the best for the football club. I wasn't a director but I knew what made the club tick and knew the people. He always asked for advice and guidance on areas where he wasn't so sure but he never, ever complained about his health.

In a matter of days his health deteriorated rapidly and I was told to expect the worst with an unexpected phone call. I do have a regret that I never got to see John during his final days but was stunned when I received a call on the morning of our home league match versus Accrington Stanley. I cannot recall who rang me, only the words- *"We've lost John"*. John passed away on the morning of the match on 22nd August 2009, 17 years to the day of our first ever competitive match. I recall writing an obituary to place on the website and found it difficult to compose myself. Arriving at the Rec for the match there was an obvious sombre mood around the whole stadium. It was a truly awful time. We won the match 3-1, I recall little about it. The passing of John hit everybody. He was that "larger than life" character that you meet from time to time. He had a connection with the supporters and it was a huge blow to the football club.

The club provided a magnificent tribute for John with an organised minute's silence before the match with players, staff and family gathered on the pitch prior to kick-off with supporters with flags gathered on the pitch side by the East Bank. This was followed by a Memorial Service after the following home match versus Hereford United at which I was privileged to be able to provide my own tribute to John in public. In truth the organisation of the event behind the scenes for the service were chaotic before myself and the Reverend Mike Pusey became involved just a couple of days or so beforehand but it was a marvellous tribute to a man whose life revolved around his family and Aldershot Town.

His grandchildren were the mascots whilst Gary and I presented John's wife Mary with a special framed shirt with "John McGinty 1" printed on it. In addition to traditional hymns there were songs too with four of John's favourite Irish songs. I was also sad to inform people within the Army FA too as John had made a huge impact with the military of which he thought so much of. My boss Major Billy Thomson and I attended the funeral in Alton. It was standing room only. I had an abiding memory of John from the day of his 60th birthday in 1997. We had been invited to his party in Alton but were skint at the time and couldn't afford it. I politely declined to John but never told him the real reason. Imagine my horror when we spoke about how it went afterwards and he mentioned the fact that it was a free bar. That was John though. I bet it cost him a fair few quid too.

To me the loss of John was the first brick of the walls coming crumbling down at the club. Don't get me wrong, the financial

Rev Mike Pusey conducts a service on the pitch to remember John McGinty. Emotional times.

woes had been evident for a number of years by now but he was like one of those old fashioned world leaders that kept a turbulent country intact for decades due to his influence and presence more than anything else. But once that individual is no more, then the liberties start to be taken and slowly but surely the danger signs start to appear and then

Gary Waddock and I making a presentation to John McGinty's wife, Mary.

it is carnage. Respected club Vice President and journalist Jack Rollin summed it up perfectly when he quoted that John was "*Unforgettably selfless. A man with a heart bigger than himself*".

Significantly John's strongest association was with Gary Waddock. The pair just had a tremendous understanding and respect of each other. Indeed the post-match interview I conducted with Gary after Accrington Stanley had to be cut short because of the distress he was in. It was a truly emotional moment which showed human feelings at their most natural. Gary said that he had "*Lost a mate*". His team certainly responded by winning the match versus their Lancashire opponents. Gary told them to "*Go out and win the match for John*". They didn't disappoint.

# Singing the Blues

1992

With John sadly no longer with us it was only a matter of time before Gary would be on his way too. By the middle of October there were murmurings that he was being sought after by other clubs. The name of Luton Town started it, followed by Wycombe Wanderers.

We played Morecambe at home and the scribe from The Sun started asking awkward questions to Gary post-match. I detected in his body language that something was brewing but, as Gary always did well, he gave nothing away and was guarded in his response. I started to fish about and was tipped off that the Wycombe interest was serious. I was down at the training ground on the Tuesday morning after the Morecambe match as Gary arrived. *"Anything to talk about?"* I joked. *"I think we'd better have a chat"* he responded, and we did. To be honest I could understand him wanting to leave the club purely because it was chaos behind the scenes and there was no strong leadership. In fairness following John McGinty as Chairman was a bit like following Sir Alex Ferguson as manager of Manchester United. Gary had lost the relationship that inspired him. He was also heading for a club that was in a higher division but in the middle of a stormy relegation battle. He was leaving Aldershot in a play-off position, the team having scored four goals in our previous two home matches and, on the pitch, with a fine bill of health.

My view is quite profound. If somebody in authority behind the scenes had shown more conviction and sat Gary down and explained where the club was heading and satisfied him that it was secure and realistically ambitious I believe he would have stayed. At the time we didn't even have a proper Chairman. Investment Boards, Operations Boards. What did it all mean?

To me the day that he departed was a sorry, sorry day for Aldershot Town Football Club. The man that had led us to the Football League against all expectations was on his way without the opportunity to say goodbye to the fans. It could have been avoided. Anybody who believes that his departure was financially swayed is misguided. It was all to do with the lack of leadership and insecurity within so close after losing his closest ally and the man that was the influence the bring him to GU11 in the first place.

I would have given the job to Martin Kuhl too. Martin knew what was needed and knew the club having been there for eight years in a variety of roles. I believe he would have jumped at the chance to be the number one and it would have ensured continuity. He eventually joined up with Gary at Wycombe but only because nobody from within gave him any assurances either.

Through the connections of Commercial Manager Nicky Banger, his former Southampton colleague Jason Dodd arrived as caretaker manager along with assistant Paul Williams. It was some roller coaster for Jason in his month in charge. Tony Taylor was his main contact when he arrived. Then, as another Boardroom restructure was announced, Simon Groves took over. Within a couple of weeks John Leppard took the helm as Acting Chairman. I think Jason could have taken the club forward too but he was more than unsure about the uncertainty behind the scenes. "*When I came I was told to report to Tony, then the next week to a bloke called Simon and now to a bloke called John. Who the f\*\*\* is John?*" he said to me. It made me laugh. He was soon on his way to a great job back at Southampton.

# I Got a Feeling

1992

To be honest this period started to disillusion me. The Boardroom situation was becoming a real concern. Too many comings and goings. Too much uncertainty.

Former Birmingham City, Portsmouth, Newcastle United and Reading midfielder Kevin Dillon was appointed as the new manager in November. He was actually the last footballer to be given his debut by England World Cup winning manager Sir Alf Ramsey during his time at St Andrews in 1977. I met Kevin along with Nick Fryer at the Holiday Inn in Farnborough at the request of John Leppard, an hour before the official press conference. Kevin and I conducted an interview in the hotel and Kevin mentioned Reading as an example of how a club should be run and how he would use it as an example. He had been on the coaching staff at the Madejski Stadium for 13 years. We stopped and re-recorded. It wouldn't have been a good way of starting his tenure due to the older supporters' disdain for the Berkshire club from when the two towns used to compete on a level playing field. This was to become something that would become a problem for Kevin further down the line but from my perspective I liked the bloke and we got on well.

His leadership was a totally different type to that previously experienced though. Kevin wasn't what you would class as a "typical Aldershot manager" in the manner that fans had previously been accustomed to and there was never a close bond with the supporters. After assessing personnel on and off the pitch Kevin worked out who he could and couldn't trust and that is important in football because so often people look after themselves and it is a business where back stabbing is the norm. It is horrible but people are protective. Kevin soon learnt that he could trust me and I respected that. We would often have conversations and, whilst his direct approach to resolving issues with personnel on and off the pitch did him few favours, I truly believe that some of the activities off the pitch would have tested the most experienced of managers.

The difficulty was that Kevin had never really experienced "shoestring" football. He wasn't afraid to say it how he saw it and he ruffled more than a few feathers in the process as he tried to make improvements. He did change the training facilities too which was a bit of a nuisance as it was convenient for me nipping down to the Army stadium to conduct interviews.

I used to enjoy interviewing Kevin too. You never quite knew what he was going to say next. He wasn't a "media savvy" manager. In fact he wasn't a great media fan at all. He wasn't the kind of guy who wanted to be in the public domain. He never hit it off with BBC Surrey's presenter Gavin Denison and it used to be good viewing watching the two of them in talk mode at the post-match interviews. Kevin didn't particularly like Gavin and I believe the feeling was mutual. In the end the "Reading" stigma was something Kevin used to use in fun. He'd end up saying *"That team down the road"* if he had to mention them.

Kevin came from a club that had the finances and structure in place to progress to a club where you are always looking for the next corner to cut to save a few bob. He was unable to adapt to that and was probably out of his comfort zone. It all caught up with him eventually.

Kevin Dillon became manager in 2009.

As far as I am concerned his eye for a player is up there with the best and if you look at the players that he brought to the club I'd be interested to hear an argument to the contrary- Jamie Young, Jermaine McGlashan, Aaron Morris and Darren Jones spring to mind for starters.

Whatever people's views on Kevin are I didn't see too many problems during his first season. When he joined the club we were actually 10th in the table and hadn't won a league match for over a month.

# Don't Stop Believin'!

1992

**K**evin and his assistant Gary Owers started well too. A decent goalless draw at Notts County whose Director of Football was Sven-Goran Eriksson (a nice photo with Oliver was taken too) was followed by a staggering recovery versus Northampton Town on a cold and windy Tuesday evening at the Rec.

We were trailing with 10 minutes remaining and going nowhere until Scott Donnelly took advantage of a rather fortunate penalty netting at the second attempt. We won the match in injury time through Marvin Morgan who chased down a ball in the left hand channel that he had no right to win. He cut inside and let rip to send the stadium into raptures. A 5-2 win at Dagenham and Redbridge extended the unbeaten run and we were rocking. Although an unexpected 6-1 reverse at Burton Albion soon put a halt to matters but only temporarily. Ironically that match was the 1,000th competitive fixture for the club; a bit like Arsene Wenger for Arsenal at Chelsea.

A match at Darlington was postponed as we were just north of Leeds before a real blood and thunder match at Northampton Town on a February Friday evening which we won 3-0 at Sixfields. The match had it all. Controversy, brawls, dismissals, the usual when Gavin Ward was in charge of one of our matches. Every club has a referee that their fans don't take to. In the former

**Referee Gavin Ward in debate with Kevin**

AFC guise a guy called Ron Challis always used to be involved in disputes. Post '92 Ward was that man and it never seemed to leave him.

Attendances were encouraging too with an initiative with Eagle Radio proving fruitful. Football needs initiatives to attract supporters. It is a never ending requirement to ensure that that next generation is enthused and encouraged to become regulars. Over 4,000 for the visit of Notts County was testament to this.

Further successes at Chesterfield, Bury and battering Rotherham United ensured that with five matches remaining there were eight teams battling for four play-off places with Rochdale, Notts County and AFC Bournemouth comfortably in automatic positions. We stuttered in successive home matches versus Torquay United and Crewe Alexandra, collecting just one point so the pressure was on for the penultimate away match at Cheltenham Town. With the match heading for a draw deep into injury time at Whaddon Road Dean Morgan, on loan from MK Dons, collected the ball on the right, lifted it between two defenders before cutting inside and connecting to fire home into the net. It was an exquisite piece of finishing from a stylish player. A la Scott Davies two years previously I was standing on my seat in the press box in celebration along with Oliver. The guy from BBC Cheltenham, a rather animated character it is fair to say, gave us daggers. I couldn't have cared less. This was such an important goal, scored in front of the near 800 travelling fans. A photo

taken by Ian Morsman of those celebrations depicts everything you could wish for about supporting your team. Crucially we were nearly there now and this was confirmed the following week when we defeated Lincoln City 3-1 at home despite conceding an early goal.

Fans ecstatic at Cheltenham as Dean Morgan's last minute winner ensures play off spot is likely.

272

The last ever league match at Morecambe's Christie Park the following week is only remembered for the fact that Kevin had a post-match dust up with Shrimps captain Jim Bentley. It was all to do with a late challenge from the defender on our striker Damian Spencer which looked particularly nasty. I was just about to start interviewing Kevin on the pitch when Bentley walked past and it started. It was comical stuff really and our goalkeeper Jamie Young had to intervene. Morecambe's victory that day ensured that they too made the play-offs but we were paired with Ronnie Moore's Rotherham United.

We were at home in the first leg on FA Cup final day. Another packed Rec crowd saw the match seemingly heading for a goalless draw.

Aaron Brown, who had been faultless and nominated the Man of the Match, then under hit a back pass to substitute keeper Mikhael Jaimez Ruiz with two minutes remaining. If ever there was a striker you didn't want to be on the end of such a pass it was Adam Le Fondre. You knew he was going to score and he did. We never recovered from that and lost the second leg at the Don Valley Stadium 2-0. Rotherham surprisingly lost to Dagenham and Redbridge in the Wembley final.

My brother, Oliver and cousin Stuart on the East Bank in the League 2 Play Off semi final in 2010.

# Pack Up

1992

For Aldershot the season was over. To reach the play-offs was an achievement not to be underestimated. The way the side was set up away from home during this season was as organised as I have ever seen from an Aldershot team whilst at home we only lost four matches. It never got any better for Kevin though and eight months later he was gone as on field matters deteriorated rapidly.

The loss of so many key players during the close season was a root cause of this and the majority of them joined former boss Gary Waddock at Wycombe Wanderers who were now in League 2. The visit of The Chairboys in September 2010 was set up as a bit of a grudge match. The build-up to the match was frenetic but the game itself was a damp squib and a goalless bore draw.

In fact I recall this match more for Nick Fryer being honoured after he had decided to step down from his role as press officer after 18 years. Nick was a terrific ambassador for the club and I worked closely with him preparing the releases which he would issue for many years.

It was a working relationship that stemmed from the days when I was secretary and it worked perfectly. We used to speak most days, sometimes two or three times and towards the latter days used to tear our hair out at some of the nonsense going on. Many thought his departure was something to do with Kevin but it wasn't. Like me Nick had a good relationship with Kevin.

Whilst we have the same passion for Aldershot I was fortunate to be employed by the club for the various roles that I provided. Nick was a volunteer throughout and that should be acknowledged.

It was also apparent that it cannot be a voluntary role in the Football League because there are too many demands and requirements on your time. Nick received a signed shirt for his service with his favourite player honouring his commitment- that man Alex McGregor- along with a montage of the former winger.

Another fundraiser. Mark Butler (far right) next to Nick Fryer.

Nick had also invited me to sample some hospitality at Tottenham Hotspur versus Aston Villa on a Monday evening a couple of years before. It was great sitting in the stands at White Hart Lane and you could be sitting next to one of a host of legends including Ossie Ardiles, Alan Mullery, Pat Jennings or Martin Chivers. I liked this process and discussed inviting an Aldershot legend to each match as our own guest of the day. Nicky Banger went for it and it went down really well for a couple of seasons or so. Involving other loyal supporters, Craig Matthews and club statistician Pete Stanford, we managed to track down most of the all-time legends who had worn the red and blue for both clubs. They enjoyed the hospitality and a meal and I would then interview them for 15 minutes or so in front of the sponsors and guests. They would then be introduced to the fans on the pitch at half-time. It was well received. The best one was trying to hunt down Jack Howarth. This guy was "THE" legend that the fans of the previous generation wanted to see. He was the record goal scorer of AFC with 196 goals, 100 or so ahead of the second placed striker, in the sixties and seventies. Craig and I tried to track him down for a couple of years before Craig eventually found success. Jack came and I was told that he was a real character. I only got to watch him during his latter days when I was a youngster but the stories were legendary. Stories that he used to have a pint or two before the match weren't dismissed. *"How does it feel to be back at the Rec, Jack?"* I asked. *"It's great, nothing changes. The grass is still green."* he quipped.

I used to get frustrated sometimes too, especially on the night games when the "corporate" guests had had a little bit

Record goal scorer Jack
Howarth with director
John Leppard.

of extra drinking time, starting from when work finished. Many corporates are just guests for the day and not interested in the actual match or club come to that. I recall one match versus Shrewsbury Town in March 2009. Gary Abbott is in "Category A" of Shots players as far as I am concerned. He was the special guest on this occasion and some of the guests were disrespectful when I was interviewing the former striker. I was about to blow a gasket and call the interview to a halt as I stopped and let everybody in the room know what a special player Gary was and the fact that they should respect that fact and listen to him. Some of those present weren't bothered. Fortunately Gary got the "proper" welcome that he deserved when he was introduced to the "proper" fans later in the evening.

After a couple of years or so Nicky said to me that the club had changed their policy and they were looking for celebrities and football players who had not played for the club to be official guests. I wasn't interested and told him so. Athlete Dwain Chambers was the first guy.

Interviewing The Class of 79 at
another fundraiser. All heroes from left
to right- Alan Wooler, Glen Johnson,
John Dungworth, Joe Jopling and
Alex McGregor

I said that Aldershot fans won't be interested in people that didn't represent us. They started to do it though and then introduce the guest onto the pitch at half-time. I felt so sorry for former Southampton striker Ian Baird. They gave him this big "jazzed up" intro on the tannoy – to silence when he was introduced. It could have been any player of a similar standard and the response would have been the same. He didn't play for Aldershot therefore the fans weren't interested. They didn't do it again.

If there is one away trip I detested it was Macclesfield Town. It all kicked-off in November 2010 when we headed towards Moss Ross.

In conversation with Colin Hancock at a fundraiser.

I always took Oliver with me in the press box in those days before he was old enough to want to stand on the East Bank or away terraces with his pals. It was a terrific grounding for him. He used to take a laptop and was an integral part of the match day media team. Most clubs welcomed him with open arms and there was never an issue, despite the fact that he was just 12. It all fell apart at Macclesfield though. I queued to get our press accreditation. Ours weren't there. I stated to the lady in charge that the request had been made but she wasn't having it. *"How old is he anyway?"* she asked pointing to Oliver. *"12."* I responded. *"He can't come into the press box. He's too young. Breaching regulations"*. We exchanged words as I told her that Oliver had been accepted into the press box at places such as Coventry City and Bradford City without any issues. I was then informed that if he paid to get in Oliver could sit in the row in front of the press box with his laptop and the wires stretching from the electrical sockets behind. *"You are joking"*. I said. *"That would be dangerous and be more dangerous"*. We never got any further. I told them that I would pay for Oliver's admission and that he would be sitting with me in the press box whatever. They asked for my name and said that they would be reporting me to the Football League. Pretty put out by this stage we then walked all the way to the press box on the opposite side of the stadium to be told on arrival at the steps that we needed to walk back to the ticket office and enter via a side gate, walk via the perimeter of the pitch and gain access that way. By this time I couldn't give a jot about the match as I was seething. They have this rickety old press box at Macclesfield too. Every year we would go there and sit in the designated seat given and then this old boy would appear with kick-off approaching and state that we were sitting in his seat and he would make us move. Every year he would say that the club were getting round to correcting their seating plan. They never did. We were pretty awful on the pitch too and lost 2-0. It summed up a pretty dour day.

I never thought anymore on the matter until the Aldershot Town club secretary Bob Green contacted me to state that I had been reported to the Football League by Macclesfield Town. *"We don't want to upset the apple cart"* he told me. I presumed that meant I was on my own on this one. Indeed the only person within the football club who said they would back me once I had explained the situation was Kevin Dillon.

A guy called Derek Johnson called me from Dataco, the company responsible for press accreditation and he informed me that I had contravened Football League rules because Oliver was under 16 and that he would no longer be permitted in the press boxes including our own at Aldershot and that my pass would be withdrawn if this continued.

I asked Mr Johnson if he was aware of the "Football League Junior Reporter of the Year Award" that was organised by the Football League? He obviously wasn't.

I informed him that it was a competition for under 14s where the three winners attended respective play-off finals at Wembley as part of their prize, sitting in the media section of the stadium amongst other matters. The winners in 2010 included a 10-year-old. Amazingly he responded to me and said, *"That's different"*. I couldn't believe it. How could it be different? We had a healthy(ish) exchange of words (not really!) and I told him that Oliver would be sitting with me at press boxes up and down the country. The next call was from Gavin Megaw, the Director of Marketing and Communications at the Football League.

He reiterated the stance that Oliver would not be able to sit in the press box and that the Football League didn't want to jeopardise the relationship it had with Dataco and other media organisations. He was pleasant enough and offered Oliver the opportunity for a day at the Football League behind the scenes which was appreciated. I never took the offer up purely because within a matter of weeks both Johnson and then Megaw left their posts. I thought just to keep quiet on the matter and say nothing. It was never mentioned again and Oliver continued to accompany me in the press box. I am a great advocate of promoting youngsters with obvious talent and was able to do this at Aldershot Town to great effect. I felt that there was just a narrow-minded vision from the powers that be on this one. I wasn't too impressed with the lack of support from the football club on this matter either.

With Oliver in the Press Box- not at Macclesfield obviously!

# When We Collide

1992

T he continued change of personnel within the Boardroom and senior employees meant that Kevin never fitted in with the hierarchy and it was quite evident that he was a "dead man walking". He wasn't a "toe the line" sort of bloke. He had his own methods of trying to professionalise the club and I believe that he made progress in certain areas. However he obviously wasn't going to fit in with the vision the club had moving forward. The pressure was on too because the club had openly stated that they had put together a break-even budget on the proviso that the average attendance would be 3,500. This was a huge gamble. No Aldershot team had attracted such a healthy average since 1979/80.

By the turn of the year we were 800 fans down per match having won just two home league matches. A decent FA Cup first round victory, after a replay, versus Andy Scott's Brentford was soon eradicated as Conference South side Dover Athletic progressed with ease in the second round at their Crabble home. The reaction to this was disturbing. The fans at the bitterly cold and damp Kent surroundings let their feelings known and it was just a matter of time really. You had to feel sorry for Terry Owens too. The former Chairman had sponsored the travel so those travelling by supporters' coaches did so free of charge. It cost him a sizable four-figure sum too.

A New Year's Day victory at Barnet saw the dismissal of Mark Stimson as Bees boss immediately at the end of the match. Kevin was furious about this as Stimson was a former colleague and friend of his. The pair played together at Newcastle United. Within a week it was Kevin's turn and I wasn't surprised at all when I received the call to prepare the statement announcing his departure just eight months after we had reached the League 2 play-offs.

The timing wasn't clever though. Chief Executive (yes, another one) Peter Duffy called me on a Sunday afternoon as Oliver and I were having a special day out watching Manchester United v Liverpool in the FA Cup third round at Old Trafford.

I actually prepared a statement in the services at Hilton Park on the M6 on the way home but Peter had a tendency to change the wording. I knew we would be in for a few drafts. The announcement was due to be made on the Monday morning. On the day we were sitting in the Boardroom fiddling about changing dialogue whilst the press release was still on hold. Then the Sky Sports ticker tape made the announcements before we did. *"Sources: Kevin Dillon sacked at Aldershot Town"*. There are no secrets in football these days.

I'll throw one into the mix though- I don't believe we would ever have been relegated from the Football League under Kevin Dillon. Two home defeats at the turn of the year versus Hereford United and Oxford United had just exacerbated the situation and the fans were demonstrating. They viewed the club in a state of disarray on the pitch and this had been enhanced when striker Marvin Morgan was substituted during the Hereford visit. There was ironic cheering from the home faithful. *"I hope you all die"* was Morgan's ill-advised response on Twitter. Particularly poor timing from Morgan as the club was in mourning at the sudden passing of popular Supporters Club Secretary Julie Beattie at the age of just 49, just hours before the match.

I rang Kevin to offer my support at the loss of his job. His response made me laugh. *"Don't start all that sympathy stuff with me. I don't do that"*. For me though he is a loyal man and this was proven when he had the chance to bring back Dean Morgan on a permanent basis at the start of the season. He wasn't prepared to renege on a verbal agreement that he had struck with Wade Small the day before. He had earned the club a few bob too especially with the future sale of Jermaine McGlashan.

Whether he fell in love with Aldershot Town is another matter but I'm not convinced we guided him in the right direction internally and I include myself in the equation here too. He had particular frustrations from within too. He had asked for the reserve team to be withdrawn from the Capital League in January 2010 for the 2010/11 season in order for him to "pick and choose" when a match could be played where he could use his contacts to arrange a game "behind closed doors" which would be of benefit instead of scraping a squad together just to fulfil a fixture on a set date; a simple request which would have also provided a financial saving too. However administrative negligence internally ensured that his wish wasn't carried through. He also experienced player registration difficulties where he was regularly given incorrect information in addition to non-existent communications regarding hotel plans for away matches which sometimes saw the squad training 50 or so miles from the designated hotel. All in all it particularly annoyed him and understandably so. He was also never invited into a Boardroom during his tenure. There was just a lack of camaraderie throughout.

By this time Kris Machala was the Chairman and owner too with a 51% stake in the club but it was Chief Executive Peter Duffy who was providing the influence.

He had extensive global experience and, after a slow start, I started to buy into what he was trying to achieve. However there

is no doubt that, given his considerable business background, we were too small a club for him and it wasn't going to last. His concentration appeared to be on the top end of the business though and not the nuts and bolts that keep it together which for a club at the level of Aldershot is, for me, essential.

Compering a sponsors launch with Peter Duffy (centre) with Kris Machala (right).

# Raise Your Glass

There was no need for interviews this time around. Duffy had pinpointed a replacement and within days former Crazy Gang man Dean Holdsworth was in the hot seat. The former Wimbledon and Bolton Wanderers striker was a high-profile appointment and a man who knew how to work the media. He arrived from Newport County who he had guided to the Conference South title accumulating over 100 points.

Dean's initial brief was to steer the club away from the relegation zone but, to be honest, we were six points clear when he arrived. I never had any thoughts that he wouldn't succeed here. Alongside his assistant Matt Bishop who also came from Newport the pair enjoyed a solid opening whilst there were more arrivals in the Board Room. This time around I never even met some of them. Indeed I worked out that from the Conference-winning season through to the end of the 2012/13 season there had been at least 19 directors.

*"Mike Smith is joining the Board"*, I was told. *"You know, the one in show business"*. I duly did my research but could find nothing about Smith's connection with football, only recollections of his time at Capital Radio, BBC Radio One and working with Noel Edmonds. I drafted the press release and was given the go ahead and was so close to releasing the statement before I realised it was a different Mike Smith.

Still involved in show business but this one had a totally different background and was married to former Tiswas star Sally James. It could have been embarrassing but such was the merry-go-round of directorships at the time. Sadly the other Mike Smith passed away in August 2014.

By the end of the campaign Dean had led the team to 14th position and a comfortable

14 points above the relegation zone. I thought at this stage we were fast becoming an established Football League club and were certainly pulling our weight. Indeed there were many, (myself included), who thought that the manager was destined for greater heights than the basement of the Football League. An opening day victory at Bradford City appeared to confirm the progress. However it was cup football that took over big time. Dean is a big West Ham United fan having grown up in nearby Walthamstow.

The Irons were in the draw for the first round of the Carling Cup after being relegated from the Premier League. Obviously this would be the dream tie for Dean and Shots fans too. Indeed it was the dream draw for any lower level club in the competition. I always received notification half an hour or so before in order to prepare the media release and website.

I rang Dean to let him know. He was just going into a meeting and had forgotten that the draw was being made. "*Who did you want again,*" I asked. "*West Ham away*" he said. "*You've got your wish*". He thought I was pulling his leg but I assured him I wouldn't do that. He was made up.

The original date for the tie was Tuesday 9th August 2011 but a couple of days before, the riots that swept the country put paid to that. The match got put back a couple of weeks. If ever a match was worth the wait this was it. Over 2,000 Shots supporters made the journey to east London to make themselves heard in an attendance just short of 20,000. They were there more for a night out than anything else. There was no expectation, no belief, just a bit of a laugh really. An evening in the media box at West Ham suited me down to the ground. You know when you have made it in football in the press world. It is when you are provided with a pre-match meal which we were at Upton Park followed by individual monitors by each seat showing Sky Sports News! We were 1-0 down at the break but Sam Allardyce's men were down to 10 just after the start of the second half when debutant Callum McNaughton was sent off for holding back Danny Hylton en route to goal. When Luke Guttridge levelled with 12 minutes remaining you felt there was a sniff that we might stretch this to extra time and, perhaps penalties. Then, with a minute remaining, the stuff that dreams are made of for lower league fans. These are the occasions that come around that you could count on one hand. We were attacking towards the stand where our noisy fans were gathered and inserting plenty of pressure. The ball was cleared out to the right edge of the penalty box where Hylton struck to guide the ball home into the corner of the net. We all went wild. It was a surreal moment. The celebrations began in earnest a few minutes later when referee Graham Scott blew for the final whistle. We were all buzzing. I took Dean into the press conference and I am sure that it was his highlight moment in football management. To think that 19 years to the week we had embarked on that first ever competitive away match just down the road to Upton Park at Collier Row. It was a special night. After the interview with the boss I tried to hunt down hero Hylton. *"He's already gone home."* I was told. *"He's with his Mum."*

This was the start of a cup run to savour. We defeated Carlisle United and Rochdale at home to progress to the last 16 for the first time in the history of any Aldershot team. The draw for the next round of the competition was held prior to our home league match versus Crawley Town. We were at home, preparing to travel to the ground and watching nervously. Most of the big

Danny Hylton celebrates with the Shots fans netting a last minute winner for a famous victory in front of nearly 20,000 at West Ham

hitters were still in the draw- Arsenal, Chelsea, Liverpool, Everton, Newcastle United.

Even Southampton would have been decent. We were drawn first for a home tie and then the patience as the opposition was drawn- MANCHESTER UNITED! We could have flown to the Rec on our carpet we were so high, as we all danced around the living room floor. The pure joy in Oliver's face said it all for me. It made it all worthwhile. I felt like a little kid again too. My mind went immediately into overdrive. This was going to be huge. Within 10 minutes of the draw my phone was awash with texts and phone calls, some people whom I hadn't spoken to for years. Many with the same question- *"Can you get me some tickets?"*

There was a pure buzz at the stadium when we arrived for the Crawley match. It also coincided with the return of our "Legends of 87" for an evening fundraiser which I was compering. It was no surprise that we lost the match 1-0, the first of four successive league defeats. Minds on and off the pitch were focussed elsewhere and if you are to be taken advantage of on such an occasion

The Class of 87 at the fundraiser. Len Walker is central in the back row. Paul Shrubb (far right) and Rosemary Aggett (2nd right).

a team managed by Steve Evans is about the worst kind of opposition you could face under those circumstances.

Accrington Stanley, Barnet and Macclesfield Town followed suit before Dean rested a number of players for the visit to Dagenham and Redbridge, three days before the United match. Ironically we won 5-2.

# The Edge of Glory

1992

Peter Duffy headed the organisation for Manchester United. I was pleased that he kept me involved and sought my input at every opportunity. Duffy called for a meeting of directors and key staff of which I was present. It was like the Italian Job with everybody responsible for their specific areas, planning for the big heist.

The first notable area of concern were the ticketing prices. Everybody had an input and the original plan was that the prices would be severely increased for the match to over £30 for adults. However what had not been considered was the fact that Manchester United had to buy into any ticketing pricing policy. They were adamant in their response. *"We're not having our fans ripped off."* They were not prepared to budge and be involved in any increase which was refreshing to see. I had every understanding that we had to capitalise on the match but, at the same time, make sure that this was not to the detriment of our regulars. There was plenty of debate where everybody had an input including one who had this cock-eyed idea that we could put all the tickets on eBay and sell them to the highest bidder. Really?

An ingenious plan was eventually agreed that the prices for the tie would remain as per normal league matches but those buying tickets on a general basis had to purchase a ticket for the forthcoming league match at home to Burton Albion too as part of the package. It worked and worked well. Supporters believed that the club had listened to the fans about keeping the prices sensible. There was no choice in the matter. Manchester United made sure of that. They looked after their fans. Who would have thought it?

I was, however, impressed with the way that the Board of Directors were working together. I didn't know some of them but

Shahid Azeem (far left) with Sky Sports
commentator Martin Tyler preparing
for the visit of Manchester United the
following week

they really seized the initiative on this one and, for me, it boded well for the future. Duffy coordinated the project well. They all used their contacts to full effect to make sure the club took every commercial advantage.

I ensured former players and those that had served our club since 1992 but who now lived away from the area were also able to purchase tickets and ended up in a pretty unpleasant debate about it on the Shotsweb forum, having to defend my actions. There are no regrets from my point of view. Remember- *"Never forget where you came from"*.

When the tickets went on general sale there were few left and they soon sold out. The messages of abuse (and it was nasty) I received on my phone from disgruntled people beggared belief. They all wanted tickets as United supporters and I wasn't too bothered. It did teach me one lesson though – to take my mobile phone number off the club website page!

The media arrangements in itself were demanding. The interest was worldwide too. I was dealing with companies and journalists as far away as India. For the first time ever I had to turn some applications away. Our usually accommodating press box catered for 22 personnel. This time around we had 150 press requests and, as a club, we hit the jackpot as Sky chose it as the live match, earning a nice tidy sum in the process.

To cater for the additional media we had to utilise the back row of the North Stand in front of the media box and inform those season ticket holders to ensure they had first dibs for an alternative seat. By the time the media box was finalised we had over 100 in attendance (including 32 photographers) plus Sky.

I made sure that all our "regulars", including the long serving and excellent journalist Carl Obert from the Farnham Herald, were looked after and placed them in their usual places in the media box alongside the audio broadcasters such as BBC 5 Live.

Written journalists including The Daily Telegraph's Henry Winter were placed in the North Stand where the supporters were and I know that this was well received by the reporters who felt that they were a part of an old-fashioned atmosphere.

There was no way we could feed all of the media so I decided to do something novel and introduce a "Goody Bag" with various nourishments included. The Good Lady, Oliver and I were up until 2am on the morning of the match filling these bags and getting them prepared alongside my mum and brother. We were one Snickers bar short too- one lucky journo received a Milky Way instead! Everybody chipped in. Everybody wanted to be a part of it. The adrenalin kept us going. In fact this whole operation was run on adrenalin.

We planned our own official media day which received an attendance like nothing I had ever seen before. The usual "Presser" as they call it consisted of Tim Durrans from BBC Surrey and me on a Thursday morning for 15 minutes or so with the manager. We were on another planet here. Everybody wanted a piece of "Aldershot Town for five minutes". You could not but enjoy this period because it was something special. Polish television wanted Kris Machala whilst there was interest in non-executive Director Shahid Azeem from stations in Asia.

I wanted it to be right from the outset with regards to the media on the day. The Good Lady was in charge of coordinating and hosting the "meet and greet" at the gate and she loved it. Jamie Redknapp, Lou Macari, Ben Shephard, Martin Tyler- she was in her element and struck up a good rapport with the large media numbers. *"You can't speak to these people like that as if you know them all"* the rep from the Football League who was monitoring proceedings said to her on the gate. Well, yes you can! The natural approach made the media present feel totally comfortable and relaxed on our manor and that is just what I wanted.

The irony was that, at no stage, up until the Sunday prior to the game, had we really discussed the football itself. On that day United had succumbed at Old Trafford to their City rivals 6-1. Would Sir Alex play a stronger side at the Rec now?

Manchester United in town with my brother , Oliver and The Good Lady

Whilst all this was going on it was difficult for the manager too. For a month the only topic of conversation was Manchester United and I know Dean was feeling a touch isolated by this, conscious that he had an important league programme to continue.

We were at the stadium all day for the United visit and it was an unforgettable experience for us all with so much activity and preparation required throughout. It was great to see the buzz as I went down at 5.30pm to see my brother, niece and nephew queuing at the turnstiles and chat with all the fans who were so excited.

I remember speaking to a fan I had known for years and was approaching his 90th birthday, Ken Moses, and just to see the pure joy in his face made it all special as he waited to gain entry, 85 years after his first visit to the Rec.

Then the United coach appeared with Sir Alex sitting in the front row. They received a welcome they were not used to as they had to drive through a tight entrance at the High Street end with fans either side of the coach providing their own welcome to this part of north east Hampshire. It was all in good taste.

Chas (without Dave), organised by Mike Smith, provided the pre-match festivities as the East Bank was rocking. It was also the biggest night for the players in the Aldershot team, some of whom were United supporters. As the players entered the pitch as "Alive and Kicking" was playing I felt an overwhelming sense of emotion thinking from where we had started in 1992 to what we were about to view. We never quite did ourselves justice on the night but certainly didn't disgrace ourselves. United included the likes of Michael Owen, Nemanja Vidic, Ji Sung Park, Antonio Valencia and Phil Jones whilst it was another household name, Dimitar Berbatov that set them on their way to a 3-0 win.

As a club Manchester United were fantastic. You hear of all kinds of stories about clubs at the top level but they were most

Dean Holdsworth walks out the tunnel with Sir Alex
Ferguson in October 2011

accommodating on all levels and provided expertise and support
to Aldershot that they didn't have to either. As a club we did it
well too. We did it extremely well and were complimented by Sir
Alex and Manchester United.

The most heart-warming story came after the match finished.
Within the Army FA, the daytime job, we have an elderly
volunteer, Major Mike Crowe MBE. *"The man with the poshest
voice I have ever heard"*. Oliver tells me. Mike suffered a stroke a
number of years previously but when he was stationed in Scotland
he was responsible for a barracks in Aberdeen when Sir Alex
Ferguson was in charge of the Scottish club and where they used
to train. They struck up a friendship but obviously lost touch over
the years. Mike asked me to speak to Sir Alex and let him know
that he was ok. I thought to myself that this was unlikely but
assured Mike that I would if I could.

At the end of the match I was in the tunnel waiting to conduct
the post-match interviews with our players when Sir Alex came
down the steps with his own media representative. I approached
him at the bottom of the stairway and introduced myself as the
Aldershot Head of Media but also with my Army links and
mentioned Mike. As soon as the name Mike Crowe was mentioned
he stopped and was fully engrossed in the conversation. *"Mike,*

*how is he?"* The international post-match interview with the world's most famous manager would have to wait as the Sky entourage were getting restless. *"How can I get in touch with him?"* Sir Alex continued. I gave him my card and said that if he contacted the said address I would make sure he would get the message. Two days later a superbly worded letter arrived for Mike at our Army FA headquarters from Sir Alex.

It was a wonderful letter with personal contents for Mike reflecting on their obviously enjoyable days in Aberdeen. Mike was made up and Sir Alex Ferguson went up hugely in my estimation too.

The one nagging doubt that I had about the whole scenario was that although we were at home we wore our all white kit, as we had done in the previous rounds. Dean was a great advocate of this kit but I believe that we should have worn our traditional red and blue. We were at home and should have taken any advantage that we could have. It didn't seem right to me that Aldershot were wearing their change kit whilst United wore their internationally acclaimed red shirts. It was another example of how strong Dean's influence was behind the scenes.

# Set Fire to the Rain

1992

It was all back down to earth from there though. After being in the public spotlight for a month we returned to "dear old little Aldershot Town" again. All those people who were keen to re-associate themselves with me disappeared and the visit of Crewe Alexandra the following Saturday saw an attendance of just 2,331 home supporters. The visit of United saw just under 6,000 "Shots" fans. The press box was back down to 16. "*Where did they all come from, where did they all go?*" I asked myself.

I believe, as a club, we took our foot off the pedal after the Carling Cup tie everywhere. My belief was that if you get it right for the visit of one of the most famous clubs in the land then you can get it right for anybody. We rested on our laurels and expected things to come to us instead of taking advantage of the furore that had surrounded the club in the build-up to the match. Soon after Peter Duffy departed. He stepped down from his role having been in the post of Chief Executive for 20 or so months. He was a touch baffling to the ordinary supporter with his philosophies and emphasis on "brand" and catchphrases. However, when he arrived at the club it was in a precarious state, having lost over £800,000 in the two years since it had entered the Football League. He managed to restructure the significant outstanding debts to a more manageable level during his tenure and strengthened the structure of the organisation. To succeed, however, it needed strong leadership and I believe that his departure diluted that. When you are at the helm of a football club you have to say no. You upset more people than you please by doing so and have to have a thick skin. Peter was always fair with me and, whatever his relationship may have been with others, you cannot ask more than that. I don't believe that some of the shenanigans that happened after his departure would have happened on his watch. It set the tone for the demise of our Football League status and worse to follow. He wasn't the greatest timekeeper mind. Waiting for his arrival for a meeting I would often ring him to find out where he was. *"At the Ash crossroads"* he would reply. I never did say to him whether he ever considered taking another route. Before his departure we had a most farcical event occur on Boxing Day when Southend United visited the Rec. Gavin Ward was the pantomime villain again.

He awarded the Shrimpers an early penalty which was converted and, it is fair to say, wasn't having a classic although there was no argument when he sent off Darren Jones just before the interval when he decked Liam Dickinson right in front of the North Stand.

During the opening 45 minutes there was obviously some problem with the floodlights as they kept flicking on and off. There was a delay to the start of the second half and confusion abounded, mainly because the associate director responsible for ground affairs, Richard Petty, was actually away on holiday. All of a sudden an announcement emanated from the Match Day Control Centre that the match had been abandoned. Almost immediately the PA Announcer Mark Taylor overrode this and informed fans that the match had not been abandoned. You can imagine the laughter amongst the fans not knowing who was correct or not. I made my way to the tunnel area where Mark said that the referee had not come out and had officially made the decision. A further announcement confirming the match was off was again followed by "Oh No It Isn't!" Eventually it was confirmed that it was but it was pure pantomime.

The following day, with the festive period meaning that there was little sporting activity, Sky wanted to make a real song and dance about it. Their reporter called me and said that he was outside the ground with a camera crew but there was nobody there. I politely reminded him that it was a Bank Holiday. Peter and I discussed the situation and I said that there was nothing we could gain out of this and to just say nothing. All staff were briefed and eventually, after numerous chase-up calls, Sky disappeared and we managed to avoid a further tarnish to our reputation after the previous day's activities.

It was quite comical really and suited us down to the ground because we could have played until the following Christmas and not scored a goal in that match.

We went from one extreme to the other in the second half of the season. After going nine hours and 36 minutes without a goal we finally ended that dour run with a 2-1 win at Terry Brown's AFC Wimbledon. This was then followed by breaking an Aldershot record of winning six successive Football League matches which also covered the period from 1932 to 1992. This included defeating Southend United in the rearranged fixture when they were in second position in the table; particularly satisfying as the fans of the Essex club never let the matter drop about the Boxing Day antics.

They actually missed out on automatic promotion by a point and fluffed their lines in the play-offs so it had a huge bearing. We were setting a tidy platform for the future on the pitch, or so it appeared.

We had a terrific evening at home to Bristol Rovers- which commemorated 20 years since the demise of AFC in March 1992. Peter Vincenti's goal was the perfect way to recognise the significance of the date and I was delighted to be able to introduce onto the pitch at half-time 27 former players and management totalling 5,852 appearances and 625 goals including the likes of Jack Howarth, Steve Claridge, Joe Jopling and, of course, Alex McGregor.

Indeed that evening rates as one of my highlights as a Shots' fan, having the honour to make the introductions to the fans of such revered characters stretching from the 1950s through to the final 1991/92 season. It was my idea and the club engaged in the plans which was encouraging and different to the experiences of April 2008 and that celebration match versus Weymouth when the plans were all at sea behind the scenes. All the players gathered in Wally's Bar (named after a terrific and excellent servant of the club, Wally Clarke). Craig Matthews and I had to take them around to their seats for the match. Jack Howarth fancied a quick fag though. A steward who had no idea who Jack was told him to stub it out. I interrupted him, *"That's Jack Howarth"*, I said. *"Tonight, Jack can do what Jack wants"*.

I was delighted to host the return of the legends of AFC
(1932-1992) to remember 20 years since the demise of AFC

We scuppered Swindon Town's title celebrations as they were put on hold after beating Paolo Di Canio's side 2-1 in the penultimate home match of the campaign in front of the engaging Mark Clemmit and his BBC crew, all waiting for a piece of the action. Di Canio signed every autograph on offer after the match despite his obvious disappointment. A point at eventual play-off promotion winning Crewe Alexandra on the final day ensured that we finished 11th in the table and, up until the Easter weekend, an outside chance of a late play-off push itself was not out of the question. For the first time in three seasons we also finished the season with the manager we started it with which should have been a step in the right direction too.

After the way the 2011/12 season finished there was plenty of optimism around the club during the summer and why shouldn't there have been? Indeed after the Crewe Alexandra match I provided interviews with Ben Herd and Jamie Young and was pretty certain this would be the last interview that I conducted with both guys. We shook hands at the end and wished each other well. It was a pleasant surprise that both agreed terms with the club for another season.

# Picking up the Pieces

1992

T he football, however, wasn't centre stage during the close season. Part of the remit I enforced as Head of Media was to hold and chair weekly meetings with senior members of staff including the Chairman and also the Chief Operating Officer, Richard Low, who had been on the Board since 2011, so we were all aware of communication methods.

On reflection they eventually became a waste of time but were productive in the early stages. At one of these meetings discussions were afoot about plans for the new season. It was then casually mentioned that the Dalai Lama was visiting the EBB Stadium in June. My ears pricked. "THE Dalai Lama", I said and was told that it was. Immediately I pointed out that this was a massive event and that the profile would be huge. Indeed as soon as it was announced I had all kinds of enquiries from national and international media. The Sun, of course, made a meal of it but I suppose it gave the club national attention.

I didn't think it right that I be the spokesman for the club on the visit of His Holiness as I couldn't take any credit for organising the event. I fielded all media enquiries to Richard Petty who had been heavily involved. He made an off-the-cuff comment to The Sun that the Dalai Lama *"Might bless the pitch whilst he is in Aldershot"*. The newspaper made the most of it and how that was to be so relevant over the next nine months! TalkSport Radio were also extremely interested. I was wondering whether they might send somebody this time around. When we played Manchester United I know they hadn't sent a reporter but I was also aware that "live" updates were made throughout the match. They weren't being broadcast from our media box!

The work was well underway in staging the event but I was nervous in the fortnight preceding it. I kept asking about media arrangements and it all appeared too relaxed. I spoke to Richard Low and said that we needed to sort this otherwise it could become a problem. I met with the members of the Buddhist Community Centre (UK) to discuss the media situation. They said it was all under control. I asked if I could see the passes that they would be producing. The guy provided me with a crumpled up piece of paper with a name written in pen. I couldn't believe it. I said that was not going to be sufficient and that if I was to be involved then the press would be organised internally by myself and that we would operate the media box as per a normal home match. This was eventually agreed but I knew it would be chaos.

On the day we arrived at the ground at 6am- the Dalai Lama was due five hours later. I had roped in The Good Lady and Oliver to help and boy was it needed. The place was heaving at this early stage. Imagine my horror when I arrived in the media box and it was stacked full of boxes of bananas! Our first task was to move them out as BBC Surrey and Eagle Radio were both broadcasting early and my first priority always was to "look after your own".

The Dalai Lama at the Rec in the summer of 2012.

As hard as we tried to keep the media box in check it was impossible. For one, many of the reporters present had little understanding of the English language. I decided to just let it run its course but by the time the Dalai Lama arrived our media box of 23 seats had approximately 50 in it with people sitting and standing on the tables. Everybody seemed happy though and it was such a relaxed occasion.

We were briefed that we could not look the Dalai Lama in the eye or officially address him as there was a protocol. What a load of nonsense this was.

He eventually turned up about an hour late and actually stopped his chauffeur driven car behind the North Stand and got out of his vehicle to shake hands with his many followers. After addressing the 4,500 assembled at the Rec (it was to prove our highest attendance of the season) he was due to attend a private function in the EBB Lounge. I had managed to make my way to the lounge and it was uncomfortably packed. They had obviously had the same ticketing problem that I had. The deal was that the Dalai Lama was to personally meet all the children that were present before receiving a specially made shirt from the club which had "DALAI LAMA 1" emblazoned on the back. This was our bit of "PR" out of the day. Kris Machala was to make the presentation with Ian Morsman making sure we had our piece of the action recorded on camera. It didn't happen. As soon as he saw how packed the room was the Dalai Lama swiftly retreated out of the room, down the stairs, into his car and out of the stadium. Richard Petty managed to run down the stairs and throw the shirt into the front of the car. I doubt it's ever been worn and one thing is for certain, there was never any photograph taken.

So with this historic visit behind us it was all systems go for the new season. There was cause for optimism. Dean had led the club to a decent finish the previous season and I was expecting a more settled squad at the start of the new campaign without the regularity of being involved in the many loan signings that we had for the previous campaign.

This had proved arduous to deal with, primarily because I was hardly ever informed in advance from within by the club administration when we had signed a player and always had to bluff it with the respective press officers from the other clubs when they made contact with me. It did frustrate me with the way the information came out for signing players. Most of the other clubs' press officers were full-time whereas I used to juggle a few balls in the air and hope for a pro-active support system from the club. As hard as I tried it just didn't seem to happen and it was a frequent occurrence. In total we had used 47 players during 2011/12.

I did have some concerns off the pitch though but put it to the back of my mind at the time. You see when we started the club in

1992 we ran it on a shoestring. After the first season I was full-time Company Secretary but the job was much more than that entailing a variety of disciplines- multi-tasking if you like although The Good Lady may doubt I possessed that talent!

We had Rosemary Aggett working in the office for the first few years. Cheryl Pearce joined in 1999 and basically that was it. Yes we enhanced it as we moved forwards. We employed a full-time "Odd Job" man on a pittance of a wage before John Humphrey, a talented player who had had his fair share of injuries, doubled up working at the club combining his playing duties. We eventually employed a Commercial Manager too but predominantly commission-based. Stalwart Norman Penny had provided this role for a number of years before on "pocket money". The better they did, the better the club did. That was how it was. What we also had too was that we all worked within the same building and everything came through my office. I knew all of what was going on at the club and could link up the communications to the wider audience when required.

My concern on the additional staffing was striking more of a nerve with me. By the start of the 2012/13 season we had listed in the programme a Chief Operating Officer, Secretary, General Manager (Richard Low's brother Danny), a full-time Associate Director, Commercial Manager and assistant plus many part-time staff too. They had even got rid of all the bar staff, the majority volunteers who had a love for the club and wanted to give their bit back. They were asked to re-apply for their positions. One barman, Steve Hall, had worked in the South Stand bar since the day it opened in the summer of 1992 when he was a member of the Supporters Club committee. He was, and is, just a Shots fan through and through. He would have done anything for the club if treated correctly. We were in Football League 2 for crying out loud! Why so many staff?

Another guy called Ryan Murrant started appearing at our weekly meetings too. Whilst it was all a bit "cloak and dagger" at first it was eventually announced that he was to be the full-time Marketing Manager; another manager. We had more bosses than ICI! As it happens the guy had some decent ideas with regard to fan engagement but he was such a complex character that even the slightest hint of negativity from somebody and he would go into one; block supporters from social media networks and stretch relationships to breaking point. He was keen to promote this hashtag Shotsfamily. I just couldn't get into it because it wasn't an Aldershot thing. At one stage or another I ended up becoming the mediator to a succession of disputes between Ryan and the majority of my media team. I felt as though I was becoming a full-time "Agony Aunt"! It was hard work and I was just starting to tire by this stage. I am sure Ryan would admit that Aldershot just wasn't the right fit for him and vice versa. Another who was in the wrong place at the wrong time really but you cannot blame anybody who is given the opportunity to advance their career. It is natural that you would accept the challenge.

Even the Chairman was on a wage. Who was I to question all of this? I wish I had now. It was quite apparent that the expenditure would be far in excess of the income. For many matches we were getting bigger gates in the Isthmian League Division 3 when our players were all on "pocket money" and part-time. Looking back it was an accident waiting to happen but what a crash it eventually would be. When I finally learned of what the wage bill was and what some people were earning I can honestly state that I felt sick with anger.

How on earth it was allowed to end up in this stage God only knows but it was allowed. The individuals concerned were given the opportunities to progress their careers by the powers that be but the club was clearly not structured to sustain such an arrangement and the overload of staff without a solid plan was a monumental error of judgement. The mounting debt had been incurred over a number of years before many of the current Board had become involved but this was just adding to the problems. Although Kris Machala was the majority shareholder my view is that if you have no sway in the Boardroom then there is no point being there.

One of the original directors, Peter Bloomfield, had stepped down during this period and I was desperately keen for him to receive recognition after 20 years of loyal service but he declined.

He wanted nothing to do with the remaining directors and told me that it would all end pear-shaped. I thought this sad because Peter had always been loyal to the club and had worked exceedingly hard for a lengthy period of time but those at the helm really thought that he was surplus to requirements. I actively encourage new blood and ideas but one thing you can never buy is knowledge and understanding and knowing what makes a football club tick. The importance of history and heritage, ignore it at your peril. Peter was the final director from 1992 to relinquish his duties and that was sad too. Related to a former Chairman of Aldershot FC, Dick Caesar, he saw earlier than me that everything we had set up to form the club was gradually being dismantled and falling apart. The ethos of what we stood for was diluted. Another, however, who returned to the terraces, so the club is in his heart.

At the weekly communications meetings there were continual problems being added to the agenda and it was clear to me that there was little understanding of what the supporters wanted and what was realistic in this quest. One of the most bizarre topics discussed surrounded the theme tune that the team ran out to. Since the year dot at Aldershot Town it had always been "Alive and Kicking" from Simple Minds. If ever a song was integral to one club then this was it. This is the only song that the fans associated the club with. It was symbolic to what we were all about when we formed in 1992 and that was never lost. You ask Steve Wignall about the song and he will still say now that every time he hears it the hairs stand up on the back of his neck and it sets off the emotions in him. It is the same for me too. However there was a call from behind the scenes that the song should be dropped and replaced with something more upbeat.

We'd had all this before when, for a period of time, the players ran out to the theme from the 1976 film The Omen, Ave Satani, just after Dean was appointed manager and Alive and Kicking was dropped to earlier in the build-up to the match being played prior to the players making their entry onto the pitch. Then we had Elbow's One Day Like This. All nothing to inspire the fans. This time, at the meeting, the call was for Alive and Kicking to be dropped completely with uplifting songs for the fans to replace it. Dean wasn't involved in this one but it was what happens when more people are employed at a football club who don't have an understanding of how it functions. *"Alive and Kicking dropped? Not whilst I'm involved at this club it won't be"*- I told them. This time I got my way.

However the focus was on the players and the pre-season friendly campaign. A match had been arranged versus Warta Poznan- an unmitigated disaster.

A Friday evening against a team that had no spectator pull at all, it was obviously arranged through Kris Machala. He believed that due to the large Eastern European community in the south of England the fans would flock in. The final attendance was 729 with a sprinkling of Polish fans. The amount of pizzas that the Polish side ordered after the match on our account could have bankrupted the club let alone anything else.

There were a lot of people involved in preparations for the season and at this stage there did appear to be a lot of hard graft being channelled but, in hindsight, was it being channelled in the right areas?

Richard Low had assured me that matters off the pitch were certainly improving and I distinctly recall a conversation we had when he told me that once a few matters within the youth section were sorted *"We will never ever experience financial difficulties again"*.

I was comforted by this statement although never really had a full understanding of how the youth structure operated. He also stated in his opening programme notes, *"It was not that long ago that achieving financial stability and control for the football club was our only goal, a huge task that we believed would take months if not a year to achieve, but I realised very quickly that under the guidance of the Chairman of the Board, the management team and the staff had already achieved so much already leaving me with the relatively easy task of applying the finishing touches.*

*"With the last game of the season done and dusted, and the solid financial foundation laid we sat down and formulated the strategy that is now a detailed 3-5 year plan that each and every*

*one of us are clear and committed to achieving."* I never did get to read that detailed plan. I would love to have had the opportunity to do so.

Chairman Machala followed up by stating, *"My main aim when I became involved at Aldershot Town was to provide financial stability for the club. It is a balance to achieve as we need to concentrate on ensuring that we have a playing squad that can compete too. Alongside stability in the Boardroom I am pleased that we have progressed in both areas and that is vitally important as we look to the future".*

Critically in the same notes versus Exeter City in the opening home league match of the campaign he added, *"My plan has always been to make the club financially sound. Many clubs have rich owners who put the money in but the repercussions can be severe later down the line. Our plan is different. It may take longer as we will only spend what we can afford but our plan is to secure our future by self-financing, playing attractive football whilst at the same time continuing to further our flourishing youth policy.*

*"As we celebrate 20 years as a football club it is important to recognise what happened in 1992 and to ensure there is never a repeat of that".*

Financial commitments had been made in various areas including the purchase of two state-of-the-art food trailers and there was a concerted effort in attempting to concentrate on engaging with supporters. I did warn the Low brothers about the dangers of opening dialogue on Twitter especially when matters on the pitch aren't quite going to plan. It came back to haunt them really.

After it having being reported that he had declined the opportunity to join League 1 Crawley Town as manager in the close season the services of Dean and his management staff were secured too.

There was excitement with the first round draw of the Carling Cup and a tie at Wolverhampton Wanderers who had just been relegated from the Premier League. It was agreed that an Insiders' DVD would be taken of the weekend starting with the team leaving Aldershot on the coach, through to the hotel overnight stay and then the build-up of the match behind the scenes. Our video cameraman, Kappadeano (Dean Martin), was tasked for this and did an outstanding job. A proper Shots fan, Dean worked way over and beyond the call of duty for the club, received a pittance for what he did and was usually taken for granted. He brought in a few thousand pounds for the club off the back of a similar DVD for the Manchester United match and never did receive any remuneration for the Wolves match. The occasion itself was pretty good. There was no pressure on the team and a Michael Rankine header ensured that the match entered extra time and, ultimately, penalties. We were eventually knocked out via the spot-kick route.

The league campaign commenced with an easy and convincing 2-0 victory at Plymouth Argyle. The performance was easier than my journey to the match. We used to travel down to Devon or Cornwall most years for a holiday. It would have coincided well with this week but instead we had chosen a holiday in East Sussex! On the day of the match Oliver and I set out for Devon at 6am in the morning. I have always had the same philosophy though. If you commit yourself to a role then you do it properly. Not going to Plymouth was never an option.

Unfortunately the bright opening subsided with our first home match of the season. Exeter were victors. Although disappointed in the defeat I was quite proud with an off the pitch project. During the summer I had been tasked with overseeing the new match day programme. The club had decided that they wished to go down a new route with regards to the publication. I wanted no part in the politics but said I would source a new editor if they were changing tack. The reason being was that I didn't want to go back to how they operated a few years ago when they had an editor who knew nothing about the club and how it operated.

When we gained promotion to the Football League in 2008 the opening home match of the new season was an attractive one versus AFC Bournemouth. It was the perfect opportunity to document the terrific 16-year story since 1992. There wasn't a mention of the achievements in the programme. Nothing. It was as though those 16 years had never happened. Why? Because the programme editor at the time had no allegiance to the club and lived miles away. He had no understanding. You need to have knowledge to do the role justice.

I approached a member of my Media team, Victoria Rogers, to become the programme editor and she did a fantastic job, winning an award from the Northern Programme Club in her first season followed up by a prestigious league honour the following campaign. I spent a period of time mapping the outline and content of the programme and then set up a Media Academy. An advertisement was produced to attract young trainee journalists to become involved in the Academy. We acquired approximately 12 members and all were assigned to different tasks within our communications including the website and programme.

Victoria was then the central contact for programme matters and we ensured that each Academy member had a specific responsibility and they delivered and delivered well. A number of the lads informed me at the end of the season that without their involvement in our Academy they would not have found the permanent employment that they were seeking within sport. I was chuffed to bits to learn that. Many of the members were able to experience the delights of match day duties within the media home and away in addition to being able to train at the local commercial radio station 964 Eagle Radio, where the Managing Director is lifelong supporter Paul Marcus and who proved a great support for the project throughout. It was extremely fulfilling.

The Exeter defeat was followed by Cheltenham departing the Rec with maximum points four days later in the pouring rain. The match was poor but we were able to commemorate the occasion by inviting many of the original players and management from 1992. They were introduced to the fans at half-time. The cheers were to become some of the loudest heard at the stadium that season!

# Skyfall

1992

By the time Chesterfield visited the Rec in early October we were already up against it. Three home defeats in five scoring just two goals but bizarrely all the vibes coming out of the club remained upbeat. This was despite the previous Tuesday evening when somehow we had allowed a 3-0 lead at Plainmoor turn into a 4-3 defeat at Torquay United. Thinking back this was a huge blow and just the kind of occasion when the manager and players don't really want to face the media and, to be honest, an occasion when I didn't particularly want to ask the questions either. 3-02 am was the time I arrived back home from Devon and off to work for the day job the next day too.

We then lost 1-0 at home to Chesterfield and followed this up with reverses at Plymouth Argyle in the Johnstone's Paint Trophy (and another long early morning journey back from Devon), Gillingham and Rotherham United.

The Gillingham match broke my heart- not because we were heavily defeated by Martin Allen's men but because it was the game where I finally accepted that my Peugeot 406 was going to meet its maker after 161,000 mainly Shots-bound miles. My pride and joy broke down on the M25 and I had to arrange for my media team to find alternative transport via the Aldershot News Sports Editor Jon Couch whilst I waited for the AA to arrive.

It was pouring with rain and I was none best pleased and felt even worse when the AA attendant told me that the car was on its last legs. He did patch it up and when he asked where I was going he suggested that I venture home because if the car broke down again in Gillingham it could be a bigger problem. Of course I ignored him and started on the road to Kent. I eventually arrived at 3.20 after the usual trial and errors attempting to find a car parking space at Priestfield. I always ensured that the visiting club media rep was provided with a car parking space inside the stadium at the Rec but this was not always replicated. Imagine my thoughts as I tuned into BBC Radio Kent and parked up as we went 2-0 down. By the time I managed to get inside the stadium a further roar erupted and the Gills were awarded a penalty. When I reached the press box we were 3-0 down and eventually lost 4-0.

As a club we were at a crossroads. Struggling in the league against a supporter base where many had only been used to mainly good times, promotions and decent entertainment. Times were getting tougher but the attendances were reducing significantly and were now comparable with attendances we were getting in the old Isthmian League Division 3 days! It was obvious something would give.

Kris Machala had publicly stated that the team and management were together and hoped that the recent misfortunes could be turned around imminently. Indeed, despite the poor sequence of results I don't recall any protests calling for the head of the manager at the time. Richard Low actually stated in his programme notes versus Hendon in the FA Cup that, "*We have produced a healthy business model in a variety of areas which has led to an increase in revenue on food outlets and venue hire whilst our Academy is now self-funding in a situation where we used to lose a lot of money historically.*

"*Our recent audit showed that we have better financial controls and reporting mechanisms than we have had before and we have a concentrated desire to succeed. However, as all football clubs must do, we have to watch the pennies and plan accordingly but we remain proactive operationally. As a football club we remain ambitious but are realistic in our goals. We continue to review what we need on and off the pitch to progress as a club*".

We appeared to turn the corner as Hendon were beaten (just) in the FA Cup and we had returned four points out of six in the league after an excellent victory at Southend United followed by a draw at Dagenham and Redbridge; the latter all the better for meeting up with George Borg for the first time in 10 years. The laughter and stories were as fresh as ever- a good night had by all.

# Troublemaker

1992

The problem was that behind the scenes the club was in a shambolic state and now the cracks were getting bigger. Firstly I was called into the club to attempt to sort out a situation that had emanated when Machala sacked Richard Low and changed the locks on the Chief Operating Officer's office. He then called the staff together to notify them of what he had done. Club Solicitor Simon Groves had been called into the club too and it was all extremely messy.

After various discussions Low was reinstated and the staff told that the morning's events should be forgotten. Morale-wise this was poor but there was a cancer within the club that was obviously spreading with different individuals having different ideas about how the club should operate.

Whatever the reasons behind the original confrontation I never did get to the bottom of it. However Low had departed by the end of the year and the club was effectively run on a day to day basis by long-term director John Leppard. I had known John for many years and, as I would state to anybody over the years at the club when they were in a position of responsibility, I was there to help, guide and support him wherever I could. I certainly kept to my side of the bargain with John.

Many clubs struggling at the foot of the table had changed their manager by this time in a hope to resurrect their season and steer themselves away from the dangers of relegation from the Football League and to have the transfer window to play with too. The Board had chosen to stick with Dean and my understanding is that at this stage there had not been any debate regarding his managerial position. As we entered the final home match before the Christmas period versus Rochdale we had the worst home record in the country, seven defeats in 10 matches, netting just three goals. However away from home we were pretty steady losing just four of the 11 fixtures completed on the road. There was no getting away from the fact that fans were not enjoying life at the Rec. The Rochdale match was, fortunately, an exception as we defeated the Greater Manchester side 4-2 with loan signing, Dani Lopez, netting inside eight minutes. I remember the Rochdale match for a totally different scenario though. Before the match I received a call from John Leppard.

He informed me that our midfielder Josh Payne had received a custodial sentence after pleading guilty in relation to two charges that followed an incident which had occurred in Guildford in May 2012. This was the first time I had officially heard about the matter and I couldn't believe that nobody within the club had the foresight to let their media man know so I could plan a statement relating to all possible consequences. I told John that we had to act because as soon as the matter was common knowledge the phone lines to me would be hot. I wasn't wrong in my assumption and the timing couldn't have been any worse as Payne's sentence was made common knowledge just as the Rochdale match kicked-off. For me in my role as Head of Media at the time it was a damage limitation exercise as the club could not benefit from this story in any shape or form even though Payne's contract was terminated with immediate effect. I was actually writing a press release on the situation as the match started.

A PR disaster and unsurprisingly the nationals wanted a piece of this too. I do believe that the players were ill-advised to dedicate the opening goal by celebrating with his shirt. I liked Josh and he was always receptive to interviews but the common denominator is that football and players going to jail simply do not mix and celebrating such a situation after a goal does not reflect well on your club. Fortunately little was made about the celebrations outside of Aldershot but there were a few rumblings within.

This was another example of the club keeping everything close to its chest. Prior to the start of the season our striker Danny Hylton had been banned for eight matches after being found guilty by a Regulatory Commission of two counts of seriously breaching Football Association regulations relating to an incident that occurred at Barnet in October 2011. I thought that the matter had been sorted and was not to be taken any further at the time only to receive a phone call out of the blue just as the FA had confirmed their decision.

It beggars belief that I sat within a communications meeting every Wednesday with senior members of staff and officials and was never informed of such a serious issue. Planning is key and you need to have all the facts at your disposal to do your job effectively.

On the pitch we progressed to the fourth round of the FA Cup with an excellent victory at home to Rotherham United managed by the Shots' fans favourite Steve Evans! After such a dull season at the Rec home performances were taking on a vast improvement.

After netting four versus Rochdale followed by an entertaining 2-2 draw versus Bristol Rovers on Boxing Day, which we threw away to be honest, Evans' men were then swept aside with ease, 3-1, and Hylton had earned the acclaim as the Player of the Third Round for netting a hat-trick. He also blotted his copybook in the final minute and was sent off by that man Gavin Ward. The FA Cup and Danny had a special bond this season with the Londoner netting seven goals in the first three rounds to head the goal scoring charts in the competition.

Danny's dismissal ensured that he was banned for three matches. This was at a period when the country had been decimated by freezing conditions and heavy snowfall.

A rearranged match versus Northampton Town planned for the Tuesday prior to the fourth round visit to Middlesbrough meant that as long as the weather held up Hylton would be clear for the visit to the Riverside at the end of January.

By this time a new Chief Executive Officer, Andrew Mills, had been employed and, as a rarity, the club had actually employed somebody with extensive Football League experience on a full-time basis. Instead of cutting corners or gambling with individuals with good business track records but no football foundations they involved somebody who knew the score within the industry. At this stage, though, it was all too little, too late.

# Try

After defeating Accrington Stanley 2-0 at the Rec the second part of the Hylton suspension was to be served at York City. We called it "Trains, Planes and Automobiles" in the end. The weather in the build-up to the weekend was horrendous with the snow as fierce as it had been all winter throughout the country. I had actually conducted the match preview with Dean on the Thursday on the assumption that the match would be called off. I was amazed and alarmed on the Friday morning when a rather dispirited Dean informed me that York City were confident the match would go ahead. An appeal for a cancellation to the Football League fell on deaf ears.

Some of our players couldn't even get out of their drives and the coach company refused to take the team due to the hazardous conditions. All the players were told to make their own way to Yorkshire. I can imagine their discontent and anger when, after arriving in York, many by train, club secretary Bob Green informed them all that they would have to make their way to Leeds as that was where the hotel was! More expenses probably wasted due to a lack of planning and basic communications!

I even took Dean back to his hotel in Leeds after the match with BBC Surrey's Steve Gibbs in my car alongside Oliver. Even loyal Ian Morsman had decided against travelling, not believing the match would be played. When it did start it was no surprise that a 0-0 draw was the outcome but it was another decent point and we were now in the middle of a run, losing just once in nine matches.

With two matches out of the way the final hurdle was the Tuesday evening visit of Northampton Town to the Rec, ironically the last club to defeat us just prior to Christmas. However this match was pure pantomime! The weather was still poor but the match had the green light when I arrived at the Rec at 4.30pm. The snow started to come down soon after and by 5pm the pitch was pure white and the snowfall becoming heavier and heavier. It was Christmas card weather. By the time referee Darren Deadman arrived it was surely just a case of calling the match off and we could all go home.

However I detected that Dean was keen to play and his discussions with the match official confirmed this. During my 10 years as secretary I had been involved in many pitch inspections and first impressions with the referee are always critical to the outcome.

The bottom line on this occasion was that if the inference to the referee had been that we had no chance of staging the game and the groundsman confirmed this then it would have been a no brainer. It was clear that the referee was going to wait and give it a go.

By kick-off time the Rec was sparse. Indeed many supporters couldn't even get out of their drives to attend the match and I know many who never made it or turned around halfway there, not believing that a match would be played. It was a farce and it made me think that there was something more to this than met the eye. The match being played was all about Danny Hylton being available for the Middlesbrough match and, to me that was wrong. We were on an upturn of form in the league and looking capable of getting away from danger.

This was a dangerous precedent being set. There was just nothing to gain out of playing this match. I do, however, understand that financially the FA Cup run was critical to the club and Dean would have been under pressure to succeed in this area.

The actual attendance was 1,191 including 142 from Northampton. It was a credit that as many as that attended. It was still the lowest league crowd at the Rec in 15 years and one of the lowest in the history of both clubs. Despite taking an early lead through Lopez we eventually lost the match and I believe this made a huge dent in our league progress for the remainder of the campaign. It never needed to have occurred but it did.

So Hylton was free for the FA Cup and we had an exciting day to look forward to away to Championship side Middlesbrough. It was the first time Aldershot Town had reached the fourth round and the first such occasion supporters of either club had experienced since the Barnsley match in 1987. There had to be a hiccup though and there was.

The day before the match Oliver was a bit peaky. I thought it may be excitement due to the match so let it go. On the morning of the game we were up and away before 7am.

Oliver was pure white. I asked him if he was ok and he said he was. We gave it a go. In my car I also took Ian Morsman and Dean Martin. The car was stacked up with all the required media gear. Cameras, tripods- you name it and it was in there. Oliver hadn't said a word on the journey and just prior to Newport Pagnell he was sick. I stopped on the hard shoulder before driving into the nearby services. I looked at Oliver and gave him the bad news- "*Son, we're going to have to turn around. You won't be able to go to the match*". I was absolutely gutted for him because I know how much he was looking forward to the big day. I felt terrible as a father having to tell a 14-year-old that he wasn't going to be able to watch his club's biggest cup match in his lifetime. After arranging lifts for Ian and Dean with the Supporters Trust coaches Oliver and I were homeward bound. We were back in Farnborough by 10am and Oliver was straight to bed. I spoke to The Good Lady and after a few minutes' thought said, "*I'm going to give it a go!*" She thought I was mad but I got back in my car and headed to the north east. I never stopped and arrived at the Riverside Stadium at 2.15pm- seven and a half hours after originally leaving for the match.

Arrangements for the media for these occasions can be frustrating at times. All the nationals are onto you, noting that there could be an upset on the cards. As the club media rep you have all possible post match interviews planned on the back burner knowing that should a shock result be recorded then you will be bombarded with requests at short notice. You also know that if you are knocked out of the competition as expected you may as well have left your phone in the car. It will not ring!

We were so close on the day too. With a draw looking more than likely Lukas Jutkiewicz put the home side in front on 85 minutes in front of 12,684 supporters.

However that man Hylton netted in the final minute of the match with an excellent finish to send the near 800 visiting fans into delirium – only for our hopes to be eradicated in the sixth minute of injury time to a controversial goal from Jutkiewicz. We deserved more and it was cruel on everybody connected with the club.

I also reflected on the possibles moving forward. Had we drawn the match we would have been nailed on for a televised replay bringing in healthy revenue in addition to a good attendance. Middlesbrough would not have fancied travelling to Aldershot on a Tuesday evening and were on a woeful run of form at the time. I honestly think we could have shocked them at the Rec despite our own erratic form. That would have set up a home tie against Chelsea and more international recognition and heightened revenue streams from television income.

It's all ifs, buts and maybes but it could have been so.

# Lightning Bolt

1992

There were some more bizarre occurrences happening behind the scenes in January too, before the Middlesbrough match. Our Army Under-23 team were playing a Shots XI at the Aldershot Military Stadium on the afternoon of the 8th January.

At the match I caught John Leppard and coach Matt Bishop talking at length in the car park but thought nothing of it at the time. Nearly a week later I received a phone call from Dean who told me that we needed to make an urgent announcement to confirm that "Bish" was leaving the club. I couldn't believe this as the pair had worked in partnership from their days at Newport County. Dean intimated that it was a cost-cutting exercise due to the frail financial situation at the club. A week before, the services of Ryan Murrant had been dispensed with for the same reason. I immediately contacted John who confirmed that "Bish" was on his way but he gave me the impression it was Dean who was keen on the termination and not the Board.

Whatever the true reasons were I never did get to the bottom of but I was sorry that we lost Bish. He had been an influential part of the staff behind the scenes and extremely approachable in my dealings with him. After a difficult few months for Bish I was chuffed to bits to learn that he had been appointed FA National Coach Educator for the West Midlands and North West. I duly drafted up a statement regarding his departure and forwarded it to the Board for any comments before it was released.

The usual lack of response was not a shock but Kris Machala responded via email and said, "It is OK with me. We have match v Middlesborough soon so pls make announcement asap." Indeed there was a pressure on me to release this urgently as Dean had already informed me that he was grouping the players together after training to let them know what was going on.

I pressed the green light and the statement was in the public domain. Imagine my shock within five minutes when the Chairman contacted me and asked me why I had released the statement.

I politely reminded him that he had sent me an email a few minutes before, giving approval.

He responded saying that I shouldn't have done what I did. I couldn't be bothered to argue but remember walking back to my offices and the "day job" within the barracks scratching my head, bemused and certainly bewildered. I asked myself how could anybody work with such people under these conditions. I called "Bish" later that evening to wish him well and express my disappointment. He put me in the picture regarding the discussion in the Army car park with John Leppard and the fact that the club didn't require his services which came as a bolt out of the blue to him. One fact is certain, I was never told the real facts about Bish's departure and I am not sure he knows either.

After the FA Cup exit it was back to league action and a fierce battle to avoid losing that Football League status that we had all worked so hard to achieve after the 1992 formation. Form became erratic again.

An agonising midweek journey to Morecambe meant the real loyal stalwarts attended. The debate about the importance of "corporate" rears its ugly head every now and then and I get the importance of it, I really do. Corporate is a necessary part of football these days. However it is NOT the heartbeat of a football club and it is not the soul either. How many of those in hospitality let the result of a match spoil their weekend? How many troop off into work on a Monday morning still beleaguered by the weekend's activities?

How many in hospitality are travelling down the M6 at 2am in the morning after a midweek fixture at Morecambe? There were 71 Shots' faithful to witness a 2-1 defeat to Jim Bentley's men on the night. However, this was followed up by a decent draw at promotion-chasing Cheltenham Town the following Saturday.

Little did I know at this stage that the Board of Directors had already discussed the future of Dean as the manager at the Cheltenham match. Andrew Mills had asked them the question- *"Are you confident Dean is the man to keep Football League status at the club?"* When they couldn't fully confirm that they were, the discussions continued.

By the time fellow relegation candidates Torquay United were the visitors the following Tuesday evening the decision had been made. Whatever the outcome, Dean was on his way the next day. It wasn't a classic but we won the match 1-0 to move five points away from the drop zone although we had played more games than those in a similar position. We did, however, look as though we may be slowly turning the corner.

I thought moving into Saturday's match at home to Fleetwood Town that we were making progress. I was stunned when Andrew called me on the Wednesday afternoon after the victory over Torquay. He informed me that he was sending me a draft statement in confidence which would be released later that day. I waited and read the said document which confirmed that the club were to terminate Dean's contract with immediate effect.

After topping and tailing the statement it was duly released as requested. I had to do it in the confines of the Army FA Committee room as we had a representative fixture that night at the Aldershot Military Stadium. It is never the best of places for wifi reception and the agreed 8pm release was in danger of not happening as I couldn't get the required reception and was in a bit of a panic. We finally got there but the release didn't happen in the manner that I wanted it to. However the bottom line was- Dean was no longer manager of Aldershot Town Football Club! It was soon ticker-taping on Sky Sports News.

I rang Dean up just prior to the announcement being made "live" as I believed I had a duty to speak to somebody I had worked with closely for just over two years. I take pride in the fact that I could call every manager I have ever worked with knowing that we would still have a positive relationship and a laugh or two. I told Dean that I was surprised at the timing.

To be honest if it had been made prior to Christmas and especially during a seven-match losing streak there would have been few eyebrows raised but with 13 matches remaining and the new manager not having the benefit of being able to use the transfer window it was a gamble. Dean's main disappointment was that no members of the Board had contacted him to explain the decision, added to the fact that some had shaken his hand the night before after the Torquay United match knowing what his ultimate fate was going to be.

Dean Holdsworth the manager? He arrived at the Rec as the highest profile boss in the club's history and I believe that some people he worked with were starstruck with him. He was also extremely image conscious too. We eventually came across a suitable portrait for his programme notes after many attempts. That said there were a fair few on the non-playing side who were equally image conscious over the years. However we got on well and never had a cross word. He made an impression in his first season and the club moved away from the relegation zone with four successive victories in March. The final match of the campaign was bitter-sweet. We battered Lincoln City at Sincil Bank 3-0 in front of 7,932 spectators but in doing so relegated the home side. In Dean's second season he led the club to its highest-ever placing in the Football League Cup reaching the last 16 before facing Manchester United on that special evening. Prior to that he was in charge of the team in what could arguably be considered one of the most successful evenings in the club's short history, that victory at West Ham United, in August 2011. League form was patchy though prior to the visit of Manchester United match although a victory at AFC Wimbledon in January started a run of six successive victories and another record stretching over both clubs and 65 years. A strong finish to 2011/12 including being unbeaten in the final five matches and victory against champions elect Swindon Town led to higher expectations the following season and a positive pre-season campaign.

It never materialised though and the form became patchy. In truth I don't believe there were too many problems on our travels. Dean had the team set up to pick up the required points on the road, similar to Kevin Dillon. However the statistics show that he couldn't get the team going at the Rec and that has to be priority. Defeat after defeat and a distinct lack of goals proved too much. If it had been Kevin Dillon in charge fans would have been outside marching with banners and demonstrating. This didn't happen whatever people may say in the cold light of day.

There is no doubt that his use of the loan market confused and frustrated supporters at times. In excess of 10 signings during Dean's tenure didn't start a league match. While there may have been legitimate reasons it didn't help his position and the small talk that would emanate out as to why these players were not playing. I remember one permanent signing, Stefan Payne, signed on a Friday afternoon, featured for the last 10 minutes at AFC Wimbledon the next day and then he was shipped out to Sutton United never to return. Dean did miss out on securing the services of Dani Lopez in the January transfer window at the last minute which, I believe, would have made a difference.

He was desperately disappointed with this and knew the importance an established striker who had netted six goals in 11 starts in a previous loan spell would be.

My own observations are that there were many who were in awe of Dean due to his reputation and background and he could certainly tap into that and use it to his benefit. He needed to be managed and, indeed, supported better from within. I don't think this happened, especially during the 2012/13 season because, for the majority of it, there was a lack of stability, strength and necessary experience in senior positions at the club. There was just too much turbulence at the club. Sometimes a manager's life is lonely and they need that guidance and to be tested. It didn't help either party in the end before the parting of the ways. Indeed the club did state when Dean was relieved of his duties that it showed appreciation for his efforts and *"Acknowledged the difficult circumstances under which Dean has managed to steer us out of the relegation places. Dean also leaves as a Football League manager with the club remaining in Football League status."*

At the end of the 2011/12 season I thought Dean possessed the qualities to go on to greater things. This clearly didn't happen and, as I have seen on countless occasions over the years, it all ended on a sour note. There is no doubt that there were some good days under Dean, notably the Carling Cup run, but something went drastically wrong during that final season because the squad of players should have been more than capable of finishing far higher than they eventually did. Indeed at the end of 2014 nine of the 18 who featured in his final match versus Torquay were plying their trade in the Football League with five playing in League One. In addition goalkeeper Jamie Young returned to Australia featuring in the top flight Australian A League for Brisbane Roar.

He was close to Richard Low too and I am not convinced that was to the benefit of either individual during the first half of the 2012/13 season. The dismissal will have dented Dean's pride for sure but he was cute enough to have outside business interests because he knew that such a day would be inevitable. He had a short spell in charge at Chelmsford City soon after but it all ended in tears with the Essex club losing eight of its opening 13 matches with a totally revamped squad and a smaller budget; perhaps too much, too soon after the Aldershot episode for Dean.

Andrew Mills was in charge of sourcing a suitable replacement. As all supporters do I looked about at the candidates that would be expressing an interest. In my heart of hearts I hoped Gary Waddock would be the man the club appointed and it would have been popular for most. The only reason being that at the time the club needed galvanising and a touch of excitement was required urgently. Many will argue that Gary had been sacked by Wycombe Wanderers, a club struggling in the same division. My response would be that the circumstances he had to endure in the latter part of his tenure at Adams Park would have been too much for some of the best in the game. Make no mistake about it, when matters are not fluent behind the scenes at any club then it does affect the manager and that can stem down further down the line to the players. I also thought that Gary had unfinished business at Aldershot too.

The longer the discussions went on the more I started to lean toward Andy Scott but only through rumour, something I never subscribe to but I hadn't been given any indication from within as to who it would be. Andy was a manager who had worked with the Chief Executive previously and who had an excellent track record at League 2 level.

He had led Brentford to the title in 2009 before taking them to a healthy position in the division above added to some exciting cup runs. Even though Andy had a relatively short and difficult period thereafter at Rotherham United he certainly fitted the bill as somebody who could take the club away from danger. Andy was appointed manager within 72 hours of the departure of Dean with the experienced Terry Bullivant as his assistant. Ironically Andrew Mills had also been the Chief Executive with the task of sacking Andy at Brentford!

We deliberately chose a low-profile announcement with the press on the Friday afternoon prior to the home match with Fleetwood Town but I was impressed with what I saw of Andy and Terry. I was surprised that an 18-month contract had been awarded though. I thought that a better deal would be until the end of the season with the target to avoid relegation. This would then have put Andy in a strong position to renegotiate in the summer.

If relegation was suffered then there would be managers more suited to Conference level than Andy who had never managed outside the Football League. They started well too and any signs of a relegation battle looked light years away. Victory versus the Lancashire club was followed by decent draws at Chesterfield and Bradford City and at home to Martin Allen's eventual champions Gillingham. I had seen more than enough already and told my brother that *"We will be OK"*. Words that would come back to haunt me. The Bradford match, in particular, I believe had a huge bearing on our destiny. The Bantams had played at Wembley a fortnight previously in the League Cup Final; a monumental achievement. I thought we could catch them on the rebound and we nearly did. We were on the way to a 1-0 victory that day until Alan Connell converted a penalty deep, deep into injury time. I truly believe that had we won that match we would have survived and the momentum would have taken us away from danger. It wasn't to be.

In addition to all the other shenanigans at the club there had also been a change of Chairman at this time. Shahid Azeem had taken the reins from the beleaguered Machala. He was no newcomer to the club, however, having served as a non-Executive Director for a couple of years previously. He stated that he had also played as a youth player for the Shots in the seventies and had experienced involvement at other local clubs prior to his arrival, especially Woking and Guildford City; he remains a Vice President of the latter. A successful businessman who came to the United Kingdom from Pakistan in 1969 and who is uncle to Boxer Amir Khan, he also possessed a healthy contact list. Importantly though, Machala remained the majority shareholder and this was to prove crippling because he had the final say in the Boardroom, irrespective of the views of anybody else.

The rot on the pitch had set in though and back to back home defeats versus Burton Albion and AFC Wimbledon meant that the writing was starting to ink into the wall. We did respond well over the Easter programme with a point at Rochdale followed by a win at the Rec versus Oxford United. A draw at promotion-chasing Port Vale in our next match gave us some hope but we had to win at least two of our final four matches to have a chance.

Backed by nearly 1,000 travelling fans at Wycombe Wanderers we let ourselves down. The fans were terrific but we never really turned up, despite a Craig Stanley leveller midway through the second half. Ironically it was a former Shots' favourite Joel Grant who put the first nail into the coffin with the winning goal. We simply had to beat Southend United on the Tuesday evening and hope for the best. If Wycombe was disappointing then the visit of the Essex Galacticos, as many Shots' fans call them, informed even the most loyal fans with the knowledge that we were trying to avoid- we were going down! We never got near Phil Brown's men on the night and they enjoyed a comfortable 2-0 success. It was our 12th defeat at the Rec that season. By the end of the campaign we had scored less than a goal a game at home!

We did beat Dagenham and Redbridge at home in the penultimate match of the season but by this time all the talk was emanating about matters off the pitch.

# Just Give me a Reason

1992

Two nights before the match the Club held its Annual General Meeting for shareholders. Don't get me wrong, I wasn't expecting an announcement that all was hunky dory and that it was in a fine bill of health. It clearly wasn't, due to the instability behind the scenes throughout the course of the season added to woes on the pitch. However a resolution to create a new class of share to be known as "B" Ordinary Shares didn't, to me, seem to be a problem especially as it was the only way to inject new income into the club which it clearly required. The green light for the deal would, in principle, have created a vehicle to provide an additional £1m worth of investment. A presentation was made by Peter Duffy, who had been recalled by the club in an honorary position to provide such a task. After the presentation a break ensued whilst the votes were independently counted.

Peter was aghast when he informed the shareholders that the resolution had not been carried through. There could only be one way this had occurred- the majority shareholder Kris Machala had obviously voted against the proposal. The meeting started to become shambolic with all kinds of accusations and insinuations being made. I asked for the Board to retire as one to discuss the situation and return to the floor to put all of our minds at rest that we could trust that the club had a viable future. They did this and, upon return, Kris stated that he had voted against the proposal because he was in discussions with a consortium which would be of considerable benefit to the club and would attract foreign players from France and Italy. He added that the deal would be concluded on the following Monday. I knew this was garbage. It was just another clutching at straws scenario that would come to nothing. I asked Kris directly from the floor. "*Can you guarantee next week's wages if the deal does not come off and ensure that the club avoids going into administration?"* He confirmed that he would.

At the end of the meeting I was asked to sit with the Board of Directors and prepare a joint statement to clarify the situation. This I duly did but insisted that everybody was in the room. It was a pretty hostile atmosphere, especially between Kris and Peter; the latter had worked excessively with the full approval of the Board collectively to provide a presentation that would be carried through unanimously. If Peter had known that there would be an objection from within he wouldn't have bothered.

Kris could have avoided the embarrassment by being up front prior to the meeting but chose silence. To me the failure to carry though the resolution was the catalyst for the downfall of Aldershot Town FC (1992) Ltd and would eventually become a costly exercise, not just to the individuals involved around the Board table but every shareholder too whose shares would eventually become defunct.

Importantly, and the overriding factor that appears to have been ignored, is that it would have a huge detrimental effect on the football club too and would eventually affect people's livelihoods in addition to the threat of extinction again!

A statement was eventually prepared by me with the approval of everybody within the room. I read the statement back twice and asked if everybody was happy with it.

They all agreed, including Kris. I said that as soon as I got home I would be releasing the statement into the public domain. I duly did so at 00.49hrs on the Friday morning. I shouldn't have been surprised that Kris responded, denying that he had agreed to the wording. He also denied that he would provide the funds the following week if the proposed deal fell through despite providing assurances to the 120 or so shareholders. He asked that, in future, I send him a note before it goes public, *"So I can agree on this."*

I responded to Kris and the whole Board stating that *"I didn't wish to get embroiled into the middle of a desperately disappointing evening for the football club"* but confirmed my requirements for the statement being released and stated to Kris that when

I asked for assurances from everybody there was no dissention from himself.

I ended informing the Board that *"I have 25 years of experience in preparing and issuing press releases and know the score."*

By the time the Dagenham match commenced the football played second fiddle to me. I started to be inundated by the media because, of course, the news that there was disruption at the top was now in the public domain. We defeated the Essex team but it was bittersweet. We started the day bottom of the table but realistically could have caught the five clubs directly above us with two victories. However points for Accrington Stanley, Torquay United and York City eliminated them from the equation. The only clubs that could be caught now were AFC Wimbledon and Barnet. The latter's match against Wycombe Wanderers had kicked off late; it was their final game at Underhill after a 106 year association. A Barnet win and we were all but relegated although not mathematically. We had to endure 15 painful minutes listening to match commentary in the media box or, for myself, pacing up and down the centre of the pitch at the Rec. There was a massive cheer and I asked what was going on. Barnet were leading 1-0 but Wycombe had been awarded a penalty in injury time. If they scored it would all go down to the wire.

Alas that man Joel Grant, a really decent bloke by the way, this time fluffed his lines and missed the spot kick. In truth we all knew we were down. It would require a mathematical swing of ridiculous proportions to turn the situation around added to the fact that our final match of the season would be at Rotherham United, themselves requiring the points to earn automatic promotion to League 1.

By the Monday the local radio station BBC Surrey were on the case and the scaremongering started with news headlines that the club could be entering into administration later in the week. I was furious. I had had no contact from the sports editor, Tim Durrans, and he was the guy I targeted in my response. In hindsight Tim was not the person I should have been contacting.

The BBC work in mysterious ways sometimes. The news and sports departments often run separate stories on the same subject and I often detected that they were not joined up together. Sometimes it can be a competition to see who covers the story the best.

On this occasion the last thing we needed was headline stories that were detrimental. I contacted Tim and said we had previously confirmed publicly that administration was not an option. I had already spoken to BBC Surrey journalist Aurelia Allen on the Friday afternoon. What had incensed me most, however, was that BBC Surrey sent their journalist Adrian Harms, to the Rec to try to gauge local opinion on the club's plight. I had always enjoyed dealing with Adrian as he is a genuine bloke but he even got our score versus Dagenham wrong, stating that we had lost 1-0 and not won. Blimey we had only won seven home matches all season. I had to put them right on that one!

What peeved me at the time is that just two days previously I had given Tim access all areas for the Dagenham match and ensured that he was given priority, even before our own club service Shots Player, to speak to Andy Scott live on the pitch just seconds after relegation had virtually been confirmed. The radio station editor, Sara David, did contact me to inform me that they ran the article after speaking to those present at the shareholders meeting regarding the administration situation. After some investigation I found out that one of those who had spoken privately to the station was Kris Machala. They had received the information from the horse's mouth even though he had gone on record to state otherwise at the meeting. I was totally embarrassed.

I was contacted by Shahid on that Monday and asked to attend a Board meeting being held in the evening which included the attendance of Kris Machala and, hopefully, news of the consortium and a buyout that would protect the future of the club. Shahid had asked me to attend as an independent witness with the best interests of the club and I was happy to do so especially as by this time I had also been offered and accepted the role as President of the Shots Trust. The evening was a long-winded non-event lasting over four hours and with another early morning finish. Kris turned up with his advisor and after some heated and detailed discussions the bottom line was that he was still in negotiations with a prospective buyer but discussions were still ongoing. Shahid did ask Kris how much it would take for him to walk away from the club and relinquish his position but there was no conclusive response.

Prior to the meeting Shahid had showed to me that he did, indeed, have proof of funds. The only factor I could gauge from the whole scenario was that Kris was not being well-advised regarding the situation. The deck of cards was in freefall in my opinion. The problem being faced though was a lack of trust in all directions. The bottom line is that the relationship between Kris and the remaining members of the Board was all but dissolved and there was no trust and could never be again.

There were more staff departures too with Danny Low and bars' manager Adam Cresswell heading for the exit door.

I thought long and hard regarding the situation and was becoming more and more concerned about the short-term let alone long-term future of the football club. Indeed with the civil war ensuing internally I seriously doubted if it had one.

I wrote the following heartfelt email to Kris Machala- the only man with influence because, although he wasn't the Chairman, as majority shareholder he had the casting vote on anything, even if he hadn't been to a home match for two months and, I know, was suffering health-wise:

---

## THE FUTURE OF ALDERSHOT TOWN FOOTBALL CLUB

*"Dear Kris*

*I compose this email in my capacity as Head of Media of the football club and, ultimately, as President of the Shots Trust; a position where I was honoured and privileged to be asked to represent the supporters of our club as its figurehead.*

*I am aware of the confidentiality agreement signed at last night's meeting but the contents of this email do not affect that agreement because I am not breaking any confidences. Indeed I have received written correspondence from yourself this week detailing your current intentions and that the fact that entering the club into administration is a serious option that you are considering. How I wish I had been made aware of this before my dealings with BBC Surrey on Monday.*

*I respect that you are also currently continuing negotiations in order to secure the future of the football club without the possibility of entering administration. Let's hope that you are able to make imminent progress. However should 4pm tomorrow arrive without a positive conclusion you have confirmed that you would contact the Chairman, Shahid Azeem, to reopen dialogue with him.*

*I also write as one of the two shareholders who set this company up in 1992. As you are aware from my discussions with you yesterday the option of administration would be a disaster for Aldershot Town Football Club. You say that it would secure a better "long-term" option. I state that you are wholly incorrect in this theory. It would be the beginning of the end and even if it were to succeed it would leave a seriously bad taste to those that have experienced the "dark days" before.*

*"The heart and soul of the club would be ripped out. Integrity, ethics, morals and everything that we have always stood for lost overnight and believe me we would never get it back.*

*Who will purchase season tickets, renew sponsorships, attend matches at a depleted football club stuck at the bottom of the Conference with -10 points and with public relations at an all-time low? Trust, too, of whoever is in charge would be extremely delicate. This is similar to how many teams that suffered relegation from the Football League started their life in the Conference. Many of them sunk lower- some never to return!*

*If this was the only course of action I would fully understand the consideration but it's not and you are aware of this. Culpability too is high on the agenda. At no time during the course of the season has it been inferred that the club is in such a "serious" financial difficulty that suggests that administration is an option.*

*Can you imagine the reaction of everybody connected at the club were YOU to place it into administration? Can you envisage the questions that YOU will have to answer? A nigh on impossible situation that I would not wish on my worst enemy!*

*However you would be the man that supporters, staff, shareholders, sponsors and the media target. Is it worth it?*

*"Is it really in the best interests of Aldershot Town Football Club?*

*My concern, Kris, is that already in the past week you have reneged on promises made in public to the shareholders. You also publicly confirmed that you would take responsibility for confirming the finances in the short- and long-term, if required, whilst you concluded negotiations with a proposed investor of which you made public at the shareholders meeting. Yet denial of this was made in subsequent correspondence soon after the meeting. This is alarming really considering that I drafted the statement in your presence alongside other directors and read it back to you. It is this kind of erratic behaviour that gives me that cause for concern.*

*I fully respect and applaud the financial commitment that you have provided to the club in the past. It is totally commendable as, indeed, it is with any individual who provides funds to the club. There is a tremendous sense of gratitude there.*

*However, my only interest is the well-being of Aldershot Town Football Club moving forwards. I cannot accept witnessing the future of the club risked without covering all angles.*

*I cannot risk finding out that you have put the club into administration knowing that I didn't do all in my capability to stop this.*

*Therefore I ask for the following guarantees by you which is in the best interests of the club and provides every flexibility with regards to the options available:*

a) *If the negotiations with your current potential investor do not meet fruition by 4pm on Wednesday that you contact the Chairman, Shahid Azeem, with immediate effect to continue previous discussions.*

b) *If possibilities with Shahid are not progressed and the route of administration is the only option that you are willing to consider a meeting is held at the club on Thursday where, in addition to current directors, other senior personnel, sponsors and representation from the Shots Trust are in attendance in order for a comprehensive assessment and explanation to be provided and for you to gauge opinion from respected people.*

c) *At NO time do YOU put the club into administration without consideration of the above two options.*

*I conclude that if I do not receive written confirmation by return email of your acceptance to the above three clauses by 10AM tomorrow (Wednesday) morning I will forward the contents of this email with immediate effect to:*

*All media outlets, staff contacts, Shotsweb independent message board and The Supporters Trust.*

*I am not willing to discuss the matter any further via telephone but expect confirmation by return of your intentions.*

*"There is nothing personal in the contents of this email but I will fail in my duties with the positions that I hold were I not to ensure that written confidences are provided by yourself to safeguard the proud history and heritage of Aldershot Town Football Club."*

Kris responded stating that he was still in sensitive negotiations with two different parties and had three options including administration.

By this time the gloves were off. I was involved in all kinds of conversations, emails and texts with so many current and former directors but just had no confidence that progress was being made. I was spending more time on my mobile phone outside my office than at my desk on a day to day basis. Others aspects of my life were suffering too and I was beginning to feel it health-wise. As far as I was concerned enough was enough. I told everybody that if this matter wasn't resolved by the Wednesday evening I was going public. I couldn't contain this information any longer. Our club was being destroyed and the very fabric of what we set out to achieve 21 years previously was crumbling before my very eyes.

Kris then produced an email saying that an offer was awaiting two signatures and would be concluded the following morning (Thursday 25th April). Whatever the offer was he was not willing to provide any further information. I had to wait, however, to give it a chance if it was going to save the club. Eventually a prospective letter of intent did arrive from the representatives of a potential buyer but that is all it was- potential. There was no detail, nothing concrete and to be honest I could have written the letter. Shahid responded- "*You can't make this up. I'm not responding*".

Despite further attempts from the individuals involved to keep this matter private I went public and called a meeting of Directors and staff and also chose an assortment of supporters and sponsors who I wanted present to hear what I had to say. I didn't want a free-for-all in a room packed with hundreds of people because it would have defeated the object of what needed to be achieved. I called the meeting "The Future of Aldershot Town Football Club" and it was all due to start at 8pm. I had planned to go to town with what I had to say with no holds barred. When I arrived I learnt that all the Board members were in negotiations to try to resolve the club's future. This, I believed, was encouraging and those present were told that the meeting would be delayed by a few minutes. Shahid then contacted me and asked me to go easy on Kris as he said that they had agreed a deal "in principle" that would secure the future of the club and would allow the remaining members of the Board to take it forward. I wasn't happy with this as Kris had a habit of moving the goalposts when you thought everything was done and dusted. They also wanted a confidentiality form signed by all those in attendance. I wasn't happy with this either.

The time of confidentiality, in my book, was way past its sell by date.

The meeting did start and I welcomed those present and spent 25 minutes talking passionately about the football club, my experiences as a youngster, the rebellious years, how proud I was to be involved in the formation of the new club and the 20 years since when we had enjoyed many highs and, of course, some lows. This was the lowest of the low though and I wanted an outcome to the meeting that would give those attending hope and that this could be fed back to the wider supporter base.

Halfway through the meeting it had to be adjourned when John Leppard informed me that Kris was playing silly games again after earlier agreeing to terms and conditions. They had to make their way back out to continue negotiations. Whilst the intent of the meeting was to make the situation public I don't believe that anything was eventually gained. In fact it probably put the fear of God into more people who now knew how precarious the situation was.

# Read All About it

1992

The weekend came and we made our way up to Rotherham for our final match in the Football League- barring a miracle that just wasn't going to happen. I was dreading the day. We arrived in south Yorkshire at the impressive New York Stadium on a sunny afternoon with all the hope and expectation with the home supporters. They knew they were going up. I said at the time that if we weren't going to be having a party then I wanted to be spoiling somebody else's. Rotherham had endured hard times over the recent past since leaving their Millmoor home, ironically just over the road from their new ground, and having to play in nearby Sheffield at the Don Valley Stadium. Of all managers to be in charge of the Yorkshire side too, it was that man Steve Evans! I felt for Andy Scott on this day. Andy's previous job had been in charge at Rotherham. It must have felt strange for him especially as it was a totally different club to the one he knew. Those two- and three-thousand gates rattling round an athletics track were replaced by some hefty five-figure capacities at the new home. This match was an 11,300 sell out. Our fans were magnificent throughout. They had accepted the inevitable and backed the players. In fact we had done well on the pitch too until Johnny Mullins put the Millers in front on 64 minutes.

What really hit home for me, though, was injury time. The exuberant home crowd were edging ever nearer the pitch waiting for the party to begin when Lee Frecklington confirmed their promotion with a second goal. As soon as the ball entered the back of the net I tweeted *"Sitting here unable to accept what we are just about to throw away. Absolutely criminal that this has been allowed to happen"*.

I got up out of my seat in the media box and walked along to the perimeter of the pitch and behind the goal to where our fans were gathered. Nobody stopped me. I felt numb inside. If the tears weren't showing on the outside believe me they were drowning me inside.

I wanted to be with our fans. I wanted to be with my son who was with them. As soon as the final whistle went I just recall fans supporting each other in the moment of doom.

We had just seen our club throw away everything we had fought for and I knew that there were even darker times ahead. I know fans were coming up to talk to me but I cannot remember who or how. I just felt nothing. Then there was anger.

Some Rotherham fans were disrespecting our own situation, gloating about our demise in addition to their own promotion. The mood was a touch tetchy and I wanted Oliver to be with me as I had to walk back around the perimeter of the pitch to conduct the post-match interviews. How I was looking forward to that! I was prevented from doing so by the stewards before our own Police Liaison Officer at Aldershot was heavy-handed in the way he dealt with the situation. I was close to losing my composure with him but, fortunately, was ushered away by our own Dean Martin before a desperate situation became intolerable. That would have looked good. The co-founder of the club and current Head of Media arrested on the day we lost everything we had fought for 21 years before!

I was forced to make an exit outside of the stadium before entering back via the reception areas to meet Andy Scott and the players. Andy spoke superbly considering the hurt he must have been feeling. I have also never conducted such emotional interviews as we did with Captain Ben Herd, Peter Vincenti and goalkeeper Jamie Young. Anybody who ever casts doubts on how much this kind of situation hurts a footballer needs to tune into those interviews. They were distraught and in tears. Good guys who deserved better. I don't recall too many words spoken on the long journey home to Hampshire. It was a sad, sad day and it wasn't going to get better anytime soon.

With the football out of the way it was now all about whether the club was going to survive. Were any of Kris Machala's last-ditch attempts to secure a future going to be successful or, indeed, could those currently in positions of authority agree a deal together?

Since the meeting of the 25th April I was aware that there had been further developments behind the scenes to secure the future of the club. I knew the McGinty family had been offered the opportunity to sell their shares and the secured debt they had on the club. The holder of this would have the overriding right to appoint an Administrator. Mick McGinty was the son of the much-loved former Chairman John. He notified the club of the situation and I was also in discussions with Mick regarding this matter. Kris had also attempted to appoint three new directors including his advisor to take control of the club without any disclosure to the existing directors. I know that a meeting took place between Kris, the remaining directors and Andrew Mills on the way back from Rotherham which I am aware became quite passionate, where Kris was given another ultimatum to secure investment by midday on the Monday or be responsible for pushing it towards administration.

Then, and without my knowledge as Head of Media, Kris spoke to BBC Surrey to give his version of events up to that point. It couldn't have been more ill-advised or timed. It was all about proof of funds again from Shahid as the stumbling block. I knew the funds were there and, upon reflection, could I have banged everybody's heads together to resolve it? Probably not because they just could not communicate effectively with each other.

There was no information coming from the club and then another bombshell- Andrew Mills resigned. It was just the wrong place at the wrong time for him. He was quite categorical in his reasons for his resignation as he stressed in his statement. Then another bombshell as the Youth Department Academy Preparation Centre became involved, confirming that the money from within their department had been *"Misused by people at the Football Club without the authorisation or knowledge of Youth Department employees and that we have been left in an impossible situation where we have to halt proceedings."* The good name of the football club I had been proud to help form was being dragged to the depths of the gutter. It was so sad and sickening.

# Let Her Go

1992

The 2nd May 2013 was D-Day- the day when the football club I co-founded entered administration. The very episode I was trying to avoid was now current. I have seen the initial documentation where the attempt to put the club in administration was made via Kris' solicitors with apologies sent from the three remaining directors. It would have been difficult for them to attend a meeting that they had no knowledge of. With administration now the only option and the initial attempt invalid, Mick McGinty was entitled to appoint an Administrator and the course of action was duly completed. Mick's actions were crucial in giving the club a possibility of survival. Any other route taken would, to me, have had a severely detrimental effect to an acceptable future of any description. Aldershot Town Football Club was now in administration. The regular phone calls were at breaking point now especially with Shahid, John Leppard and Kris. It was intense but we were just going around in circles. Once it fully sank in what had happened I was utterly speechless.

So how did Aldershot Town Football Club end up in this mess? Let's get this straight from the start- the financial pressure was building prior to entering the Football League but that first season adjusting to life at the elite level came at a huge cost. There was a never-ending sequence of events aimed to ease the pressures but they just continued to grow. Eventually they would grow out of control. When the lifeline of that Carling Cup run came to ease the problem in 2011 I believe it was at this stage that wrong decisions, policy and direction just added to the plight.

It is quite apparent that there was an overspend of unnecessary proportions during the close season of 2012 added to a disregard of the strict budget guidelines at the time and only those at the

337

helm at the time will know why this was allowed. The seriousness of the financial situation should have been highlighted to the wider domain far earlier than it was and, perhaps, influence and common sense could have prevailed and administration avoided.

The staff bill at the club was horrific. I calculated that the non-playing staff administrative bill at the club was over £200,000. When you take into consideration that when we started in 1992/93 our players' wage bill was £44,163 (including the manager's wage) and the staff administration wages was just £7,916 it puts it into perspective.

As you progress the opportunity for wider income streams and sponsorships obviously increase but attendance wise there was little difference. In 1992/93 we averaged nearly 2100 per league match. 20 years later in our epilogue from the Football League we averaged 300 fewer home fans through the turnstiles and with the addition of visiting supporters an average in total of just 96 extra spectators per match. It was crazy. It is all about control and it is quite apparent that it was all out of control.

That, alongside what was happening on the pitch, is unforgivable with no firm control. When we started the club Steve Wignall could account for every penny he spent. I remember the days when the manager was invited to attend the start of a Board meeting to explain his position and answer questions from the Board. That certainly happened in my time as company secretary through the Wignall, Wigley and Borg years. As a club we took the finger off the pulse and the consequences reached fruition in damaging ways. We tried to be something that we weren't. We were a small fish in a big pond but too many in positions of authority over a period of time believed we were bigger than we actually were.

No longer being members of the competition that we all dreamed of reaching when we formed the club hurt me and I could not accept that we allowed it to happen and never will, because to reach the Football League was what we had all worked so hard to achieve. We had blown it big time and it left a huge scar.

I had told Shahid that as soon as administration was confirmed I was out of the equation. This chapter had seriously affected me and I needed to concentrate on my health, career and family. I also knew that I would always be involved in any negotiations that would occur over the next few months and, indeed, used as a vehicle as a respected spokesman for differing consortiums. I wasn't prepared to do that either. I issued the following statement:

---

## Resignation Statement

*"Aldershot Football Club was liquidated in March 1992. It was a sad, sad time to be a supporter of the football club. It was like a bereavement. It appeared terminal. It was.*

*However I was proud to be involved in the formation of a new football club soon after. Proud to own one of the two shares that formed the club.*

*We formed Aldershot Town Football Club the following month. A structured club built on morals, ethics, integrity and sheer hard graft. The aim was to give the supporters a football club they could be proud of. To be part of something special.*

*"A club that was part of a community committed to what it could give and not what it could take.*

*When we formed the club it was my directive with Terry Owens that there would be a supporters representative on the Board of Directors and this occurred in the first few years but eventually this was lost in the translation.*

*We enjoyed the most fantastic occasions. We had fun, it was great to be involved.*

*The supporters had their football back, they enjoyed coming to games and we achieved five promotions in 16 years to reach that ultimate dream of the Football League.*

*"We earned a reputation of all that was right in football, especially in those early years. We did it in the right manner.*

*I sit here today wondering how it could all fall apart in such a rapid fashion. The day the club that I was so proud to be a part of forming has headed into administration. How can it be? Where did it go wrong?*

Every supporter of Aldershot Town Football Club deserves an answer. Every player, member of staff, sponsor, creditor and shareholder deserves an answer. Our community deserves an answer.

Since the AGM of 18th April the club has entered a period of rapid decline and embarrassment. This emanated from the majority shareholder who has continued to mislead the supporters, change the rules on a daily basis and has blatantly provided untruths and who has so much to answer for. His actions are unforgivable. I have never been involved in dealing with such a complex character than I have over the last fortnight. I never want to see the man again.

However our club entering into administration has been caused by a sequence of events over a period of time. In truth was the club ever really ready to compete in the Football League?

Did we ever really take advantage of our Football League status?

Despite continued efforts to restructure the finances it never really had any breathing space. We "hit the jackpot" 18 months ago with a tremendous run in the League Cup and the dream of playing Manchester United in the fourth round. Did we ever capitalise on the profile that match provided?

Too high a changeover in personnel within the Board of Directors and within the non-playing staff of the club has been unhelpful too. No structure, no guidance, no purpose and no accountability.

"During the course of the close season of 2012/13 all control evaporated as expenditure was made in the most ridiculous of areas. Who controlled the spending? Who gave the green light for these decisions? Who takes responsibility?

In the early days of our club everything went through my office. We responded and we knew how to deal with the fans. We communicated. I spoke to the two Chairmen I served under, Terry Owens and Karl Prentice, frequently every day. We weren't perfect but we did our best. Do you know what? We did ok!

I saw a letter in the Aldershot News this morning from a frustrated supporter about the current situation the club is in *and it brought back memories. I can recall when the gentleman concerned wrote a letter of complaint into the football club. He had a genuine gripe. I took the time to contact him and met him at his house. We had a cup of tea and a chat and all was well. That was what the club was all about and it is what we did. We listened.*

*These days there are staff in the front office, portacabins, hospitality boxes, back rooms, front rooms. It is all fragmented. There has been no direction. Nobody really has known what their responsibilities have been for a period of time now. It is unacceptable.*

*People try to tell me that entering administration will be the best thing that could have happened considering the murky nature of the club's structure and finances. It's not for me however.*

*I cannot look people in the eye, those that I have brought to the club over the years, who may have to agree a revised payment, if at all, for services they have provided to the football club.*

*I speak to players, staff and supporters and this hurts like nothing we have ever experienced before. We are all suffering. We are all numb.*

*"There will be a process now to preserve the future of Aldershot Town Football Club through the administrators. I sincerely hope that the club is able to secure a healthy future. That is paramount.*

*For whoever takes control of the club I plead with you the following:*

- *Respect the supporters. Listen to the supporters.*
- *Please ensure that there is representation on the Board of Directors from the Shots Trust.*
- *Please provide clear communications and engage with the supporters from day one.*
- *Value your fans and don't take them for granted.*
- *Get back to basics and please do not provide ridiculous "plans" that are not achievable.*
- *Do not mislead the supporters under any circumstance.*
- *Just live within your means and explain why you are doing so.*
- *Just tell the truth as it is.*

"*Communications moving forward will be essential for whoever takes control of the club. Administration has severely dented the club's reputation. It has jeopardised the values and relationships that we spent years to build. It has tarnished our trust and respect.*

*Serious work will be required to rebuild the club's reputation within the community and with the supporters too. There is a lot of work ahead for whoever the successful bidder is.*

*I truly hope that whoever takes control of the club in the future they have the best interests of Aldershot Town Football Club.*

*For me however, it is back to the terraces. I have spent 21 years at the heartbeat of our club. I am not willing to be fighting fires anymore.*

*I have enjoyed the good times and there were some great times too. I have enjoyed the characters I have met. I value every relationship and friendship I have built over the years. Lifelong friends. Good people. The club will always be so special to me. I will always look back with pride on what we achieved. I cannot look back with pride over the sequence of events over the last two weeks though. It is rotten to the core.*

*I have confirmed to the club that I will be stepping down as Head of Media with immediate effect. I want no more to do with the internal organisation and running of the club.*

*What I am also not prepared to do is become a mouthpiece for potential investors keen to purchase the club. I know that my name will be used as a credible source to interested parties and that is not fair to me as an individual.*

*I have sacrificed so much over the years in my career because I wanted to keep my link with the football club in a variety of roles. I always thought it was essential to have somebody involved who was there at the formation. I have always put the club first. My family and career come first now and I leave with my head held high.*

*To me this feels like a bereavement all over again. I never anticipated that we would ever have to experience such a situation again. This is a tale of woe and destruction on a huge scale and it leaves a scar with me. For me this is the saddest of sad days.*

*"There are plenty of supporters who will have that passion, desire and determination to ensure that your voice is heard. Make sure it is. Make sure that people listen. Don't ever be fobbed off again about your football club. Go back to the values we had in 1992.*

*Remember- The fan comes first!*
*Up The Shots!*
*Graham Brookland"*

---

Some of the responses I received from the statement, especially from supporters really touched me. The period had been the most difficult I had endured, feeling additional pressure day by day, wanting so desperately to save something that was really outside of my remit. Many well-wishing messages will be kept forever too.

Ironically I had all but made my mind up at the Dagenham and Redbridge match and it stemmed from the most ridiculous of circumstances. With relegation a distinct possibility that day all the media vultures had descended on our part of north east Hampshire waiting for the storyline.

Prior to the match I accommodated all and sundry including the Late Kick-Off Show. I had had a strong but healthy exchange of views with their producer Andy Steggall in the build-up to the match, the reason being that I was disappointed with the coverage they had given the club during the course of the season considering it was a regional show. They hadn't been near the place but there they were when the going was getting tough for us. However after dealing with the media scrum before the match I came back to the media box that I was in control of and was stopped from entering by a Steward. I explained that I was the Head of Media but had left my pass in my car. She wasn't having any of it. I started to lose control of my own thoughts and knew then that this was becoming ridiculous.

# Do I Wanna Know

1992

I needed a break and played no part in anything that occurred up until 1st July when a creditors' meeting was called.

Shahid and Andrew Mills, who was helping the transitional period behind the scenes, did ask if I would stay on to assist with the administrators, a company based in Southampton called Quantuma Restructuring. I was adamant it was a no but was happy to speak to the Joint Administrator Carl Jackson and, subsequently, their press agency to offer advice.

Of course I kept abreast of matters and did speak at a public meeting of the Shots Trust in June at the old Royal Aldershot Officers Club, the same building (now known as Potters Hotel) where we held the memorable inaugural public meeting to set the club up in 1992. The Trust wanted to see if there was enough public interest to be one of the bidders to buy the club. There were plenty of positives to come out of the meeting but I knew it would be too much, too soon, even though Terry Owens was now their Chairman and Peter Bridgeman, the Trust Secretary.

Terry and I had been speaking on a daily basis prior to administration as he was also heavily involved in trying to bridge gaps that were required. I said I would speak at the meeting, mainly as a favour to Terry more than anything else and I kept to my word.

I did also help compere with Terry "An Evening with Steve Claridge" in aid of the Trust soon after administration. Considering mine, and everybody else's state of mind in the room it was an evening full of laughs and reminiscing. Steve was in fine form too. I was also touched by receiving a standing ovation from the fans attending when I walked into the room. A bit embarrassed to be honest but I knew that it was from the true people of the club and that meant so much to me.

We had a funny incident at our local newsagents too. The proprietor is a Hereford United supporter. We have always had plenty of banter over the years but, on this occasion, he got on the wrong side of The Good Lady. He tried to come out with some humour regarding going into administration and it didn't work. The fact that the situation had cost me a wage too. The Good Lady responded and an argument ensued. My dog, Alfie, was the only dog "on the manor" allowed into the newsagents. Not anymore. The last words said to The Good Lady were *"And don't bring your dog back either. He's banned"*. However an "Alfie Is Innocent" campaign commenced and fortunately common sense prevailed and, eventually, we were all happy again.

Although not directly involved I was still learning of tales of woe from others surrounding the club. We held our own Army FA Cup Final on Wednesday 8th May at the Aldershot Military Stadium. Traditionally over the past few years we had always invited youngsters from the Aldershot Town Juniors section to attend. As per usual we had purchased 22 sweatshirts and an assortment of other merchandise for the youngsters only to learn an hour before kick-off that they wouldn't be in attendance due to disgruntled parents who were upset at the club's situation.

Also it was revealed that many of the coaching set-up had left the club to join Crawley Town whose Chief Executive at the time was Richard Low.

Just over a week later we had our Army FA 125th Anniversary match at the Madejski Stadium, Reading. The Army team was managed by Stuart Pearce with the opponents, an FA Legends team, managed by England manager Roy Hodgson. Sir Trevor Brooking, then FA Director of Football Development, was also in attendance and in a conversation I had with him he informed me that he was also aware of the Aldershot situation having received less than complimentary correspondence from parents regarding our plight. All rather sad.

On 1st July I attended a sparse gathering of creditors (of which I was one) in the EBB Lounge. It was the first time I had been in communication with Shahid and fellow former Directors and consortium colleagues Tony Knights and John Leppard since administration. Shahid had been the driving force to form a consortium. Despite reputed interest from other parties to be involved he and his colleagues were the only people who stepped up to the plate and I respect that.

The picture portrayed at the meeting sounded as though there was still some work to be achieved. Quantuma informed the floor that there was just one bid on the table- that of the previous Board minus Kris Machala. They had all, apparently, agreed to write off their loans and personal or business funds owed. It was also stated that there was still some work to be done with regards to creditors, players and ex-directors to reach suitable agreements. The administrators confirmed that everything needed to be in place by the Thursday of that week when a shareholders meeting would take place.

Indeed in a joint statement from the administrators and consortium issued after the meeting the following was reported, *"Working with the administrators, the consortium had believed that they could take the club out administration this week.*

*"However, there are still some major hurdles which, if unresolved, will prevent the only bid proceeding.*

*"Primarily these hurdles revolve around creditors (both football and non-football) accepting compromises in order to reduce their debts to match the offer received.*

*"The administrators have made it very clear that unless a deal is completed by Thursday this week, the prospects of saving the football club are slim as there is little or no cash left to meet ongoing trading and there are no other offers on the table.*

*"In the event that the club fails and goes into liquidation, there will not be any dividend payment to creditors whatsoever.*

*"The next few days are critical in terms of the survival of the club and we urge all supporters and creditors to get behind the bid put forward by the consortium.*

*"Unless that bid proceeds, the club will stop trading and will enter into liquidation."*

Wow! The worrying aspect for me was that Carl Jackson was adamant when he stated that if all talks were not concluded then the funds would have run out and that consideration to liquidate the club was a serious option.

It was also acknowledged that the current consortium bidding were not prepared to invest any additional funds above their bid as they needed to concentrate these funds on the business development of the club. It was quite clear the future of Aldershot Town Football Club was in the hands of those outstanding creditors yet to agree terms.

Within an hour of leaving the meeting Shahid had called me and we had a chat. I knew that I could help once learning who some of the outstanding creditors were and I told him I would do so. Within 10 minutes John Leppard had made contact too. I told him I would help too. Ironically after the initial chat with John he then spoke to me about the fact that I was a creditor. I told John that I didn't think my few hundred pounds was going to be the difference in Aldershot Town FC being saved and that he should be concentrating on bigger sums of money. I thought no further regarding the conversation.

The next day I received a call from Richard Petty, thanking me for agreeing to write off the amount due further to my conversation with John and asking me to complete a form to confirm this. To be honest I was annoyed although there appeared to be confusion regarding my situation and Richard had not been given the full facts. I explained the situation to him.

I had not agreed to anything but never expected that I would receive the money anyway – but it was the principle of being taken for granted- something I had put up with at the club for too long. I gave Richard an alternative. How about offsetting the amount I was owed with two terrace tickets for a period of time for Oliver and me? He spoke to John and informed me that John was not willing to make the agreement. I left it at that but was more than put out at the way the matter had been concluded. Basically what the club had agreed to was that for a couple of seasons I would be paying through the turnstiles only for them to return all the money that I spent during that period at the end of the deadline for all payments through the administration. Crazy, but it was their call.

The following day I still had concerns about whether the club had a future, despite the tones emanating elsewhere. Talk is cheap but action counts for everything. I'm not one of these "It kept me awake all night playing on my mind" usually but on this occasion it did. All kinds of scenarios were swirling through my mind.

I called Shahid and said I wanted to meet him. I also spoke to Richard Petty, who was working tirelessly behind the scenes, and said I would come in and go through the list of creditors and help where I could negotiate an agreement.

Conscious of the delicate and sensitive situation and the huge pressure on certain individuals involved I sent an email to all members of the consortium and a guy called Russ Howell who was involved and eventually became a director.

It said,

---

*"Dear All*

*I know how much work you have all undertaken over the last two months and personal sacrifices made too.*

*To me it appears that you are so close to the finishing line and that the bulk of the work to get you into the position you are in now has been completed.*

*The last part is always the most difficult but for the club to be liquidated now after all these efforts would be a disaster and something that I believe can be overcome. If it happens it will never be overturned.*

*I know that the process has been a tiresome and weary one but the ultimate goal to cross that line is close and the legacy that this could bring for the current and future generations of Shots supporters could be exciting. Your role in this is that legacy. Once gone it will never be possible again.*

*"There are so few obstacles remaining I plead for you to carefully consider the future that we all want to see for Aldershot Town FC above the few people who are holding out for a better deal.*

*I truly hope that the next 24 hours will see common sense prevail with those individuals.*

*Shahid- we spoke earlier. I want that vision we discussed of Frank Burt celebrating his 100th birthday next year with the players honouring him as they enter the field of play and the crowd on all four sides of the ground emotional in their applause and loyalty to our oldest fan. What a day that will be.*

*I make one plea to you all that if you believe that liquidation is the only option remaining to contact me before any final decisions are made. I will help knock any heads together if it comes to it for the future of our club to be guaranteed. We can still come through this.*

*I wish you all well.*
*Best Regards*
*Graham"*

---

The response from Russ Howell was less than gratifying and it was clear that he had no understanding about the fans and what made them tick. He actually stated in his email that the consortium *"Had lost the will to continue"*. I think that Russ had become too embroiled in the fans' message boards and that is a dangerous game to play at the best of times.

I tried to educate him with my response and also put him straight with regards to some issues surrounding the Shots Trust. Indeed in addition to the problems around the consortium bid there were divisions within the Trust too and Terry Owens had actually resigned from his position the night before.

I contacted Terry and said that this was the most crucial period regarding the future of the football club and it was imperative that he remained as Chairman because the Trust needed him as a figurehead. If there was any public knowledge of dissention in the ranks it could prove disastrous. Fortunately Terry continued in the role for the critical period.

I met Shahid at his offices in Woking on the Wednesday morning. We had a frank conversation and he was open about matters to me. I could see that the stress of the situation was catching up with him too and it was obvious that there were still obstacles to overcome. Shahid said that there was likely to be a shortfall between what the consortium was prepared to offer and what would be required once all the creditors' agreements were reached. The consortium was quite clear in their stance that they would not be in a position to put in additional funds as this would be to the detriment of the business model which would suffer as a consequence.

I said that if this was the case then I would make an appeal at the shareholders meeting the following day and that we would be able to raise the required funds through the floor and also via a wider appeal to supporters.

Upon discussions with Shahid it was obvious that there was also a lack of empathy with the consortium and certain members of the Shots Trust, some of whom seemed to be operating behind Terry's back. Terry was in an extremely difficult situation and coped with it well. Shahid wanted an assurance that the Trust was behind the bid. I spoke to Terry and explained this to him and said that a statement of some kind would be preferable at this stage with the consortium the only option. I could see no alternative. At this stage I was prepared to do anything to help secure the future.

I left Shahid with the words *"Don't give up at any stage after everything you have been through over the last few months. If at any stage you feel that it is not going to happen contact me immediately and I will use my own influences to sort the situation out"*. The bottom line was to let him know that I was there if needed and I knew I could help.

From Woking I drove to Aldershot to meet John Leppard, Richard Petty and Russ Howell. We looked at the creditors list and I agreed to make some phone calls and report back.

Progress was made in many of these quarters which was good news although I don't believe that some of these deals were followed up swiftly enough from within which meant repetitive calls being made to the same individuals later down the line. More savings could have been made with a touch more proactivity. What has to be realised in this kind of situation too is the sensitivity of the matter when it comes to finances. £1,000 may be pocket money to some people but for others it is the difference to putting food on the table for the children as it was for some of the players and staff who had not been paid.

What it also means is that for a period of time you are robbing Peter to pay Paul and it has all kinds of consequences that take time to deal with and heal. Plenty of time added to the stress and pressures that these situations create. Indeed the £1,000 or so hit home harder for some than the sizeable five-figure sums that others lost in the sorry mess that occurred.

Upon learning that the shortfall was likely to be no more than £50,000 I informed the other three people in the meeting that I would make an appeal to the shareholders at the meeting the following day.

# Blurred Lines

1992

Terry Owens and I were at the shareholders meeting. As the two people with the shares that started the club up we agreed that it would be fitting to make the appeal jointly. Terry started to speak to the floor and I followed up with a passionate speech about how much the club meant to me and how desperate I was for it to continue for Oliver. The appeal raised in excess of £85,000. Everything was ticking over nicely and all was positive apart from a rant from one confused shareholder who actually didn't vote in favour of the CVA. If this hadn't been carried through then the club would have ceased to trade.

I couldn't work out what he was trying to achieve but, then again, he was a former councillor and I have often wondered what goes on behind council walls! Even the important proxy of Kris Machala was safely in the hands of Terry to vote in whichever way he saw fit. I thought my dealings with Machala were over. How wrong I was though!

Then, in front of a packed EBB Lounge and attending media, the floor was given to a former director who aired his own views regarding the recent events. Indeed it got to such a stage that I could see that Shahid was at boiling point. I went straight over to him to attempt to calm him down and ushered him out of the room because I knew how critical this meeting was. Any negativity now, one phone call and it was all over. The individual may have had a point relating to some of the issues he spoke about as I had not been involved in the matters he was describing. However, at the time, I was only concerned for the future and not the past. In the kitchen next door I had hold of Shahid who was trying to make a phone call to an investor to call it all off whilst Terry Owens was also restraining him. I told Shahid, Tony Knights and

John Leppard to sit down and try to cool off after the spat and they did so, ironically in the away dugout at the Rec. It all calmed down and I returned to the room where there still remained many shareholders concerned at what was going on. Steve Gibbs had collected the names of those who wished to make a donation whilst I was dealing with the situation outside the room and already it was an impressive list. I knew it would be.

I was encouraged to learn that the appeal for funds was making a huge impact but also clear in my mind that it was best not to reveal the amount raised because there were still creditors who were negotiating. An inkling that there may be more "in the pot" would defeat the object but the figures were eventually released which may not have helped the situation short term.

The repercussions of the conclusion of the shareholders meeting did have a detrimental effect and suddenly the goalposts changed as some of the original investors backtracked. John Leppard contacted me and said that more work was now required and a revision of the plans was needed. He asked if the Shots Trust made a payment of £40,000 would they consider a seat on the Board. I said that he needed to speak to Terry as Chairman. He wasn't prepared to do so and asked if I would act as the "middleman" which, of course, I agreed to, eating up more pressure. Terry agreed in principle but said he would have to put this to the vote and also that there would be no agreement until the two parties had sat down to further discussions. I let John know of the matter and left it to them to take forward but knew there must have been some desperation for this to be even considered because a few days previously the option of a fans rep on the board was a non-starter.

It soon became apparent to me afterwards that although this was a proposed consortium, the individual dialogue between those concerned and how they communicated with each other was not great.

Then came the bombshell! One of the creditors who had not come to an agreement was Kris Machala. I couldn't believe this as I presumed it had all been sorted.

I was asked by the administrators to intervene and decided to involve Terry Owens too. The reason being is that, in my opinion, Kris was by now just way out of his depth and panicking. I thought that he would listen to Terry and me and also knew that there would be no further possibility of speaking with the consortium, especially Tony Knights. Whenever I would have a conversation and Kris' name came up with either a member of the consortium or club personnel they all stated the same thing-"Don't tell Tony!"

Whilst I knew there was a chance I also knew that it would be difficult, especially as the last correspondence I had had with him was that I stated "I never wanted to see him again".

The administrators were now classing the situation as extremely delicate and that Kris, on the advice of his solicitors, was continually moving the goalposts. In fairness to him he was trying to recoup as much money as he possibly could because whatever the final outcome he was going to lose an awful lot.

I spoke to Kris and, indeed, his first words were regarding the fact that I had publicly stated that I didn't want to see him again. We had a long conversation regarding the state of the club and that he now held the trump card. All that stood between Aldershot Town Football Club and its survival was Kris Machala. After continuous conversations and emotional pleas from Terry and me to Kris he finally agreed to the terms and conditions. *"Please think about my son Kris"*, I said. *"Aldershot Town is his life"*. *"What about my son?"* Kris responded. *"What about the things I won't be able to provide?"* I genuinely felt for Kris but he had got himself deeper into a mess over a period of time. When the going got tough I even said to Kris that if the club was liquidated then he would be known as the person who caused the downfall.

I knew that he would have never wanted that but this was not the time or place to gamble on such matters, especially if there was an element of doubt.

I duly informed Carl Jackson at Quantuma and spoke of my relief. I thought that was the end game and that we were there.

Imagine my horror half an hour later when I received further correspondence from the administrators who had, by now, received an email from Kris' solicitors. Additional stipulations had been included which were not in the original agreement between Kris and me. Some of the conditions were just unworkable. Carl's email included the line of which made me freeze- "*In reality Kris is playing a very dangerous game- does he not realise I am potentially hours away from closing the club?*"

# Don't Forget Who You Are

1992

The conversations continued between Kris, Terry and me for what I call "The Missing 48 hours". This period was extremely stressful. At no time was any of the consortium involved in these discussions. I was asked by the administrators whether the Trust would agree to making the payment with Kris.

I was uncomfortable about this as the fund set up by Terry and me was specifically for outstanding creditors and had the Trust been involved in such a payment there would have been all kinds of administrative and legal nightmares that would have had to be overcome in a short space of time. I explained this to Quantuma and they understood the situation.

At one stage Kris's solicitor had asked me to be a guarantor to the CVA amount that he was due. I duly responded stating that there was no chance of this. Furthermore I didn't have any money anyway. This was way over my head and I was feeling it too! The Good Lady will vouch for the stress and anxiety this situation was causing. My phone was glued to my ear throughout the many conversations held in my garden but I was isolated. There was nowhere to turn to.

I had to change the rules a touch and introduced a lifelong supporter and friend who had confirmed to me when the appeal was made that he would help in whichever way he could to secure the future of the club. He remains anonymous by request but his involvement was a key factor in the situation being resolved. Supporters should be forever grateful for his involvement.

The consortium would have no idea who this individual is and never will but do you know what- he is Aldershot through and through and has been all of his life and will be on the terraces forever.

Kris eventually agreed to the proposal but there still remained drama. He needed to sign the CVA agreement and return it to the administrators. I spoke to him regularly during the afternoon of 10th July. He said he would sign the document and fax it over to Quantuma. Late in the afternoon I received a call from the administrators to state that all they had received was the signed back page but not the whole document. Kris then told me that he would put the original document in the post and that it would arrive the following day. I was still nervous until the document had been received in full.

I was out of the equation on Thursday 11th July due to a Board of Trustees meeting in Andover for the Army FA. I had my phone on silent and had told everybody that I was unavailable on the day. Imagine my horror when midway through the meeting the name "Kris Machala" flashed onto the screen. I literally froze again. What was he playing at now? When there was a natural break I immediately phoned Kris. It was as though I was speaking to a different person.

He was polite, courteous and explained that he had had enough and that he had sent the completed forms and would not pose any further obstacles regarding the future of the club. That all he had been doing was to protect his family and own finances. The following day a relieved Richard Petty confirmed receipt of the document at the club.

I had more than a touch of sadness regarding Kris Machala though. He was a genuine man who got involved in the football club for the right reasons and had always promised to follow the legacy left by John McGinty to guarantee the future of the club. He arrived from Poland in the 1980s and had suffered hardship in the Eastern Bloc country. I used to speak with him frequently and have no doubts that he was sincere in his affection for the football club.

The problem with being involved with a club the size of Aldershot which owns nothing is that if you put money into the club you have to accept that you are unlikely to see it again. I think that Kris believed that he would get a return but this never happened and was never likely to. By the end of his tenure he was just so far out of his depth it became dangerous. I can see, however, that he would have been easily persuaded by other members of the Board of Directors and that he wasn't strong enough to make the crucial decisions that leadership at a football club needed. The bottom line is that he had the opportunities to help himself but didn't take them. It all ended sadly for Kris and he will, no doubt, rebuild his own life elsewhere, scarred by his involvement at Aldershot. It was never meant to be that way. I have seen countless Chairmen over the years suffer hardship either emotionally, business-wise, financially or through family issues. Kris joined that unfortunate list as this experience affected his health and finances. So sad. Whatever he does in the future and wherever he goes, I truly wish him well.

There were still some matters that required attending to but by this stage I knew that the football club was safe although you are never totally confident until you see it in writing. On 16th July the news was confirmed although there were still some issues between the football club and the Conference League that would require rubber-stamping. For me though this was the opportune moment to bow out for good this time and revert to my original decision when the club entered administration and also step down as the President of the Trust. There was just no way I could go through the upheaval and turmoil that the season would bring. I issued an additional statement commending the consortium naming Shahid, John and Tony plus the role that Russ Howell had played too. I also added the role of the Shots Trust but, above all, the part that the supporters had played towards the end of the administration process.

I ended it by re-emphasising how, in the dark days when a positive conclusion appeared remote, I had reminded Shahid and his colleagues of my dream which was to see supporter Frank Burt celebrate his 100th birthday which would be during the course of the season- "*What an occasion that will be*", I said. I thought the statement was fair and covered all topics that were relevant. Shahid contacted me and I confirmed that I couldn't be involved.

We then discussed a logo for a new badge that the consortium was planning which would have more of a relevance to the Army involvement within the town. I told him frankly that there was no requirement to change the badge. I had been informed that there was a need to take out the 1992 from the badge but nothing else. Of course that obviously disappointed me immensely because "1992" was an integral reminder to all of us about what our club was all about. It was removed pretty quickly from the club's history as was the share I owned to help form company "2711473".

I make no secret that to lose "1992" from the club badge and that share absolutely crushed me and I am sure that it did the same to Terry too. Indeed I am certain that good men such as Karl Prentice, Peter Bloomfield and Malcolm Grant, who were appointed onto the Board for the inaugural 1992/93 season, would have felt the same too. Shares were issued for a new company and somebody else possesses numbers one and two for company number 08362929. It is not known as Aldershot Town FC (1992) Ltd anymore.

As relieved as I was that football in Aldershot had been saved part of me started to accept that the club I had been so involved in forming had slipped away to another guise.

Apart from the call from Shahid I never received one phone call from any other members of the consortium. Not a word of thanks- nothing. It really disappointed me.

# Wrecking Ball

1992

My job was done now though and I was looking forward to returning to the terraces. However I was so disappointed with regards to the lack of respect received from within the Football Club from the day it was taken over. Let me put it straight- I didn't expect the royal treatment or anything like that but I did believe that I warranted something for 21 years' loyal service as a member of staff, especially considering some of the situations that I had been involved in during that period and, of course, being a co- founder of Aldershot Town FC (1992) Ltd. To me it just seemed to be a natural process that something would occur. Nothing did at the time. A thank you would have been a starter. At least three years previously I had received a "25-Years' Service to Football Award" from the Hampshire FA nominated by the Aldershot Football Association but, from my club, nothing!

The feedback I received since is that some members of the consortium believe that the Trust held them back by holding the public meeting back in June with a view of becoming a bidder should the financial position be viable. My take on it is this. I was President of the Trust and not involved in the decision making process, just a figurehead. However if the Trust had not made an attempt to bid then it would have been neglectful in its duties to the supporters. Especially considering that the only other "bid on the table" was from a consortium which included the directors of the club when it went into administration. The Trust had no alternative in my opinion.

Terry was still dealing with the administrators, keen to tie up all loose ends and, furthermore, ensure that everything was done correctly with regards to the £85,000 raised by the fans through our appeal. It was agreed with the administrators that a joint statement be issued to acknowledge thanks to the fans for their contribution. I re-wrote the original draft and, after liaising with Terry, it was returned to the administrators who would forward it to the football club for an official release. When it was issued my name and Terry's had been omitted from the original statement.

I found that totally disrespectful as we were the two guys who made the appeal in the first place and, without sounding blasé about matters, not one of the consortium could have stood up and made a similar appeal and received the same kind of response. Why? Because they didn't have the history, recognition and respect from the supporters that was required.

I felt comforted a few months later when the administrators report was issued and Joint Administrator Paul Goddard addressed at length the detailed circumstance of events that led to the club being taken out of administration. He explained that at the meetings of 4th July 2013 – *"At this time it remained apparent that the sole offer still remained slightly short of the funds required to ensure that the Football Conference's regulations were satisfied.*

*"However at the meetings a plea was made by certain individuals in attendance at that meeting for supporters to rally support and make donations to the joint administrators so as to bridge the gap between the offer available and the funds required. The results of this plea were far more significant than anticipated ultimately resulting in £85K being raised. Having passed this significant milestone, I continued detailed discussions with the proposed purchaser and various classes of creditor and was able to exchange on a conditional sale and purchase agreement with the purchaser on 16th July 2013."* My name may not have been mentioned but I'll take the "certain individuals" title knowing that it referred to Terry and me.

The first competitive match was on Saturday 10th August at Grimsby Town. It was a day to celebrate although I must admit I felt a bit like a fish out of water sitting with the fans at the match without any responsibilities but I was proud watching Oliver and all the younger supporters at Blundell Park singing to their hearts content, backing their team to a deserved point. That was what it was all about.

The first match at the Rec was on the Tuesday evening versus Dartford. This was when I seriously expected that I would be contacted and invited as a guest as a thank you, not just for the antics of the summer but to recognise 21-years' service. Nothing! I know that The Good Lady had attempted to contact some directors and senior personnel to ask what plans they had. They never responded to her. I believe that was another disrespectful episode by their not doing so.

My total feeling was one of apathy and disdain to proceedings. Had I really been involved in finalising some of the most difficult creditors in the latter stages? Had I been the primary focus in ensuring that the major creditor acquiesced to his agreement? Had I stood up at a shareholders meeting to instigate an appeal that raised the £85,000 required to help secure the club and ensure a future? Had I been the middleman for the consortium and Shots Trust and some delicate times when a time bomb was ticking and I managed to use my diplomacy on a huge scale to avoid the explosion? Had I continued those rallying calls to the consortium in a plea to ensure that they never gave up? Had I really provided all of the above when my own doctor had stated that I needed to avoid any stress-related matters due to my own circumstances at the time? It was as though this never happened. I had every right to be angry.

Imagine how I felt the night we played Dartford? I know everybody in the Directors Box were praising each other and taking plaudits for a job well done and rightly so too. The sense of feeling when "Alive and Kicking" was played as the players entered the pitch. A job well done! And there was I queuing up at the turnstiles without a word of acknowledgement. I even purchased a ticket for the wrong area.

I felt absolutely numb as I witnessed members of Rushmoor Borough Council including the Mayor, specially invited to celebrate the occasion. Thanks for the memories!

We defeated Dartford 3-0 but I could have easily walked away and never returned to the football ground that had been my spiritual home for nearly 40 years. I am so pleased I didn't. I had to use the principles that I have told others to use so often down the years that a football club is about the "CLUB" and not the people that run it. You are there to support your team. Not those sitting in the Directors Box.

When we played Cambridge United the following Saturday fortunately it all clicked for me and I rekindled my love for the club. Despite the defeat I enjoyed the occasion watching the match from the East Bank with my brother and other friends, including that mystery man who showed such loyalty when the going was getting tough just before the consortium took the club out of administration. I just had a pure loyalty to the football club.

To make matters worse Terry Owens had his seat for life in the Directors Box taken away from him; an unnecessary course of action. Terry was in a perilous situation in the summer juggling a number of balls in the air as Chairman of the Trust. It was nigh on impossible. We spoke every day and everything we did was always in the best interests of the football club. Terry was granted his seat in honour by John McGinty. There was no need to take this privilege away from him. It's not as though the Directors Box is full to the brim in the Conference. To have a future you have to have had a past and those of us involved in 1992 will always know what was achieved to reinstate football in the town. Terry was the conductor and deserved the honour. Why take it away? I understand a policy regarding "free" tickets. The club was trying to set its stall out from the start regarding the issue of "complimentaries" and I encourage that but this was different.

It was not the first time this kind of situation had occurred. A number of years earlier a decision was made to withdraw the role of Patron. An honour bestowed on a number of individuals including Dave Tomlinson and my brother taken away. Why? These kind of decisions only damage the very fabric of the club. These things have a minimal cost element to them and the negative PR of such decisions far outweigh any of that. I could name countless former playing and management staff who have been treated with a lack of respect upon returning to the club over the years and spoken to rudely. One such individual, who served eight years at the club, had arranged a car park pass with his new employers, who were in the same division, to attend a match. Upon arrival he was not permitted to enter the Rec with his car and made to reverse out of the stadium with a trail of vehicles waiting to get into the stadium behind him. Another who was an excellent servant for over a decade at the club arranged a ticket representing another club scouting to view a player that we were happy to move on. When he arrived he was told that his ticket wasn't there. "*What should I do then*"? he asked. "*You know where the turnstiles are*"? he was informed. Totally embarrassing and unnecessary and it leaves a stain on the club too. Word gets around on the circuit and it is a truly negative one of the club and it really annoys me.

What hurt me more than anything though was the scurrilous conversations emanating with regards to my own situation. I may not have been involved officially anymore but you obviously get to know many, many people over a lifetime of being around a football club. Word gets back! My circumstances changed at the end of the 2010/11 season when Peter Duffy approached me to offer me a full-time job at the club heading up the administrative and media department with a directive to improve internal and external communications – and boy did it need it. I told him that I never had any intention of returning to a full-time role within the club. In addition I was not comfortable in the knowledge that my returning would affect the positions of people who I had known for years including secretary Bob Green and who would lose their livelihoods at my expense. What I did agree to was changing my own role to head up the media department with full responsibility for overseeing a variety of roles including the programme, website, develop external relationships with the media and to attempt to improve communications internally (a thankless and impossible task as I was about to find out).

My part-time remuneration was agreed by Peter, Kris and John Leppard. John and I went back many years and his company was always enjoyable, especially at the bar. One certainty is that he is an out and out Aldershot Town fan and I acknowledge that. The football club has also undoubtedly cost him a lot of money over the years. He could have walked away this time but to his credit, he didn't. I had always responded to his requests during the summer too, getting involved in activity to help save the club where he wouldn't have been able to use his influence. It disappointed me intensely when I heard feedback from friends that John was stating that my "earning a wage" had been wrong and that I should have been providing the service for nothing. I never cost Aldershot Town FC a penny. Indeed the income from the "Shotsline" years alone would have covered my wages during the 21 years. It was a "full-on" role given the time and dedication it deserved. In addition to the day by day responsibilities on a match day my team and I would be at the relevant stadium two hours before kick-off and, more often than not, the last to leave an hour and a half afterwards. I am sure John Motson and Martin Tyler have never experienced these problems. It's the same job, same role but just on a smaller scale. I cannot lie and say that these comments didn't hurt because, whilst I know there was no malice, it upset me, adding to the other disappointments over a short period of time.

Furthermore many years before when premium rate phone lines were profitable I also had the opportunity to add Southampton and Portsmouth to my repertoire but put the football club first as I would never have been able to have conducted this time-wise. The times that I could have furthered my career but chose not to in order to remain loyal to the football club because I believed they needed my input. I did operate the AFC Bournemouth line for a few years. Believe me interviewing their then manager Mel Machin is an experience in itself whilst Eddie Howe, as skipper, always spoke eloquently and showed signs that he would progress to a managerial role. However this involvement was of great benefit to me but also the club as I learnt a great deal from a Football League set up.

As Head of Media at a Football League club I was one of a handful of people across the 92 professional clubs who was not full-time in such a position.

Indeed there were clubs in League 2 who actually had more than one full-time employee within their media department. I had to juggle a lot of balls in the air but I know I did it well.

The Good Lady will tell you that it was every evening, every Sunday during the football season without fail. There was always football club activity, phone calls, press releases, website articles in addition to the role of "mediator" which became a regular occurrence. It was more than just a media role. It covered every aspect, every department of the club. Everybody wanted a piece of me and I never said no. I should have done, there is no doubting that now. All of these isolated incidents just widened the gap as to whether I could ever strike up a relationship with the Board of Directors again.

# Somewhere Only We Know

1992

I decided to just concentrate on the football and ignore anything occurring on an official basis at the club. Whatever was going on in the Boardroom or "upstairs" wasn't my concern anyway. I had decided to return to the terraces and that was where I would be.

I had started a blog regarding club activities and, now not being officially involved, was able to be a touch more flexible and opinionated with my views. It was like rolling back the years to my youth and I found it enjoyable but my over lasting impression is always to ensure that the football club comes first. It was always going to be a tricky opening to the season with the aftermath of administration fresh in people's minds.

Andy Scott had a tough task assembling a squad on what would obviously be a far reduced budget and with a negative -10 points tally before a ball was kicked. Indeed he was still signing players on the coach journey up to Grimsby the day before the season opener in August. It all started well and the points' deficit was erased after just seven matches which set a false dawn of expectation. The loss of key players to injury started to raise concerns especially after a shock exit in the FA Cup in a fourth qualifying round replay at home to Calor Gas Southern League South and West side Shortwood United who were 65 places below us in the league.

This was followed soon after by successive four-goal defeats away at Cambridge United and Halifax Town; the first time this had happened to any Aldershot team in my living memory.

Just prior to this period the Board had given Andy a new three-year deal. I raised the matter in my blog stating that I didn't think this was a wise move. Nothing to do with Andy. I liked his integrity but my view was that no manager should be given a contract when they are sitting in a relegation zone even if it is by default because as soon as the announcement is made the pressure is raised on him. Unfortunately, this became the case. Not because his job was in jeopardy but when you tackle such a period as administration I believe it is important to be able to work below the radar with freedom without any unnecessary distractions.

There were a few comments inside and outside the club at the time after the heavy defeats and they paid dividends because all of a sudden some of the younger group of players stepped up to the plate whilst the experienced lads started to show their worth too until they fell back into decline after the turn of the year.

I don't regret one word of the blog because sometimes you need to test the waters and make people aware of the significance of what is going on. When I sat in the stands on a cold afternoon at The Shay and saw my team capitulate as soon as they went a goal down I felt desolate. After all the turbulence we had gone through I saw signs that there could be more murky periods ahead and that could not be afforded. My actions in writing the blog were that of a fan. One of 140 who travelled to West Yorkshire. The fan I was in the seventies and eighties and not the club official anymore. I thought to myself that is how it should be. Freedom of speech is always a touch regimented when you are in a position of authority. It didn't have to be anymore. I quite liked that. I said it as I saw it.

As a fan on the terraces you view things differently. Two matches in a week and it hits the pockets. You have to pick and choose if you can attend some of those away matches now whereas before, of course, I was working. People say to me how fortunate I have been to have had a pass to gain access over the 21 years I was an official. I don't think so. It was work and hard work at that. However I do fully get the fact that fans pay their money and have the freedom to voice their opinions when they wish. It is hard-earned money and I understand that much more clearly now than previously.

You sometimes lose touch with reality the longer you are away from the terraces and I would urge any director to queue up at the turnstiles, toilets and park their car at an away match where they can find a space. Find that vantage spot on the terraces after being body searched and then aim to buy a burger and cup of coffee at half-time in the driving rain without a programme to view because they have sold out.

January 2014 saw that special occasion to celebrate Frank Burt's 100th birthday. The day that I had set the vision to the directors six months previously when I thought that the end could be nigh.

The opponents were Kidderminster Harriers and the club, and Shahid in particular, had moved mountains to make it a special occasion. Unfortunately the rain put paid to the match itself but it was agreed to hold the celebratory luncheon in the sponsors lounge. What an occasion it was too, just like I said it would be in the summer.

I had been approached to compere the festivities by Paul Marcus for the club and, after consideration, agreed to do it because this was all about Frank and nothing else. Quite honestly I would do anything for Frank Burt, the most wonderful man you could meet and who had attended the first ever match at the Rec in August 1927 versus Grays Thurrock. It was an occasion befitting such a gentleman. When I arrived I made a beeline straight to Frank who I hadn't seen since the summer as I had not partaken in the Directors Box during the season.

He was talking to the Chairman of Chelsea, Bruce Buck, but as soon as he saw me he shouted *"Graham"* and we embraced. I truly loved that moment. You see the survival of the football club was all about people like Frank and to see the joy on his face said it all. Of course it was all worth it. I did speak to other directors and exchanged handshakes in a diplomatic manner. It didn't change my views at the time though.

After the event I suggested to the Board of Directors that Frank should be offered the position of President of the Football Club on the day of his 100th birthday purely because I saw it as a great opportunity for Frank and also for the club. In my view they missed a trick as it didn't happen.

The season started to wane again. After a tidy victory at Barnet the team went eight matches without a win including

**Proud to compere Frank Burt's 100th birthday celebration**

a torrid FA Trophy quarter-final defeat at Havant and Waterlooville. If ever there was an occasion a club needed to take the initiative in a competition this was it. A visit to Wembley would have galvanised the club in such a special way and could have set a firm foundation for the future. Not only did we lose, we were hammered 4-1 and it was a woeful evening. We really fluffed our lines on this one. Failure to beat bottom placed Hyde United in Greater Manchester was followed by a last-gasp Brett Williams' equaliser at Dartford on a late February Tuesday evening in Kent. There is a photo of the fans celebrating just as the ball enters the net. Oliver is included in the centre of it and if ever a photo epitomises why it was worth helping to save the club this is it.

I love watching Oliver so excited, looking forward to the matches and building his own group of friends from people he has met through the club. I recall a time when he was much younger when I looked across at him during a match and his face was blank. *"You alright, son?"* I asked. *"You do enjoy coming here, don't you?"* He responded, *"Not really Dad."* I felt awful and he stopped coming for a short while. I would never take him somewhere that he didn't want to be. He eventually asked me if he could come to a match with me again and has never looked back since. Aldershot Town is his club. There is no other and, fortunately, the events of the administration and relegation from the Football League have not jeopardised that. Indeed he now has a freedom that he has never had before and can express himself how he wishes to.

We just couldn't edge clear of the danger zone though and defeats in March at Tamworth and then Braintree Town started to suggest that we had a serious problem. The latter was a "Tour of Duty" for Shots fans which is where a rallying call is made to attend

Oliver (central above cross bar) celebrates vital last minute
equaliser at Dartford in 2014 before ball has crossed the line

a specific match each season. The fans did their bit in their hundreds
and travelling with them on the train the level of affection for the
club was noticeable. Unfortunately we conceded within three
minutes and never looked as though we would recover.

The cries of support and appeals for the players to "wear the
shirt with pride" were over. Only they could get us out of this
mess now.

# To Make a Dream Survive

1992

By the time April came around we were in serious difficulty and there became a realisation that we could end up suffering a successive relegation back into regional football. We had six matches to save our season and one of those was at runaway league leaders Luton Town. Despite a terrific effort we returned pointless from Kenilworth Road.

Shahid actually stood on the terraces on the Tuesday evening match at Alfreton Town. I told him that it was a good move and, in time, he would be able to build relationships and awareness with supporters. That is all fans want- a touch of familiarity. Performing against a club who had a serious opportunity to reach the play-offs we started the match with a tremendous energy to it and won 4-1. The following Saturday we travelled to that destination that still makes me sweat- "Macclesfield Town". Nothing less than a point was acceptable due to the circumstances surrounding other clubs. All was calm until with 13 minutes remaining the Cheshire side took the lead through Scott Boden. All of a sudden attention turned to the other matches, "*Are still losing*"?- "*What about Dartford?*" The situation was just so tense. Then that kind of experience that only a football fan can describe occurred. Time was running out as we entered the 95th minute of the match. With our last attack Brett Williams was felled inside the penalty box. The referee didn't disappoint. We all started celebrating as though we had scored before it suddenly dawned on us, "*Hang on, he's got to score it now.*" Brett possessed sheer bottle and resolve to slot the spot kick away. Cue the scenes- 40- and 50-year old blokes (me included) acting like lunatics hugging anybody in the vicinity, tears of joy streaming down the faces of men and women young and old. That point took us out of the relegation zone. Our destiny was in our own hands with three matches remaining.

Teddy Sheringham, who had that all-so-brief loan spell at Aldershot nearly 30 years previously, stood on the East Bank for the Good Friday visit of Salisbury City and witnessed his son Charlie level for the visitors in the first half as they clawed back a two-goal deficit.

Fortunately Joe Oastler netted the winner for Shots and it meant we went into the penultimate game of the season at local rivals Woking in the knowledge that victory would secure Conference status. Anything else and it would set up a rather worrying last day showdown with fellow relegation contenders Hereford United.

My brother came over from Jersey specifically for the match. It is difficult to describe just what was resting on this fixture. Forget your multi-million pounds shoot out for the play-off finals for the Premier League. To any Shots supporter this was so much more.

They announced that 1,436 Shots fans had made the journey to Kingfield. There were far more within the stadium. And did they back their side? Did they make a difference?

Another penalty from Williams set them on their way midway through the second half and the place erupted. Despite former Shot Brett Johnson levelling soon after it was fitting that Mark Molesley secured the original target of survival with seven minutes remaining. There were "scenes and limbs" at the final whistle. Yes it was right to revel in the celebrations. Not just to celebrate avoiding relegation against the odds but to celebrate the fact that together on and off the pitch we had all played our part in ensuring that we had a football club to support. We had all done it together and it was an outpouring of emotion and relief. Ironically Hereford beat us on the final day with a late goal from the much maligned former Shots striker Michael Rankine and celebrated their own party at the Rec as the victory should have ensured survival. Six weeks later though their own financial situation ensured that they were expelled from the Conference. Another former Football League club to hit hard times- an ongoing trend. It was sad to see and, on this occasion, I had every sympathy with the local newsagent. Hereford United was eventually liquidated in December 2014 and those fans can now enjoy the planning of setting up their own phoenix type club for 2015/16 and beyond.

Andy Scott (left), Coaching team and Paul Shrubb celebrate Conference survival after defeating Woking.

Celebrating at the final whistle with Coach Matt Gray as relegation is avoided at Woking in 2014.

# Let Me Go

1992

Since December 2013 I had been in contact with Shahid too. He called me to arrange a meeting. I was apprehensive at first and sent him a strong and detailed email covering my displeasure over the matters I have covered but agreed to meet. We had a heartfelt two and a half hours. I admired his honesty and his subsequent apology that he made public in a future programme. He said that "*He got it wrong*" and I respected that and it certainly built part of the bridge with me and gave me some comfort. It did not alter my feelings about some of the activities that had occurred as they cannot be changed but it was enough to be able to "move forwards" but never in any previous capacity that I had served in because I didn't want that anymore. Time moves on and life does too.

We continued to meet on a regular basis and struck up a rapport. Strangely we kept bumping into each other at Warwick Services on the way to or from an away match and would always start a dialogue. I started to realise that his intentions and vision of the football club and its place within the community was not too dissimilar to that of Terry Owens and me in 1992. Indeed he had some excellent initiatives planned especially involving the Army and was determined to see them through. The problem being, of course, is that the baggage that had occurred before, during and after the administration process had caused a discomfort amongst supporters where many remained upset that their football club had hit difficult times again after not heeding the lessons of the past.

I explained to Shahid that it would take time, careful planning and an assurance to the supporters and it would have to be a patience game. As a Chairman it is imperative that he had a strong

Shahid Azeem (right) and Paul Shrubb (left) raising funds for the Phyllis Tuckwell Hospice

Board of Directors around him too. I am not convinced that the balance of the Board is right though.

Shahid expressed a keenness to rectify the situation of Terry and me to ensure that we were recognised for the role that we had played over many years. The three of us eventually met in April 2014 and, after consultation with the Board of Directors, a meeting was arranged with them. I was honest and forthright in my views and expressed my dismay at some of the activity that had occurred over the past year or so. After a healthy exchange with Terry, me and the members of the Board we duly shook hands with each and every member and departed.

A few days later we were both offered the role of Club Ambassadors and a seat, should we wish, in the Directors Box. With our experience, knowledge and love of the football club it is a role that we both accepted although my place remains on the terraces once the match has started. The club said in its statement that Terry and I *"Symbolise the values and ethics that are Aldershot Town"*. Shahid commented that his year would have been *"That much harder without our support, advice and co-operation"* and that our appointment was *"to be a fitting recognition of that support, not just for this season but for many years previously"*.

As the 2014/15 season started though there was still much to do and by the time the FA Cup had started the team weren't exactly pulling up trees in the Conference. Victory in the fourth qualifying round tie at home to Torquay United set up the plum first round draw though- away to Hampshire neighbours and 2008 FA Cup winners Portsmouth. If ever a club needed such an opportunity this was it and it would be on Remembrance Sunday too.

This was an occasion that all fans who had been "through the mill" in the previous couple of years could savour and why not? This was a draw to ignite the flames. When we were paired with

Portsmouth at Fratton Park Oliver danced around the room like a lunatic with excitement but even I, more reserved and guarded these days, felt a buzz of anticipation upon learning the news. It was a draw to get the tongues wagging. To talk about Aldershot Town in positive mode again. We could not have asked for a better fit. We could not have asked for any other possible draw to ensure that the lapsed supporters returned to enjoy an outing to the south coast- only if we put a performance on though.

The players needed to show their capabilities in such an environment. They needed to "have a go" from the outset. They couldn't afford to let themselves down. The club couldn't afford it either. That was all that was asked for and they didn't disappoint and did those fans certainly did show their respect too.From the moment the two sets of supporters paid their own immaculate Remembrance Sunday tributes to befit the military history of both towns prior to kick-off you just sensed that this could be a special day.

The unity of the 2,500 sell out Shots fans packed behind the Milton End was as exuberant as I have experienced. It was great to be a part of that. It was great to see real heartfelt passion for their football club overflowing with pride.

Fans on display at Portsmouth in the FA Cup in November 2014

Portsmouth had endured their own major problems since their Premier League heyday with a kamikaze slide through the Football League to the basement division amidst all kinds of turmoil and, similar to ourselves, administration. However it was also a fact that on the day they played Chelsea in the FA Cup final in 2010 we were preparing for a Football League 2 Play-Off semi-final versus Rotherham United. We were, at the time, a decent established side only to hit our own rock in the middle of the stormy seas that lay ahead to eventually lose our Football League status and more.

There was actually a sense of disappointment that we didn't go on and win the match after Jordan Roberts' leveller then Mark Molesley edging us in front, deservedly so at the time.

However a 2-2 draw gave the club the opportunity to take advantage of. Indeed a draw was the best result we could have envisaged.

The replay was a certainty for live coverage on BT Sport and the additional revenue from the FA Cup run was significant where the club could make solid foundations to enhance those that had been built slowly due to the adversity of the turbulence of the recent past.

The replay was special too. That man Molesley ensured a special conclusion with a late winner and the only goal of the game in front of 5,374 fans. It was a fantastic atmosphere and a unique night at the Rec. I honestly thought that the club had turned the corner but, even I, with all my years of experience, should have known better.

# Got No Fans

Since the Portsmouth victory the team had started to struggle again. A second round defeat at Rochdale after a replay saw FA Cup exit but this was no embarrassment. Indeed there were enough chances to win at the Rec and set up a home tie with Nottingham Forest. However a home defeat to Isthmian Division One South Burgess Hill Town in the FA Trophy and five league defeats in six coming up to the end of 2014 saw all the hope and jubilation of Portsmouth extinguished as quickly as it arrived. The visit of Macclesfield Town in December saw the first ever sub 1,000 league attendance in the history of either club whilst the following Saturday's 870 for the Burgess Hill visit confirmed the lowest ever league or FA competition attendance. In addition, one of the original consortium members, Tony Knights, had stepped down as a director too.

Indeed as we headed for the final fixture of 2014 the morale of the fans was at rock bottom after the recent run of results, especially at the Rec. A visit to the "new" local rivals since the formation of the Phoenix club, Woking, was a tough ask.

Managed by the experienced campaigner Gary Hill he had guided the Surrey side to a play-off spot and, over a period of time there had developed an edge between the two clubs.

It was typical Aldershot though and it encapsulated everything there is about following the Shots. Fans arriving at Kingfield had little or no expectation for the match especially after the disappointment of recent weeks. Andy Scott's men then produced a terrific performance full of energy, drive and commitment to race into a two-goal lead at the interval. Despite their dominance though it wouldn't have been Aldershot without the injury time drama as the nerves jangled and Woking pulled a late goal back.

Even holding on for dear life in stoppage time felt right because it was what Aldershot fans have been accustomed to over the years. Rarely has anything been achieved the easy way. Win the match they did and it was a vital victory as the club continues to find its feet since administration.

Just prior to the festive period I had been involved in organising the Army Football Association's Game of Truce where the British Army and German Bundeswehr commemorated the 100th anniversary of the Christmas Truce of 1914. It had been a difficult period trying to secure the Rec as the venue. Major Billy Thomson and I were desperate for the match to be played in Aldershot as the home of the British Army and conversations with Shahid were held as we felt the opportunity was slipping away. Indeed it was due to the tremendous support of Chelsea FC, who have had an agreement to use the stadium since the club exited administration that the match could be staged as they rescheduled some of their youth and Under-21 fixtures and were extremely co-operative. This was a good decision as it was a wonderful occasion, fitting for such an event. To spend time in the company of our guest Sir Bobby Charlton CBE, was a privilege. He was an absolute gentleman. Indeed over 2,500 spectators attended too and the occasion graced the international stage as the Army won 1-0.

However it also meant that I had to deal with organising a match with the football club for the first time since my departure. It made me realise that after the experiences of the summer of 2013 there remains so much more work to be achieved and still so much to learn before the club is ever ready to return to past glories on and off the pitch. In truth it was hard work because the infrastructure just is not there. It was always going to be difficult and that is exactly what it is. It is not about quantity within your organisation, it is about the quality.

Oliver with Sir Bobby Charlton at the Army Game of Truce in December 2014

# Blame

1992

Results on the pitch continued to deteriorate to an extent that by the visit of Kidderminster Harriers in January in addition to four successive home defeats in all competitions there had been nine defeats in 11. The crowds were continuing to diminish to an extent that just 1,035 attended the visit of the midlands club. Demonstrations were planned to protest before and after the match and Oliver was involved in this. Who was I to dissuade him with my previous form?

One of the plans was for the fans in the East Bank not to enter until 15 minutes after kick-off. "*You need to be careful, son. What if we are 2-0 up by the time you all enter? It will be embarrassing for you all*", I told him. "*Dad, When was the last time Aldershot scored twice in the first 15 minutes?*" he responded. He was correct too. We lost 1-0 on the night. The locals were restless after the match and the demonstrations and numbers increased. The departure of Andy Scott was inevitable and occurred the following morning.

It is never pleasant to see the departure of a manager but sometimes it is a necessity. Andy Scott came to the club at a tricky time as the battle to avoid relegation from the Football League was on. He was unable to steer the club away from danger but he would have been aghast at the events of the summer of 2013 and administration. Indeed when he joined the club there had never been any inkling that financial problems were rife. I am sure if he had known he would have given the place a wide berth. However I believe that he conducted himself with great dignity during the process and that should be acknowledged. He also sent me a touching email when I stepped down from my role. Andy also had to build a playing squad from scratch at short notice after the club exited administration and, in my view, despite some low points during the campaign, achieved by keeping the club in the Conference during 2013/14.

The Portsmouth FA Cup matches gave the club a lift at the time but we were treading water in the league not looking up and, at that time, not looking down either. However the sharp decline in results thereafter saw another relegation battle looming after the Kidderminster defeat. Any manager whose side has lost 10 out of 11 league matches is under pressure whether they feel they are or not. Andy paid the penalty for that and became the third managerial casualty in four years at a club who had only sacked one manager in the first 19 years of existence. That tells its own story. As this book concludes the Board of Directors have the most critical decision they will ever have with respect to making the next managerial appointment.

There are still tough times ahead for the club but at least it can move forwards. Rather tough times than no times at all. At least it still has the opportunity to experience those days such as Portsmouth and, indeed, at Woking. The club has, since administration, produced plenty of good community focus work in its short tenure. However the most important ingredient to me is for the powers that be to have an understanding of what makes the club and the fans click and an understanding that the vast majority of fans just want to see their club produce on the pitch. At a club such as Aldershot Town that doesn't mean winning every week, it means knowing that your team has given it everything and put in a performance. Until that is perfected it will remain a long and winding road to continue the journey we started in 1992 and those that started the inaugural story in 1926. But, over a period of time, this can be achieved.

You cannot buy the experiences I have gained over the years but the heartbeat of a football club remains on the terraces (and we are fortunate to still have them at the Rec). I have learnt how important Aldershot Town FC is to so many people and what it means to the fans too. What I also know is that the closer you become involved within the operation and structure of a football club you learn about matters you'd rather not know about and see personalities represent your club you'd rather not be involved. That is not good but It is a fact of life within football at all levels. Sometimes it is best to just watch the football and be totally separate from the politics.

Few have had the opportunity to swap the terraces of their boyhood club. To have had the years as a teenager growing up on the terraces, then to be the Chairman of the Supporters Club during turbulent times. To see the club I followed be the first in 30 years to lose their status mid-season in the Football League was traumatic enough. Then to have the honour as a co-founder of a new club and see the terrific rise through the leagues to regain that Football League status only to then play a major part in ensuring that liquidation was avoided 21 years later is something that I will always be proud of. I am, first and foremost, a fan. None of this would have been possible without the support of The Good Lady. There has always been a drama a day when the name of the football club is mentioned and it always caused a debate. She always knows that Aldershot was my first love way before we met. It remains Alive and Kicking!

By the way- there has still never been a player to grace the Recreation Ground surface better than Alex McGregor. He remains the greatest player there ever was!

It always will be- whatever it says on the badge